Ebenezer Josiah Newell

St. Patrick

His Life and Teaching

Ebenezer Josiah Newell

St. Patrick
His Life and Teaching

ISBN/EAN: 9783743330733

Manufactured in Europe, USA, Canada, Australia, Japa

Cover: Foto ©ninafisch / pixelio.de

Manufactured and distributed by brebook publishing software (www.brebook.com)

Ebenezer Josiah Newell

St. Patrick

The Fathers for English Readers.

ST. PATRICK:

HIS LIFE AND TEACHING.

BY

E. J. NEWELL, M.A.,

Head Master of Neath Proprietary School;

AUTHOR OF "A POPULAR HISTORY OF THE ANCIENT BRITISH CHURCH," ETC.

PUBLISHED UNDER THE DIRECTION OF THE TRACT COMMITTEE.

LONDON:
SOCIETY FOR PROMOTING CHRISTIAN KNOWLEDGE,
NORTHUMBERLAND AVENUE, CHARING CROSS, W.C.;
43, QUEEN VICTORIA STREET, E.C.; 97, WESTBOURNE GROVE, W.
BRIGHTON: 135, NORTH STREET.
NEW YORK: E. AND J. B. YOUNG AND CO.

PREFACE.

This little book is an attempt to supply what has long been an evident want, by furnishing a cheap and accurate sketch of the life and teaching of Britain's first missionary and Ireland's great Apostle. The life of a saint, if wisely studied, will foster saintliness; the life of a hero will lead to heroism. St. Patrick was both saint and hero, and yet was beset by infirmities and sins, like the weakest. But he overcame, and his victory may encourage others.

I have consulted modern authorities, and have illustrated the customs of St. Patrick's age and church from all sources at my command, but have based my narrative of his life and conception of his character upon his own writings and upon ancient records. Thanks to recent criticism and research, it is now possible to distinguish among early documents between the false lives and the true: between the legendary impostor who has been dignified by Patrick's name, and the historic Patrick, the saintly Apostle of Ireland. Two great scholars especially have rendered invaluable service to seekers after the truth—the late Rev. Dr. Todd in his "St. Patrick, Apostle of Ireland," and Dr. Whitley Stokes, who, in his edition of "The Tripartite Life of Patrick, with other Docu ments relating to that Saint," has fully demonstrated the Tripartite Life to be a comparatively late composition, and has exhaustively treated the whole subject in a manner which places all subsequent students of St. Patrick's life under the deepest obligations of gratitude and respect. I have made use of both these works, as also of the valuable edition of St. Patrick's writings in "Councils and Ecclesiastical Documents relating to Great Britain and Ireland," edited by the late Rev. A. W. Haddan and the present Bishop of Oxford, and of many other authorities to which references are given in my foot-notes.

There are many details of St. Patrick's life which are still matter of discussion, and it would be unwise and scarcely possible absolutely to ignore this fact in any biography. I have not attempted the impossible, but have aimed rather at making discussion interesting where it is inevitable, and have in such cases taken my readers into my confidence, declaring what I believe to be the truth, and indicating by notes or in the text the grounds of my belief. The character of St. Patrick's teaching and of St. Patrick's church is an integral part of the history of his labours; and in treating thereof I have felt it incumbent upon me to show the difference between the legendary and the historic Patrick, and the necessity of discriminating between them.

I hope that this book may give help to some, and lead to a fuller knowledge of the life of a saint who is well known, indeed, by name, but whose marvellous personality is not so generally appreciated as it deserves to be. At a time like the present, when Celtic problems are prominent, if not predominant, the study of the history of the Celtic Saint who, by his self-devotion changed the beliefs of the Irish people, and for ever won their love, may have a certain opportuneness. Mr. Ruskin, in a letter on the Choice of Books, has said :—" There are many saints whom it is much more desirable to know the history of [than St. Augustine]—St. Patrick to begin with—especially in present times."

E. J. NEWELL.

July, 1890.

CONTENTS.

CHAP.		PAGE
I.	—Birth and Boyhood	1
II.	—Captivity and Escape	21
III.	—Training by Adversity	32
IV.	—The Source and Date of St. Patrick's Mission	47
V.	—The Religions of Ireland	55
VI.	—Landing in Ireland and Early Successes	75
VII.	—St. Patrick at Tara...	87
VIII.	—Work in Meath and Journey to Tirawley	99
IX.	—Training of Pupils and Founding of Churches	110
X.	—Work in Connaught	131
XI.	—Completion of the Great Journey— Founding of Armagh, and Death of St. Patrick	140
XII.	—The Writings of St. Patrick	152
XIII.	—The Two Patricks, Historical and Legendary	165
XIV.	—The Teaching of St. Patrick	189
XV.	—St. Patrick's Church	204

ST. PATRICK:

HIS LIFE AND TEACHINGS.

CHAPTER I.

BIRTH AND BOYHOOD.

THE saintly life should frequently be the subject of study, as it presents an example which reflects in a measure the ideal life of the Divine Son of Man, of which it is an Imitation. All Christians are "called to be saints," but there are various types of the saintly character. Some are called to pursue "the trivial round, the common task," and to find in the quiet, unselfish fulfilment of small duties, even in the sweeping of a room, "as for His laws" and "for His sake," the blessing of their holy calling; others have to prove that "even in a palace life can be lived well." Some again find their vocation in the patient endurance of sickness, or of ill-success and contumely; others suffer the keener trial of worldly honour and prosperity, and hide the sackcloth of penitence beneath the brave garments of noble rank. Some are called to a life of ascetic rigour; there are others,

> "Whose sweet subdual of the world
> The worldling scarce can recognise."

Each has his vocation, and those who would lead the saintly life therein may have it fostered within them by the study of the lives of the saints of old, the Church's militant heroes, who like the followers of Columba had minds prepared for the red martyrdom of a violent death, or for the white martyrdom of continual mortification. Few of these early saints are likely to attract sympathy so widely as the loving and loveable St. Patrick. The stained may learn from him, for his record is not stainless; he is one of those who have risen to higher things " on stepping-stones of their dead selves." Those who are disappointed and failures may be encouraged, for his life was not a life of uniform success—for thirty years after boyhood it was in large measure a discomfort to himself and was to all appearance of little use to others. But in the end all things were his,—holiness, success, usefulness, and even what he little prized, worldly renown and the veneration of posterity—and he attained these rewards because he sought first the kingdom of God, and had a firm faith in the Invisible.

Patrick is the first great missionary whom Britain sent forth, and, if only for this fact, his life should be studied well by all Britons. There are but few names preserved of Christians of the British communion who lived before him; we find twelve in all in calendars, martyrologies, and council records;[1] and to most of

[1] Alban, Aaron, Julius, Socrates, Stephanus, martyrs; Augulus (otherwise Agulus, Augulius, Agabus, Aygulus), bishop and martyr; Mellon, bishop of Rouen; Eborius, Restitutus, and Adelfius, bishops at Council of Arles; Sacerdos, priest, and Arminius, deacon, at the same council. I omit more doubtful names, as Lucius, Amphibalus, etc.

these the addition of the words martyr, bishop, or priest exhausts our knowledge of their history. How little indeed we know even of St. Alban and St. Mellon! Students still discuss whether the British Church of the Roman occupation was mainly composed of Roman slaves and freedmen, "the poorer class of that mixed race of immigrants which clustered round the chief Roman colonies;"[1] or whether it was from the very first an essentially native church.[2] It grew in silence, like the temple of old; it has left no gorgeous buildings, no relics of greatness; the luxurious villas of the wealthy knew little of it;[3] it was long the church of the poor, but it was pure in doctrine.[4] "Happy the nation which has no history" is not a motto which can ordinarily be well transferred and adapted to a branch of the Church Militant, but it might be fitly applied to the British Church. Its obscurity is no sign of any lack of vitality; but when history begins to throw some greater light upon it, it tells the story of the Pelagian heresy, from which, however, the Church quickly recovered to become greater and nobler than before.

Patrick "the sinner," as with true humility he calls himself in his "Confession," was born some time towards the end of the fourth century, and probably about the

---

[1] *The Churches of the British Confession* in Haddan's "Remains," 218.
[2] So Dr. Brewer, *Quarterly Review*, vol. 147, 518, &c.
[3] The lack of remains led Mr. T. Wright even to deny its existence. See "The Celt, the Roman, and the Saxon," 2nd ed. 300-3.
[4] According to the testimony of Athanasius, Hilary, &c. Haddan and Stubbs, "Councils," i. 7-11.

year 394. His father was Calpornus or Calpurnius, a deacon, and also a decurion, of a Roman colony. His grandfather was Potitus, a priest, the son of Odissus.[1] Of his mother and her family he says nothing, but his early biographer, Muirchu, states that her name was Concessa.[2]

Patrick was born somewhere in "the Britains," or the Roman provinces of Britain, for he calls these his native country, and says that he had relations there. " How could I," he says in one place, " leave these and go into the Britains, though I wished to do so; though I was most willing and ready to go, as to my native land and relations;[3] and not this only; but also as far as the Gauls to visit my brethren, to see the face of the saints of my Lord!"[4] In another place he says, " And again after a few years I was in the Britains with my parents,[5] who received me as a

---

[1] *Confession*, in Haddan and Stubbs' "Councils," ii., 2, 296. There may be a doubt whether the word "priest" in the "Confession" refers to Potitus or Odissus. The words "son of Odissus" (filii Odissi) are introduced in the margin of the " Book of Armagh " between " Potitus " and " priest " (Potiti presbyteri), but occurs in no other MS. The " Hymn of Fiacc " states that Patrick was " son of Calpurn, son of Potitus, grandson of Deacon Odisse."

[2] In Brussels codex of Muirchu's life. Later stories make her a Frank by nation, and a sister, or near relation, of St. Martin of Tours. The " Book of Leinster " (W.S. 549) says " Ondbaiuin or Gombauin of Britain was mother of Patrick and of his five sisters. Or Concess or Cochmas was her name." Todd ("St. Patrick, 354, *note*) reads " Gondbaum." The sisters of Patrick were said to be Lupait, Tigris, Darerca, Ricend, or Richell, or Cinnenum, and Liamain. A brother, Deacon Sannan, is mentioned. All this is late.

[3] *Parentes*.

[4] *Confession* in H. and S., ii. 2, 309.

[5] Or "relations," *parentibus*.

son, and prayed me earnestly that then at least after so great tribulations, which I had endured, I should never depart from them."[1] Patrick also states that his father was of the village Bannavem Taberniae, and had a farm near there, from which the saint was carried away captive when he was nearly sixteen.[2] He does not in so many words assert that this village was his birthplace, but this is probably implied.[3]

There has been much discussion of rather an unprofitable kind about the place of Patrick's birth. It ought to be admitted that Patrick knew best, and in particulars as to which he leaves us in doubt it is probably safer to follow early traditions than to accept modern guesses. The identification of Bannavem Taberniae with Bononia Tarvannae or Tarabannae, which is said to have been an ancient name of Boulogne,[4] is just sufficiently ingenious and sufficiently baseless to lead astray that uncritical class which is attracted by a false etymology, or a rash emendation of a text. Patrick's statement that he was born in "the Britains" can hardly be extended so as to include Boulogne, and the theory gains little support from the late stories which connect the saint's family with Brittany. It will chiefly recommend itself to such as would prefer that Ireland should receive

---

[1] Ib. ii. 2 303.   [2] Ib. ii. 2 295.
[3] Dr. Todd (St. Patrick, 355) expresses astonishment that this inference is so generally drawn. His theory is that Patrick was born at Dumbarton, but sailed to Brittany with his parents on a visit to relations there; that Bannavem Taberniac was in "Armoric Britain," and that Patrick was carried off from thence. All this is based upon the *late* authority of the Scholiast on "Fiacc's Hymn."
[4] This is the theory Dr. Lanigan.

benefit from France rather than from Britain. A still bolder claim has been advanced on behalf of Ireland itself,[1] and a highly rhetorical passage has been quoted in its support from Patrick's Epistle to the Subjects of Coroticus, in which the saint identifies himself with his people. "Perhaps," he says, "they do not believe that we have received one baptism, and have one God as Father; to them it is a disgrace that we have been born in Ireland."[2] But with regard to this, as to some other statements of Patrick, it is necessary to bear in mind that the saint was full of Celtic fervour, and that a strictly literal interpretation of his language may sometimes be misleading.[3] In the very same Epistle, as also in his "Confession," he speaks of himself as a foreign resident in Ireland. "Did I come,"[4] he says, " to Ireland without God, or according to the flesh? Who compelled me? I am bound by the Spirit not to see any of my kindred . . . . . I am a slave in Christ, delivered to a foreign nation on account of the ineffable glory of everlasting life, which is in Christ Jesus our Lord."

In any inquiry respecting Patrick's birthplace, we must first accept his statement that he was born in one of the Roman provinces of Britain, and we must

---

[1] Usher, *Antiq.* 820, 821, mentions an author, Matthæus Florilegus, who calls Patrick in one place a "Scot" *(Scotus)*, and in another, an "Irishman" *(Hibernensis)*. Before the 10th century, "Scot" always means Irishman.

[2] H. and S. ii. 318.

[3] One of Patrick's rhetorical expressions gave rise to a ridiculous story that he was a Jew by descent. See Todd, "St. Patrick," 362 *note;* Dr. W. Stokes, 357 *note*, and 668.

[4] H. and S., ii. 316.

seek for Bannavem Taberniae on the west coast. A Welsh tradition, recorded in the Silurian "Catalogue of Saints," states that he was the son of Mawon,[1] and a native of the beautiful peninsula of Gwyr, now Gower, in Glamorgan. His name is said to have been Padrig Maenwyn. The authority for these statements is not a very high one; and the further tradition related in the "Pedigrees of the Saints," that Padrig, the son of Mawon, was the first principal of the college of Illtyd, now Llantwit Major, in Glamorgan, and that he was carried away captive thence by the Irish, is refuted by Patrick's own statement that he was nearly sixteen at the time of his captivity, which would be rather young for the principal of a College.[2] Welsh writers, however, have done their best to connect Patrick with their country. The ancient Lives of St. David state that the future Apostle of Ireland sought to settle in the valley of Rosina, where St. David's Cathedral now stands, but was warned by an angel that the place was reserved for a boy who was to be born thirty years afterwards. This boy was St. David. Patrick then by a miracle was shown the whole of Ireland, whither he was to go, from a spot in the valley which was afterwards pointed out as "Patrick's Seat."[3] Near this place in ancient

[1] This name is curiously like Maun, which Nennius says was Patrick's name before his consecration, and which seems to correspond with Magonus, the name which late writers say was given him by St. German.
[2] See further for these stories, Professor Rees' "Essay on the Welsh Saints," 128, where they are examined and rejected.
[3] *Vita Sancti David* in Rees' "Cambro-British Saints, 118, 119; *Buchedd Dewi Sant*, ib., 102, 103. The same story is re-

times there stood a chapel dedicated to St. Patrick, the only instance of a Welsh dedication to the saint.[1]

These stories rather indicate Welsh interest in the saint than any connection on his part with Wales, though if he were a British Celt and of the Brythonic branch, he would be of the same race as the Welsh. The earliest traditions place Patrick's birthplace in Nemtria or at Nemthor, which seems to have been on the coast of Northern Britain. This was the opinion of Muirchu, who wrote in the seventh century, with Patrick's "Confession" before him, and whose Life of St. Patrick, together with another early Life by Tirechan, is contained in the "Book of Armagh."[2] "Patrick," he says, "who was also called Sochet, was a Briton by nation, and born in the Britains, sprung from Calpurnius, a deacon, the son, as he himself says, of Potitus, a priest, who was of the village of Bannavem Taburniae, not far from our sea, which village we have uniformly and without doubt discovered to be of Nemtria." The copyist who wrote the existing manuscript probably did not understand the word "Nemtria," but there is little doubt that Nemtria, or Nentria, is the true reading of the passage.[3] An early poem, the date of which is pro-

---

ferred to by manuscript B of *Annales Cambriæ*, which has under "XIV. *Annus*" (supposed by the editor to be A.D. 458), "St. Dewi is born in the 30th year after the departure of Patrick from Menevia."

[1] Llanbadrig ("Patrick's Church") in Anglesey is said to have been named after another Padrig, the son of Aelfred ab Goronwy. Rees' "Essay on the Welsh Saints," 129 *note*.

[2] For a description of the "Book of Armagh" and the writings of Muirchu and Tirechan, see chapters xii. xiii.

[3] This passage is only contained in the Brussels codex, for the

bably the eighth century, states that "Patrick was born at Nemthor."[1] The later legends repeat these statements, and one author[2] follows closely the words of Muirchu, but with a slight addition, and says that Patrick was of the village of Bannavem, of the region Tiburnia, in the province of Nentria,[3] "where giants are said to have lived formerly."

Nemthor, otherwise spelled Nempthor, would be equivalent to an original Nemptodurum or Nemetoduron,[4] and Nemtria or Nentria is evidently a Latin form coined from the Celtic name. Nentur or Nevtur occurs as a place-name in a very ancient Welsh poem preserved in the Black Book of Carmarthen,[5] and this has been supposed to be the same as Nemthor.

---

first page of the "Book of Armagh" is lost. Dr. Whitley Stokes reads "Nemtrie," viz., Nemtriæ, and adds in a note, "MS. uentre prius venitre (?). Hogan." See W.S., 494.

[1] The so-called "Hymn of Fiacc." W.S., 405.

[2] Probus, author of Colgan's "Quinta Vita," of the 10th century, according to Dr. Whitley Stokes. Colgan's "Quarta Vita" (of the 9th century) makes Nemthur a town in the Campus Taberniae, the "Secunda Vita" (10th century) and "Tertia Vita" (10th century) state both that Patrick was born in Nemthur, and that he was born in the Campus Taberniae, placing these statements side by side without explanation.

[3] In another place, Neutria. Dr. Lanigan, in order to satisfy the necessities of the Boulogne theory, conjectures Neustria.

[4] Whitley Stokes, cxxxvii. This was in the fifth century the name of Mont Valérien, at the foot of which now stands the town of Nanterre.

[5] Dr. Whitley Stokes reads Nentur, but Mr. Skene reads Nevtur or Neutur, and justifies this as the Welsh equivalent for the old Irish Nemthur. See "Celtic Scotland," ii. 437 note, where he refutes the idea that the name is properly Entur, and that the initial N belongs to the article. See also Skene's "Four Ancient Book of Wales," ii., 3; also i., 222; and ii., 321.

If this be indeed so, it may perhaps be inferred that in early times the place was fairly well known. A commentator informs us that Nemthor was the old name of the place which was afterwards better known as Alt-Clut, Ail Cluade, or Alclud, "the Rock of Clyde,"[1] the same which the Goidelic Celts called Dunbrettan, "the fortress of the Brythons," and which we now by a slight change speak of as Dumbarton. The commentator probably wrote in the eleventh century,[2] but the memory of an ancient place-name may have lasted until that date, for such names frequently linger on long after all trustworthy history of the early inhabitants has perished. The author of the "Tripartite Life of St. Patrick," who may have been contemporary with the commentator,[3] states that Patrick was "of the Britons of Ail-Cluade," and that he was born in Nemthor; and in the fabulous narrative of his childhood the same author uses the two place-names as interchangeable.[4] The still later Lebar Brecc Homily on St. Patrick[5] similarly identifies the two places, and until a comparatively modern period it was universally accepted, except, perhaps, by the Welsh, that Patrick was born either at Dumbarton or in its neighbourhood. Local tradi-

---

[1] "*In Nemthor*, that is a city which is in North Britain, namely, Ail Cluade."—Scholiast on "Hymn of Fiacc," W.S. 413.

[2] According to Dr. Whitley Stokes, cxxxi.

[3] Dr. Whitley Stokes places him also in the eleventh century.

[4] "In Nemthor that boy was reared." "Trip. Life" in W.S., 9. "Once the reeve of the King (that is, of the Britons) went to announce to Patrick and his foster-mother that they should go to cleanse the hearth of the Palace of Ail Cluaide," ib. 15.

[5] Of the 13th century, according to Dr. Whitley Stokes.

tion points out Old Kilpatrick on the Clyde, near Dumbarton, and close to a small range of hills called the Kilpatrick Hills, as the exact spot. Opposite Old Kilpatrick there is a large rock in the river, visible at low water, which is called St. Patrick's stone, and concerning which there is a legend that the vessel containing the saint struck thereon in full sail on setting out for Ireland and received no damage.[1] The chapel of Dumbarton Castle was dedicated to St. Patrick, as were also the parish church of Dumbarton, East and West Kilpatrick, Chapel Hill, and the parish of Dalziel in Lanarkshire ; and in the last-named the Holy Well of St. Patrick was long an object of veneration and a place for the resort of pilgrims.[2]

The only difficulty in the way of accepting the traditional site of Patrick's birthplace is a doubt whether at the end of the fourth century there could have been a town with decurions so far north as the estuary of the Clyde. The difficulty is grave, but perhaps not insuperable, for our knowledge of the condition of affairs in Britain at the time is far from exact. The position of the Dumbarton district excellently fulfils all the necessities of the narrative furnished by Patrick in his "Confession," and also corresponds to Muirchu's description of Nemtria, and the majority of modern students have agreed in following the old tradition.[3] No other district of

[1] Innes, *Origines Parochiales*, ii. 20.
[2] Moran's "Irish Saints in Great Britain," 133.
[3] Among others the Bishop of Oxford and the Rev. A. W. Haddan, "Councils," i. 12 ; Dr. Todd, " St. Patrick," 355 *et seq.* ; Professor G. T. Stokes, " Ireland and the Celtic Church," 36-7 ; Prebendary Scarth, " Roman Britain," 211 ; Dr. Whitley Stokes also inclines to the same opinion, " Tripartite Life, etc.," cxxxvii.

Britain presents so good a claim. Glastonbury[1] was rather the Celtic paradise than the birthplace of Celtic saints; no tradition asserts that Patrick was born there, though it is said that he, like the hero Arthur, like his own pupil Benignus, and like St. Indract and St. Brigid, "no mean inhabitants of Ireland," "passed" to that quiet retreat when the chief labours of his life were over.[2] But "the island valley of Avilion" is the home of myth and romance, as beautiful, perhaps as baseless, as a dream. A site near the Wall of Hadrian,[3] and the town of Usk in Monmouthshire,[4] have each had an advocate, but neither suggestion is likely to win general acceptance, and if the old tradition be rejected, it will be extremely difficult to establish any other claim.[5] We may, I think, conclude that on

[1] It has been suggested by the editor of the Senchus Mor (vol. ii., pp. xiii., *et. sq.*) that Nemthor was St. Michael's Tor near Glastonbury.

[2] William of Malmesbury, *Gesta Regum Ang.*, i., 22-4. "Avalon," says Mr. A. Nutt, "is certainly the equivalent of the Irish Tir na n-Og, the land of youth, the land beyond the waves, the Celtic paradise. When or how this Cymric myth was localised at Glastonbury we know not. We only know that Glastonbury was one of the first places in the island to be devoted to Christian worship. Is it too rash a conjecture that the Christian church may have taken the place of some Celtic temple or holy spot specially dedicated to the cult of the dead, and of that Lord of the Shades from which the Celts feigned their descent?" "Studies on the Legend of the Holy Grail," 223.

[3] Banna, placed by the Ravenna Cosmography between Æsica and Uxellodunum; also mentioned in an inscription on a bronze cup found in Wiltshire.

[4] It has been suggested that Bannavem Taberniae may be *Bona venta Burrii*, "the street Bona Venta of Usk."

[5] Bannavem ("Book of Armagh"), Banavem (three other MSS. of the "Confession"), Banaven (the MS. followed by the *Acta*

the whole it is probable that the scenery of the Clyde estuary was familiar to the boyish gaze of Patrick.

But the view which met Patrick's eyes fifteen hundred years ago was very different from that which now meets ours. The modern Kilpatrick gives its name to a railway station. Its site in Patrick's days marked the western termination of the Roman Wall of Antoninus. There was no city of Glasgow then; there were, perhaps, a few huts around the Molendinar Burn, for Ninian, the Apostle of the Southern Picts, consecrated a cemetery there a few years after

---

Sanctorum,) has been supposed to stand for Bon or Bun-Amhain, "river foot." So Todd, 357, but this is not universally accepted by Celtic scholars. The old lives translate Bannavem by *campus.* Dr. W. Stokes says (p. 494 *note*), " Bannavem Taburniae seems to mean " campus tabernaculorum," see Tertia Vita, c. 1." *Taburnie* and *Taburne* are found in some of the old lives in place of Taberniae, the reading of all the MSS. of the " Confession." A very ingenious explanation of Bannavem Taberniae has been advanced by the Rev. Edmund McClure in the " Academy," October 20, 1888, " Somerset and Dorset Notes and Queries," vol. i., pp. 150, 151. He says:—"'Bon' or 'bun' is the Irish form for base or foot, and is frequently applied to the foot of a river, *e.g.*, Bun-doran, Bun-an-Dall (the foot of the river Dall), etc., etc. ' Aven ' is beyond doubt the Irish Amhain, pronounced Avon, and the genitive case of the form Amhan, meaning river. ' Taberniae ' is, I take it, the genitive case, with the initial eclipsed, of the old name of the Severn, known to the Welch now as Hafren, but heard by the Romans from lips which made the first letter an S. ' Sabern,' ' Sabrina.' The River Severn. ' Bun,' I might add, is cognate with English Bottom (properly Botten), German *Boden*, Latin *Fundus*. As to the eclipse of ' S ' by ' T ' after the nasal ' n,'' see Zeuss' *Gram. Celtica*, Ebel's edition, p. 185. Familiar instances of this will occur to many—*e.g.*, Mac-an-Saor, Son of the carpenter, becomes the family name MacIntyre. Mac-an-Sagart (*sacerdos*), Son of the priest, becomes Mac-an-Taggart, or simply MacTaggart."

Patrick's birth;[1] but long after his time Cathures, as the place was called, was still small and unimportant, when Alclud, or Dumbarton, was the capital of the kingdom of Rhydderch the Liberal.[2] The water of the Clyde was still clear and pure; Renfrew, Port Glasgow, Greenock, Gourock—all those manufacturing and seaport towns, which now pollute the air with their smoke and the water with their sewage—were non-existent. A few Roman galleys, or a fleet of boats manned by Irish pirates, were all the craft that ever navigated that estuary which is now so busy; and Roman watch-towers, built to protect the district against piratical incursions, diversified the scenery of the southern bank.

The Roman road, running northward from Carlisle, reached the estuary of the Clyde beyond Paisley, at Camelon, on the water of Carron, where there was a Roman town. Probably on the southern bank, and beneath the shelter of the Wall of Antoninus on the northern side of the Clyde, might be seen pleasant farms and fertile crops; but much even of the Lowlands of Scotland must have remained what it was in the time of Agricola, a country of shaggy woods and watery fens. Patrick's birthplace was close to the Highlands. Loch Lomond and its mountains are a very little way off, and the Highlands were still in their primitive condition. Lollius Urbicus, the lieutenant of Antoninus, had carried the Roman

---

[1] *Vita S. Kentigerni*, "Historians of Scotland," v. 179.

[2] Rhys' "Celtic Britain," 142-143. Rhydderch made Alclud his capital after the Battle of Ardderyd A.D. 573. Kentigern was his contemporary, and founded his see at Cathures, where Ninian had previously consecrated his cemetery.

arms in his day as far as the Moray Firth, but civilisation had since receded. Perthshire, now the lovely garden of Scotland, to which so many resort each summer for health and enjoyment, was covered by the Caledonian Forest, and much of what is now Dumbartonshire was probably similarly wooded. To Patrick "the forest dark," "savage and stern," must have been from boyhood a very evil thing, as it was to Dante, for man usually dreads unconquered nature; and the dense forests of Caledonia, from which only the summits of the mountains emerged, constituted the most impressive and appalling feature of its scenery. The love of nature, which has been a characteristic of the mediæval and modern Celt, showed itself first in an affection for the sights and sounds of the sea, which finds expression in an early Irish poem ascribed to Columba; the land, except where tilled or otherwise claimed by man's labour, presented in that early period too repellant an aspect to inspire any feeling but dread. Wild beasts were numerous; the Scotch bear is mentioned by Martial; wolves abounded, and in hard winters probably scoured the country in packs, as they do now in Russia; the wild ox, the wild boar, and the stag were hunted by the Romans and the natives.[1]

Even now Britain appears to foreigners to be in the winter a land of the Cimmerians.[2] In Patrick's days the climate of the Clyde district was probably worse than it is now; the rainfall was greater, and the air moister; there was more fog and less bright sunshine. The rivers

[1] Scarth, "Roman Britain," 187, 188.
[2] Taine, "Notes on England."

were swollen by the rains, and formed larger estuaries than they do now; remains of Roman barges are found far inland on the banks of the Firths of Clyde and Forth. So inclement a climate was naturally detrimental to the health of the Roman legionaries, and the inscriptions in Northern Britain show that deaths at an early age were common, in spite of the warm clothing generally worn and other precautions taken against the cold and dampness. Titania's picture of an unhealthy year might, with a few changes, be transferred to the climate of Northern Britain during the Roman period :—[1]

> " Therefore the winds, piping to us in vain,
> As in revenge, have suck'd up from the sea
> Contagious fogs, which falling in the land
> Have every pelting river made so proud
> That they have overborne their continents.
>
> * * * * *
>
> Therefore the moon, the governess of floods,
> Pale in her anger, washes all the air,
> That rheumatic diseases do abound."

Bannavem Taberniae was a colony, and Patrick's father, Calpurnius, was one of its decurions, or a member of its town council. It was a Christian town. Patrick's family was clerical, and Calpurnius himself was a deacon. Accordingly Patrick had a Christian training,[2] and received that measure of culture which

---

[1] See for justification of this picture: Elton, "Origins of English History;" Scarth, "Roman Britain;" Ferguson, "Diocesan History of Carlisle."

[2] It is a little curious that no legend-writer has had the imagination to connect Ninian's traditional visit to Cathures or Glasgow with the early life of Patrick. An interesting picture might be made of a visit of Ninian, the friend of St. Martin of Tours (see

a gentleman's son could acquire in a town subject to Roman law and connected with Roman civilisation, but, at the same time, on the very edge of a country of barbarous savages, and far distant from the refined society of those luxurious and elegant villas which were numerous in the districts farther south. The son of the decurion, clergyman, and farmer grew up, as he says himself, "most rustic" and "unlearned," but with a full consciousness of his gentle birth, and with an earnest desire to act up to the motto which antiquity might practise, but moderns had to invent, *Noblesse oblige.* "I was *ingenuus*" (that is, a freeman born free), he says, "according to the flesh; I am the son of a father who was a decurion: for I sold my nobility (I blush not, neither do I repent) for the advantage of others."[1] Like St. Paul he was proud of the name of Roman, and of being a fellow-citizen of the Roman saints. But if Muirchu and Tirechan are to be believed, besides his Roman name Patricius, he had a Celtic name, which is variously written Sochet, Sucat, Succat, or Succet. This is said by some to have been his name with his parents, and is equivalent to the modern Welsh *Hygad*, warlike. It was the appellation of a Cymric war-god.[2] Perhaps

"Vita S. Niniani," ii. Baeda, "Hist. Eccl." iii. 4) to Concessa (whom some traditions make St. Martin's sister or kinswoman) and to her husband Calpurnius at Bannavem Taberniae, and from this meeting might be traced the first awakening of a zeal for Christian missions in the mind of the boy Patrick. There is indeed nothing against this fancy but the total lack of evidence in its favour, and yet how many historical theories have been built up on no more solid basis.

[1] *Ep. ad Christ. Corotici T.S.* in H. & S., ii., 316.
[2] Tirechan says that he found in a book of Bishop Ultan, a bishop

we may imagine that the fervour which is so conspicuous in Patrick's writings has Celtic characteristics, but Roman civilisation was at least a most important factor in the education of Britain's first missionary. Celtic enthusiasm may have incited him to undertake his mission, but Roman discipline and obedience helped him to endure hardness as a good soldier of Christ Jesus, and Roman doggedness and perseverance sustained him in carrying out his plans to a successful issue. He was a Celt in those winning manners which made him so acceptable to the sensitive Irish, who rejected his Roman predecessor, Palladius ; he was a Roman in those powers of control and organisation which enabled him to create a Church adapted to the nation with which he had to do.

In that wild, remote spot of North Britain Patrick had ever before his eyes a monument of the power and of the skilful organisation of Imperial Rome. In his time her hands were growing feeble, but he could see in this specimen of their work what they had formerly been able to effect. The great northern barrier extended from Chapel Hill, near Old Kilpatrick, eastwards as far as Bridgeness, near Carriden, on the Firth of Forth. Agricola had first drawn a line of forts between the two Firths of Forth and Clyde; and Lollius Urbicus, the legate of Antoninus Pius, about

---

of Ardbraccan, who died 656, that Patrick had in all four names, Magonus, Succetus, Patricius, and Cothirthiacus, of which he gives fanciful interpretations. The last, which is written Cothraige in the Irish lives, is probably the Celtic Caturigios. It is said by later writers that the saint was called Patrick by Celestine, Magonus by German, Cothraige by his master, and Succat by his parents.

A.D. 140, enlarged and repaired these, and built others also, and connected them altogether by means of a deep fosse, averaging about forty feet wide and twenty feet deep, and a rampart of earth and stone intermingled, strengthened by sods of turf, which was twenty feet high and twenty-four feet thick. This rampart ran close along the south side of the fosse, and "was surmounted by a parapet, having a level platform behind it for the protection of its defenders." To the south of this again was the military way, twenty feet in width. The forts were placed at intervals of about two miles, and were eighteen or nineteen in number, and between them were smaller watch-towers.[1]

So solidly was this work constructed that it was not destroyed by the assaults of the barbarians or by peaceful encroachments in later ages, but existed in a state of good preservation down to 1726, when it was described, and even later. Men's surroundings have an influence on their destiny; consciously or unconsciously we receive inspiration or discouragement from the sights we see and the sounds we hear. To live in the presence of that great work was a liberal education to a liberal soul; it taught lessons of the greatness and the power of simple indefatigable toil, and those lessons, in after years, Patrick trans-

Possibly these various names may hint that the legendary Patrick, as distinguished from the historical, was a compound of various persons, real and mythological.
[1] Skene, "Celtic Scotland," i., 78. Scarth, "Roman Britain,' 83-87.

lated into action. No great soul could remain "untaught" and "most rustic" in the midst of Roman civilisation, even of an inferior type, and with such a memorial of Roman perseverance and strength ever before its eyes.

CHAPTER II.

CAPTIVITY AND ESCAPE.

THE decline of the Roman power in Britain was already far advanced at the time of Patrick's birth. Not many years previously the adventurer Magnus Maximus had taken away the army and fleet, including the flower of the native youth, when he set out for the continent on his attempt to make himself sole master of the empire ; and, as Gildas sorrowfully relates,[1] those who went with him never returned, for, after a brief career of success, he was overthrown by the Emperor Theodosius, and perished at Aquileia, A.D. 388. Shortly before his departure Maximus had beaten back the unconquered Picts, who with their Scotic allies had, for some time past,[2] been a continuous pest to the Roman governors and to the British provincials ; but the relief thereof afforded was not of long duration, for as soon as his troops had departed the marauders renewed their attacks. These were again checked in the reign of Honorius, about 396, but in 402 the Romans again left the island, and again the barbarians poured into the Roman province.

[1] In the "Historia."
[2] The Scots first joined the Picts in A.D. 360. Rhys' "Celtic Britain," 92.

The son of the farmer of Bannavem Taberniae would hear of all these events, and himself at times might be a witness of a plundering expedition. The colony was an outpost of civilisation, on the very edge of the hostile district, and Rob Roy's county was doubtless full of Rob Roy's prototypes, eager to pursue "the good old rule, the simple plan," and drive off the cattle of the farmers of the Dumbarton district. Patrick must have regarded the marauders, whether native Picts or Irish pirates, in much the same way as Gildas did, with mingled feelings of dread and hostility, and it was by no slight effort of Christian charity that he was afterwards enabled to regard the Scotic Irish as his brethren.

With fighting without there were fears within. The Britons at first showed much weakness in their resistance to the enemy; and this failure on their part was, says Gildas, the consequence of sin. Gildas greatly exaggerates, and throughout acts the preacher rather than the historian, and in some parts is far from accurate. "A monk," remarks the haughty Gibbon, "who, in the profound ignorance of human life, has presumed to exercise the office of historian, strangely disfigures the state of Britain at the time of its separation from the Western Empire." But Patrick's account of himself and his companions is very similar to the lamentation of Gildas over the faults of his fellow-countrymen. "I knew not the true God," says Patrick, and he and his fellow-countrymen who were carried into captivity suffered thus according to their deserts; for, he continues, "We had departed from God and had not kept his precepts, and were not obedient to our priests, who admonished us for our salvation."[1] In another place[2] he repeats the same confession about himself. " I did not believe in the living[3] God from my infancy; but I remained in death and in unbelief until I was greatly chastised." These passages need not be interpreted of any relapse into paganism among the provincials of Bannavem Taberniae, and Patrick's ignorance cannot possibly have been an intellectual ignorance of the truths of Christianity, but was rather a spiritual ignorance. It must not be assumed that Patrick's words are only the unconscious exaggeration of a devout man who abhors himself and his wasted opportunities in the past, and regards his " boyish scrapes and tricks " as gross immoralities.[4] For there was one sin which Patrick committed when he was about fifteen years old, which was to him a bitter memory all through his life. He had done it, so he confesses " in one day; nay, in one hour," and God had forgiven it ; but it was long a burden to him, and once, on account of anxiety and in sorrow, he confessed it to a very dear friend, and that friend felt it his duty to declare it when Patrick sought consecration. The anguish of mind which that revelation caused him is apparent in the short, broken sentences of emotion with which he chronicles the incident in his " Confession."[5] It

[1] *Confession*, H. and S., ii. 2, 296.
[2] *Ib.* 304.
[3] " *Deum vivum non credebam.*" So three MSS. One MS. has *unum* for *vivum*. " I did not believe in *one* God."
[4] Professor G. T. Stokes suggests this interpretation of Patrick's words. " Ireland and the Celtic Church," 43.
[5] H. and S., ii. 2, 304, 305.

was the hand of a very dear friend that dealt him that deadly thrust, which nearly ruined his missionary plans, and filled him with shame and confusion of face before his brethren. He does not tell us what the sin was, and it would be vain to inquire, but it must have been a gross transgression; and if his acknowledgment of his own sinfulness is not an exaggeration, his statement regarding others is without doubt also literally exact. "I knew not the true God, I withdrew from God, I kept not his precepts, nor obeyed my priests," is the true confession of many a soul upon whom "the wrath of God's indignation" has come, only to show itself later, as to Patrick, in the guise of constraining love.

For every year the state of affairs at Bannavem Taberniae grew darker and darker. Constantine the usurper was chosen emperor by the troops sent against the Picts and Scots; and he, like another Maximus, carried away the army and the Britons serving in it to Gaul in 407. The Britons were tired of these succours, which deprived them of their best men, and the Roman emperor was tired of a distant possession which fostered usurpers. Honorius bade the provincials shift for themselves, and they replied by dismissing such Roman officials as yet remained, A.D. 410.

In one of the forays of Irish pirates, which took place about this time, Patrick was made a prisoner. He was carried forth, as he himself says,[1] when he was nearly sixteen, from Bannavem Taberniae, with

---

[1] *Confession.* H. and S., ii. 296.

many thousand others,[1] into Ireland. There, so his
biographers inform us, he was sold to Miliuc,[2] a chief
of Dalaradia, a beautiful district of southern Antrim,
and, like the prodigal son, was sent forth into his
fields to feed swine. The place of his servitude was
the valley of the Braid.

" From the sea it slopes
Unfinished, savage, like some nightmare dream,
Raked by an endless east wind of its own,"

says Mr. Aubrey de Vere :[3] and such may be its
winter aspect; but in summer it is beautiful, and in
Patrick's time the country was covered with woods of
oak. It has been thought that the name of Ballyligpatrick, "the town of Patrick's hollow," near the hill
of Slemish,[4] preserves the memory of the place of
Patrick's abode, and near it are remains of an ancient
rath or fort, which may have been Miliuc's.[5] Opposite the hill of Slemish, and on the other side of the
Braid, is the basaltic hill of Skerry ;[6] and here local
tradition still points out, near the ruins of an old
church, an impression on a patch of rock which is
known as St. Patrick's footmark, but which, according

[1] Dr. Whitley Stokes says that this and similar expressions are
" mere Celtic exaggerations." W.S. cxxxiii.
[2] This is the form of his name in Tirechan, the Tripartite Life,
etc. He is sometimes called Milchu. Tirechan calls him Miluc
maccu-Boin ; *i.e.*, Miliuc, descendant of Buan. On the word *maccu*
see Rhys' " Welsh Philology," 407-412.
[3] Or rather Dichu, in Aubrey de Vere's "Legends of St.
Patrick."
[4] Sliab Miss or Sliabh-mis. " Mons Miss " (Muirchu and
Tirechan).
[5] Professor G. T. Stokes, "Ireland and the Celtic Church," 59.
[6] Anciently Scirit (Muirchu and Tirechan).

to a story as old as Muirchu, was left by the angel Victoricus when he ascended into heaven, while Patrick stood on the opposite hill of Slemish.[1]

In his captivity Patrick began to think seriously; "the Lord opened the perception of his unbelief."[2] He prayed frequently by day as he kept his cattle,[3] and also in the night; so that in a single day he would offer up a hundred prayers, and almost as many in the night; and when he was in the woods or on the mountain, he would rise up before light, in snow, frost, and rain, and felt no evil nor indolence in himself, because the Spirit was burning in him. As he was in this frame of mind, he had a dream, which caused him to leave his master.

"One night," he says, "in sleep I heard a voice saying to me, 'Thou fastest well, thou shalt soon go to thy native land.' And again, after a very little time, I heard an answer saying to me, 'Lo, thy ship is prepared.' And it was not near; but perchance it was two hundred miles away; and I had never been there, nor did I know any one of the men there. And afterwards I betook myself to flight, and left the man with whom I had been six years, and came in the strength of God, who directed my way for good, and[4] I feared nothing until I came to that ship. And on the day on which I came, the ship set out from its place, and I said that I had wherewithal to

---

[1] "Life by Muirchu." W.S. 276; G. T. Stokes, 58; Todd, 374.
[2] "Confession." H. and S., ii. 2, 297.
[3] "Pecora."
[4] "I came to Benum," says one MS., which omits "for good" (*ad bonum*).

sail with them.¹ And it displeased the captain, and he answered sharply and angrily, 'By no means seek to go with us.' And when I heard this, I removed myself from them to go to the hut, where I was lodging,² and on the way I began to pray. And before I ended my prayer, I heard one of them, and he was calling loudly after me: 'Come quickly, for these men call thee.' And forthwith I returned to them, and they began to say to me, 'Come, for we receive you in good faith; make friendship with us in what way you may wish.' And in that day I refused to make friendship with them on account of the fear of God, but in very deed I hoped of them that they would come into the faith of Jesus Christ;³ for they were heathens; and this I obtained from them.⁴ And forthwith we set sail. And after three days we reached land, and for twenty-eight days we journied through a desert. And food failed them, and hunger prevailed over them. And one day the captain began to say to me, 'What, Christian, sayest thou? Thy God is great and almighty; wherefore then canst thou not pray for us, for we are in danger from hunger, for it will be difficult for us ever to see any man.' But I said plainly to them, 'Turn ye with

---

[1] This is the reading of most MSS., but perhaps the reading of the "Book of Armagh" may be rendered as Wright, "Writings of Patrick," 43 (R.T.S.): "I asked them (the sailors) that I might go away and sail with them."

[2] Probably some place in the neighbourhood: Todd (368), seems to prefer to interpret it of a return to his master.

[3] This is Dr. Wright's translation. The Latin is very obscure. See Todd, 368, *note*.

[4] So Hennessy. Dr. Wright, 43, "on account of this I clave to them."

faith to the Lord my God, to whom nothing is impossible, that He may send you food into your path, even till ye are satisfied; for there is everywhere abundance with Him.' And by God's help so it came to pass. Lo, a herd of swine appeared in the way before our eyes, and they killed many of them; and there they remained two nights and were much refreshed. And their dogs were filled, for many of them were left half dead along the way. And after these things they gave great thanks to God; and I was honoured in their eyes. From that day forth they had food in abundance. Also they found wild honey, and offered me part; and one of them said: 'It has been offered in sacrifice.' Thanks be to God, I consequently tasted none of it. But on the same night I was sleeping, and Satan greatly tempted me, as I shall remember as long as I shall be in this body; and he fell upon me as a mighty rock, and I had no power in my limbs. But whence it came into my mind to call Helias, I know not. And in that moment I saw the sun arise in the sky; and while I cried 'Helias, Helias,' with my might, lo, the brightness of that sun fell upon me, and forthwith removed the weight from me. And I believe that I was helped by Christ the Lord, and that His Spirit then cried out for me; and I hope that it will be so in the day of my oppression, as the Lord saith in the Gospel, ' It is not you who speak, but the Spirit of your Father which speaketh in you.' "

The meaning of Patrick's cry in his dream has been much discussed, and if the manuscript reading be followed which I have adopted, the saint himself seems to have been puzzled as to his reason for calling "Helias." "He invoked Helias the prophet to his aid," says the author of the Tripartite Life, "and Helias assisting him freed him from all oppression and attack of the enemy." The mention of the rising of the sun immediately after his cry suggests a connection in his thoughts between Helias and Helios, the Greek word for the sun, an association of names made by the early Christian poet, Sedulius,[1] who may himself have been an Irishman. The Welsh in like manner connected one form of the name of a favourite bishop and saint, Teilo, with the same word Helios.[2] It has even been suggested that Patrick really cried out, not Helias, but "Helios," which might in that case be an involuntary reminiscence of pagan sun-worship, such as was practised in Ireland. One[3] of the writers of the legends of Patrick states that Patrick invoked "Christ, the true Sun, and forthwith the Sun arose upon him." Two other Lives reproduce the exclamation as "Eli," which might have been borrowed by Patrick from the cry of our Lord on the cross.[4] It matters little which of the words was really used by Patrick, as in any case he cannot be fairly charged from this passage either with paganism or with a superstitious invocation of saints.

The extreme rusticity of Patrick's Latin has

---

[1] See Dr. Whitley Stokes, 669.
[2] "Ancient British Church" (S.P.C.K.), 63.
[3] Probus.
[4] Todd (371-3) prefers this as the original reading of the passage.

tempted copyists to correct his expressions in many places, and their corrections sometimes create a fresh difficulty. It is impossible to determine with any certainty what followed after the vision in which he uttered the cry which has been so much debated. The usual and probable interpretation of his language is that he suffered a second captivity, but whether this happened "many" or "not many" years after the first is again a doubtful point. Muirchu, in his Life of the saint, relates that it happened many years after, and on the first night he heard a divine message, "For two months thou shalt be with them; that is, with thine enemies." On the sixtieth day the Lord delivered him from their hands. The divine message and the subsequent deliverance are certainly related by Patrick; but the manuscripts are confused and contradictory; and it is sometimes supposed that the second captivity was the time spent with the pagan sailors, while another supposition is that Patrick refers to a spiritual captivity, a captivity to his Lord.[1]

---

[1] Sir Samuel Ferguson says:—"It was the first occasion on which he had experienced what he conceived to be the presence of an indwelling coercer of his will, in obedience to whose promptings all his subsequent life was to be conformed." The Rev. C. H. H. Wright (pp. 46 and 47) renders the passage as follows, adopting the readings of most MSS.: "And again, after many years, I was taken captive once more. On that first night, therefore, I remained with them. But I heard a Divine response saying unto me, 'But for two months thou shalt be with them,' which accordingly came to pass. On that sixtieth night the Lord delivered me out of their hands. Even on our journey He provided for us food and fire, and dry weather every day, till on the fourteenth day we all arrived. As I stated before, we pursued our journey for twenty-eight days through the desert, and the very night on which we all

arrived we had no food left. And again after a few years I was in the Britains with my parents.'

One MS., printed in the *Acta Sanctorum*, makes everything clear, but perhaps improves matters with an excess of boldness, for it changes altogether the arrangement of the sentences. After the narrative of the vision it continues thus:—" But in our journey He provided for us food and fire and dry weather every day, till on the fourteenth day we came to men, as I stated before. For twenty-eight [days] we pursued our journey through the desert. And the very night on which we came to men we had no food left. And again after a few years I fell into captivity once more. On the first night, indeed, I remained with them. But I heard a Divine response saying unto me, ' For two months thou shalt be with them,' which accordingly came to pass. On that sixtieth night, therefore, the Lord delivered me from their hands. Again, after a few years, I was in Britain with my parents."

Some words are lost in the " Book of Armagh " at the end of the narrative of the dream in which he cried " Helias." It then continues, " Multos adhuc capturam dedi," which seems impossible to be translated without the addition of other words, such as are found in the other MSS.

CHAPTER III.

TRAINING BY ADVERSITY.

PATRICK left Ireland when he was twenty-three years of age; he did not return as bishop, according to his own statement, until he was about forty-five.[1] The interval is the obscurest part of his life, and little light is thrown upon it either by himself or by his biographers. It is clearly impossible that he can have spent thirty years in study, as Muirchu says and

[1] This age is fixed by his statement in the "Confession," that when he was about to be ordained bishop, the fault was brought up against him, which he had committed thirty years before, when he was about fifteen. H. & S. ii, 304: "For after thirty years they found me, and brought against me a word which I had confessed before I was a deacon. Under anxiety, with a troubled mind, I told my most intimate friend what I had one day done in my boyhood, nay, in one hour; because I was not then used to overcome. I know not, God knows, whether I was then fifteen years of age." (Wright's translation, 48, 49.) From this it has been concluded by Dr. Todd (392), Mr. Haddan, and Bishop Stubbs ("Councils," i. 12), and Dr. Skene ("Celtic Scotland"), that Patrick was consecrated at the age of 45. The common story of his biographers is that he was consecrated at the age of 60; and this is followed by Dr. Whitley Stokes (" Trip. Life," &c. cxxxviii.) This computation, however, is part of the fictitious scheme of the chronology of Patrick's life, to which I shall have occasion to refer afterwards (chapter xi.).

TRAINING BY ADVERSITY. 33

Tirechan appears to imply;[1] otherwise he would have learned better Latin than he wrote, and could not have complained of his lack of learning. "I have not learned," he says in one passage of the "Confession," "like others who have drunk in, in most excellent wise, law and sacred literature in both ways equally, and have never changed their language

[1] Tirechan says of the interval (W. S. 302): "In seven other years he walked and sailed among waves, plains and mountain valleys, through the Gauls, and the whole of Italy, and in the islands which are in the Tyrrhenian Sea (*in mari Terreno*), as he himself has said in the account of his labours. Moreover, he was in one of the islands, which is called Aralensis, for thirty years, as Bishop Ultan testified to me. But all things which happened to him you will find plainly written in his history." Tirechan appears here to quote one of the so-called Sayings of Patrick, viz.: "I had the fear of God as the guide of my way through the Gauls and Italy, and also in the islands which are in the Tyrrhenian Sea (*in mari Terreno*)." The *Insola Aralensis* has been conjectured to be the island of Lerins, off Cannes, where Honorat founded a monastery, and where Vincent of Lerins, the brother of St. Lupus, and author of the Commonitorium, dwelt. So Todd, "St. Patrick," 336 *note*. Lerins and its monks are described by Montalembert ("Monks of the West.") But Dr. Whitley Stokes considers Aralensis to be a mistake for Aretalensis, *i.e.*, *Arles*, at the apex of the delta of the Rhone. "Island" in Tirechan's "Life" frequently means "monastery," and "islanders" meant "monks" in Southern Gaul in the time of Patrick. The islands of the Tyrrhenian Sea may therefore be the monasteries of Southern France near the Mediterranean, including both Arles and Lerins. (See W. S. 421.) But whether this is the history of St. Patrick or of Palladius, his predecessor, who also, according to the "Book of Armagh," bore the name of Patrick, is exceedingly doubtful. See Todd, 308 *et seq*. Skene, "Celtic Scotland," ii. 430: "The mission from Pope Celestine and the thirty years' study in Gaul and Italy are entirely inconsistent with St. Patrick's account of himself, and no doubt truly belong to the acts of Palladius."

D

from infancy, but have added ever more and more to its perfection."[1] This would be false modesty, if he had had opportunities of thirty, or even twenty, years of study in the best colleges of Western Europe.[2]

Some modern writers,[3] whose opinion is worthy of the highest respect, have thought that Patrick laboured for some years in Ireland to little purpose as a priest, and then left the country, and sought consecration as a bishop. There is one passage in Patrick's "Confession" which appears at first sight to favour this theory. "You know," he says, "and God knoweth, how I have conducted myself among you from my youth,[4] both in the faith of the truth and in sincerity of heart, even in the case of those nations among whom

---

[1] H. & S. ii. 298.
[2] See W. S. cxxxviii.
[3] Dr. Whitley Stokes, cxxxviii.-cxli. Skene, "Celtic Scotland," ii. 14-26, discusses Patrick's mission and his writings, and considers that he went to Ireland when he was between twenty-five and thirty years old. "If he was taken captive in his sixteenth year, and remained six years in captivity, he was twenty-two when he escaped, and was probably now between twenty-five and thirty years old. He had early been made a deacon, and must at this time have gone into Ireland, probably in priest's orders, for he tells us that he had lived and preached among the Irish from his youth up, and given the faith to the people among whom he dwelt." This is perhaps a little more than Patrick absolutely says, whatever he may be considered to imply. Dr. Todd ("St. Patrick," 391, 392) does not declare himself definitely. "In another passage," he says, "which is also one of those omitted in the Armagh copy, he is made to say that he began his ministry among the Irish whilst as yet a young man. This, if we can credit Probus, was whilst he was still only a priest, and consequently before he was forty-five years old."
[4] "Qualiter conversatus sum inter vos a juventute mea."

I dwell; I have kept faith with them, and will keep it."[1] But such a passage as this must be interpreted in conformity with the general tenor of Patrick's narrative of his mission. Patrick is here borrowing from St. Paul, and appeals to the Irish, just as St. Paul, when he stood before Agrippa, appealed to the knowledge of all the Jews respecting his "manner of life from his youth." It would be quite in accordance with Patrick's usual style of writing, which is highly rhetorical, with a tendency towards hyperbole, to employ terms somewhat loosely when he had such a parallel before his mind; and here, as elsewhere, his language must not be construed too literally.[2] With

---

[1] "Ego fidem illis praestiti [v. L. praestavi] et praestabo." Wright translates as above; Hennessy renders, "I have given the faith to them, and I will continue to do so."

[2] Patrick says that he was carried to Ireland from Bannavem Taberniae with "so many thousand men." Dr. Whitley Stokes says: "His captors took him to Ireland, *with several others*," and adds a note—"Patrick says (in his rustic Latin) *cum tot millia hominum*. So in the Letter to Coroticus (p. 378, l. 22), *cum tot millia solidorum*, and in the Confessio (p. 372, l. 8), *baptizavi tot millia hominum*. Such phrases are mere Celtic exaggerations." (W. S. cxxxiii.) Dr. Whitley Stokes is chiefly led to accept the theory that Patrick laboured first as a priest in Ireland, because he accepts the tradition that he first came to Ireland in the sixtieth year of his age. He argues that he would have forgotten Irish in the interval of thirty-seven years, and that his ardent nature would not have allowed him to postpone his attempt so long. But if Patrick came to Ireland at the age of 45, as is inferred by Mr. Skene, Dr. Todd, and in Haddan and Stubbs' "Councils," much of the difficulty is removed. It is not a very great strain upon language for an old man to speak of the age of 45 as his "youth," and the classical use of the Latin word *juventus* would justify, or almost justify, such an expression.

one exception all early writers deny by implication any knowledge of such a mission; and the only one who mentions it belongs to the tenth century, and connects it directly with an appearance of the Lord to Patrick, when the saint was invited to the Lord's right hand, and was commanded to go to Ireland, and preach there the word of eternal life. The islanders, we are told, spurned his preaching; and accordingly Patrick felt the need of a commission from the Roman Pontiff, and prayed the Lord to lead him to the see of the holy Roman church, that the tribes of the Irish might become Christians through his instrumentality, after he had received the authority of preaching Christ's word with confidence. The sole purpose of the story, as given by this writer, appears to be the exaltation of the Papal commission above that given by the Lord Himself.[1]

What is more important even than the ignorance of ancient writers is that the general sense of Patrick's writings is strongly against an early mission. He confesses that he neglected the call of God for some time. "I did not quickly yield, according to what had been pointed out to me and the Spirit was, nevertheless, suggesting." The Lord had pity on him for his negligence, and recognized his readiness

---

[1] This is the story of Probus. He says that Patrick was ordained priest by Bishop Senior. Mr. Skene quotes a statement in the Epistle to the Subjects of Coroticus, where Patrick says he had sent a letter by a holy priest, "whom I have taught from infancy." "If he had taught this priest from his infancy, he must himself have been long in Ireland." But he may have been there many years as a bishop. Here again the word "infancy" seems slightly rhetorical.

of heart, for he knew how many hindered his mission and disparaged himself, saying, "As for this fellow, why does he put himself in danger among enemies who know not God?" This they said, not through malice, but because of his rusticity. "And," says Patrick, "I did not quickly recognize the grace which was then in me; now I know that I ought before to have obeyed the call of God."[1] In another place he says that he did not willingly go to Ireland until he was almost worn out,[2] for he was chastised and humbled by hunger and nakedness.

We may conclude that the twenty-two years of Patrick's life after his escape from his master were not years of peaceful study, nor of missionary work in Ireland; they were years of much suffering and privation, of hunger and nakedness, of many great tribulations. After his escape from Miliuc he probably suffered a second captivity, and on his deliverance from this he did not return to Britain immediately, for it was a few years before he was with his relations in the Britains, and all these years had been years of hardship. Where he was during this time we know not. Possibly he was wandering about the Gauls, in Italy, and among the "islands" of the Tyrrhenian Sea;[3] but if so, it was not necessarily as a student. When again he returned to the Britains he had formed the plan of being a missionary to the Irish, but his relations opposed him, and begged him not to leave them again. He was, probably at least,

---

[1] *Confession*, H and S., 309-310.
[2] Ib. 304. Donec prope deficiebam.
[3] *Sayings of Patrick* in the "Book of Armagh," W.S. 301.

in deacon's orders, but he received no encouragement from his clerical brethren; they despised his rusticity; if Ireland was to be converted, Patrick at least, so they thought, was not the man for the work. Some of "his seniors" were offended by his presumption; and, overborne by the general opposition, he doubted the heavenly call; he feared that he was really, as they said, too rustic and too unlearned to do any good : he postponed the undertaking from day to day and from year to year. Meanwhile he may have laboured as a missionary among the forests of Cumbria.[1] But still he could not rest contented with clerical work in his own country; his mind was ever full of thoughts of Ireland; he would doubtless take every opportunity of talking with Scotic captives, in order to keep his memory of their language

[1] "Three churches in Westmoreland and one in Cumberland have the title of St. Patrick : those of Patterdale, the old name of which was Patrickdale, Bampton Patrick and Preston Patrick. We are told that near the Chapel in Patterdale is St. Patrick's Well, which confirms the dedication in that case. Some doubt is thrown upon the other two dedications by the fact that both of these places belonged to Patrick of Culwen, or Curwen, the great-grandson of Gospatrick, son of Orme, son of Ketel."—Rev. E. Venables in "Transactions of Cumberland and Westmoreland Antiquarian and Archæological Society," vii. 123. See also ib. vi. 328. "Diocesan History of Carlisle" (S.P.C.K.), by Chancellor Ferguson, p. 32. The Cumberland dedication, that of the Church of Ousby, is doubtful. If the Church of Patterdale were really founded by St. Patrick, I should be inclined to place his missionary work thereabout in the earlier part of his life, rather than, as suggested by the Rev. T. Lees and Chancellor Ferguson, in the latter half of the fifth century. I have elsewhere explained the Celtic custom of calling a church after the name of its founder. "Popular History of the Ancient British Church" (S.P.C.K.), 25, 181.

fresh. If by day he could keep his thoughts fixed on his own work, by night upon his bed the thought of Ireland recurred to him; he saw visions, he heard voices calling to him, as his great hero St. Paul heard the man of Macedonia; they begged him to come over and help them, and he saw a messenger with letters containing their petition. Moreover, he had visions of comfort. The church thought him too mean to be a missionary, and he felt grievously his own deficiencies, and acknowledged that the thought was not malicious on the part of his brethren; yet the visions told him that the Lord was on his side. Then he heard of the visit of German of Auxerre and Lupus of Troyes to Britain; he learned how they had put the Pelagians to the rout at the Synod of Verulamium (A.D. 429), and how the soldier-saint routed, too, the Picts and Saxons [1] in another kind of combat. Perhaps he saw that gallant king of men, that ascetic saint, who breathed new life into the dead bones of British Christianity, and raised up the "exceeding great army" of its later saints. At any rate Patrick went out to Gaul and received (probably from German) all that measure of instruction for which, as a slave turned student in middle age, he was qualified. If he learned "small Latin and less Greek," he at least learned his Bible well, and became mighty in the Scriptures. He learned, too, to

---

[1] Some suppose from this mention of Saxons by Constantius, in his "Life of St. German," that Saxon irruptions took place at an earlier date than Beda mentions. So also Prosper says that in 441 "Britanniæ usque ad hoc tempus variis cladibus eventibusque latæ, in ditionem Saxonum rediguntur."

love the brethren in Gaul the saints of the Lord, and long afterwards in Ireland he looked back to the happy days he had spent among them, and longed to see their faces.[1] At last he was consecrated bishop, but not by German, and only after a renewal of opposition, at this time on the ground of his boyish sin.

This is not a fancy picture; in all its main incidents it may be justified by the language of the "Confession," save that the education by St. German is derived from Muirchu's Life. It is quite different, however, from the romance of the later legendary lives, but these are confuted by their absurdities, their anachronisms, their mutual contradictions, and their total inconsistency with St. Patrick's own statements in the "Confession."[2] The aim of their writers was to glorify the saint, and they had not the

---

[1] *Confession*, H. and S., ii. 2, 309.

[2] *Absurdities.*—Story that Patrick, when desiring flesh meat, was reproved by a man with eyes in the front and also in the back of his head, and that the flesh was then changed into fish. Also story of his visit to an island where there was a young man who had been there since the time of Christ, and his grand-daughter was there also, a withered old woman. Story of the gift of the Staff of Jesus by the Lord on Mount Hermon. *Anachronisms.*— Patrick (according to Jocelinc and the "Tripartite Life") studied under German and then under Martin. Now, Martin died about 401, and German was not a priest till 418. Also, we are told that Amatho was king of the Romans when Patrick was consecrated. *Contradictions.*—These are too many for enumeration. The story of Probus, with its third captivity, the ordination as priest by St. Senior, the mission to Ireland as priest, &c., differs in many respects from all the rest. Some make Amatorex consecrate Patrick, but Joceline makes Celestine. See Todd's "St. Patrick," 321-332, "Tripartite Life," in W.S.; Usher, *Britannicarum Ecclesiarum Antiquitates*, c. xvii. &c.

taste to perceive that he would be more glorified by the patient endurance of adversity and struggle against difficulties than by having his way smoothed in all respects by sympathy and by miracle.

Of his spiritual trials and consolations during this period of training Patrick gives an account in his "Confession." He thus continues his narrative, after mentioning his second captivity and his final escape :[1] "And again after a few years, I was in the Britains with my parents (or relations), who received me as a son, and prayed me earnestly that then at last, after so great tribulations, which I had endured, I should never depart from them. And there in the dead of night, I saw a man coming as it were from Ireland, whose name was Victoricus,[2] with innumerable letters, and he gave me one of these, and I read the beginning of the letter containing the words, 'The Voice of the Irish.' And whilst I was reading aloud the beginning of the letter, I thought that I heard in my mind the voice of those who were near the wood of Foclut, which is near the Western Sea,[3] and they cried thus : 'We pray thee, holy youth, to come and henceforth walk among us.' And I was greatly pricked in heart, and I could read no more ; and so I awoke. Thanks be to God, that after very many years the Lord granted to them according to their cry.

"And, on another night—I know not, God knoweth, whether it was in me or near me—I heard distinctly

---

[1] *Confession*, II. and S. ii, 303.
[2] This is the original from which arose the later stories of the angel Victor, who is called the angel of the Irish nation.
[3] The Atlantic. See below, pages 101, 138.

words![1] which I could not understand, except that at the end of the speech he thus addressed me: 'He who gave His Life for thee, He it is who speaketh in thee!' And so I awoke rejoicing.

"And again I saw in myself one praying; and I was[2] as it were within my body, and I heard him above me, that is, above my inner man, and there he was praying mightily with groanings. And meanwhile I was astonied,[3] and marvelled, and pondered, who it could be who was praying in me. But at the end of the prayer, he said thus, that he was the Spirit.[4] And so I awoke, and remembered the words of the Apostle: 'The Spirit helpeth the infirmity of our prayer; for we know not what to pray for as we ought, but the Spirit Himself maketh intercession for us with groanings that cannot be uttered or expressed in words.' And again: 'The Lord our advocate intercedes for us.'"

Patrick then proceeds to relate, but in a somewhat obscure and confused manner,[5] that some of his seniors brought against him, when he was about to be consecrated bishop, that fault which he had committed

---

[1] So Todd, 378, translates. The Latin text is perhaps corrupt. Wright, "The Writings of Patrick," (R.T.S.), 47, renders, "with most eloquent words which I heard," which is a literal translation of the reading of three MSS. Todd's version makes sense and better English, but is a mere conjecture.

[2] Wright, 48, "He was." So one MS.

[3] Todd, 378, "I was in a trance" *(Stupebam)*.

[4] Todd, 378, "He became so changed, that he seemed to be a Bishop." This is a translation of another and less probable reading. Wright, 48, "He so spoke as if He were the Spirit."

[5] All this part of the "Confession" except the vision is omitted from the "Book of Armagh."

thirty years before, when he was only fifteen, or not quite fifteen, a fault which he had confessed before he was a deacon. His very dear friend to whom he had told this fault, " done in his boyhood one day, nay, in one hour," revealed it on this occasion, although formerly he had said " Behold, thou art to be promoted to the rank of the Episcopate," and had even contended on his behalf, when he was not present, nor in Britain at all. At the time when he was reproached for his early sin, and was in much mental trouble, he had another vision, which he thus relates:—

" I saw in a vision of the night, there was a writing opposite to my face,[1] without honour, and meanwhile, I heard one saying to me in answer, ' We have seen unfortunately,[2] the face of the designate without a name.' He did not say 'Thou hast unfortunately[2] seen,' but 'We have unfortunately[2] seen,' as if he had joined Himself, as He said, ' He who toucheth you is as he who toucheth the apple of Mine eye.' "

> " It said not, ' Thou hast grieved,' but ' We have grieved ;
> With import plain, 'O thou of little faith !
> Am I not nearer to thee than thy friends?
> Am I not inlier with thee than thyself?'
> Then I remembered, ' He that touches you.
> Doth touch the very apple of Mine eye.'"[3]

Eventually the difficulty was overcome, but Patrick gives no further information, either how this was accomplished, or where or by whom the consecration was performed. Muirchu, who mentions St. Patrick's study under German, furnishes us with a

[1] Wright, 49. "a writing against me."
[2] Wright, 49. "with displeasure" (*male*).
[3] Aubrey de Vere, " Legends of St. Patrick."

narrative of his consecration, which is eminently reasonable, and probably correct; for here at least there can scarcely be that confusion with Patrick's predecessor, Palladius, which seems to have marred much of the common narrative of Patrick's years of training. Patrick's avowal of affection for the saints of Gaul points to that country as the place of his education, and German's close connection with the British church made him the most likely person in the Gallican Church for Patrick to consult. According to Muirchu, when Patrick left German, after having studied under him, the bishop sent with him an aged priest, named Segitius, that he might have him as a witness. German would not consecrate Patrick bishop, because Palladius had been sent out as a bishop to Ireland already by Celestine, the bishop of Rome, and German was unwilling to do anything which would seem like starting a rival mission.[1] Patrick accordingly went on his way to "the work of the gospel," apparently with the idea of joining Palladius, and working under him. But before he left Gaul, he heard of the failure of the earlier mission, and the death of its leader; for certain of the disciples of Palladius had returned with the news, and related it in a place which Muirchu calls Ebmoria. Patrick felt that he was called to fill the vacant post, and accordingly with his companion turned aside to "a certain wonderful man, and very great bishop, Amatorex by name, living in a neighbouring spot; and there St. Patrick, knowing what would happen to him,

[1] This is Muirchu's explanation, but German may have been influenced by the statement concerning Patrick's early sin.

received the episcopal rank from the holy bishop Amatorex. Moreover, Auxilius, and Iserninus, and the rest of inferior rank, were ordained on the same day as St. Patrick. Then benedictions were received, and all things were finished in due form, and also this verse of the Psalmist was sung, as it were with special suitability to Patrick, 'Thou art a priest for ever after the order of Melchizedek.' Afterwards the venerable traveller embarked in the prepared ship, in the name of the holy Trinity, and came to the Britains," and thence immediately to Ireland.

As the new bishop with his party set sail from Gaul, with what gratitude must he have looked back upon his past life of trial and tribulation, and with what hope must he have looked forward to the future. It was his Lord who had guided his way, and had prepared him for the work which he was appointed to do. His impetuosity had been checked and chastened, his besetting sin had been burned out of him in the hot furnace of affliction, and his pride had been humbled to the dust. But in the darkest hour he had seen before him the guiding light; in the loneliest path he had been conscious of a Presence abiding with him; and when his dearest friend rose up against him as an adversary, his Master had identified Himself with his cause. But for the firmness of his faith he could not have stood the last and keenest trial, coming, as it did, at the end of a prolonged period of trouble, after the physical sufferings and humiliation of captivity and servitude, after the buffetings of Satan, the indifference of friends, and the reproofs of his seniors. But that faith had never failed, and he now was starting on his journey, fully equipped for his work, with a wisdom gained, not in the schools, but in conflict with the world, a self-restraint taught him by disappointment, and a fortitude gained by adversity, for "the virtue of adversity is fortitude." Few missionaries have been kept so long from their work by various hindrances as was Patrick; few have finally been so successful. The secret of this success is to be found in the years of lonely communion with his God upon the mountains and in the valleys of Antrim, and in the long years of waiting in Britain and Gaul. He had been schooled both by the solitude which is the nurse of great ambitions and by the conflict with mankind which teaches wisdom and prudence in carrying out one's plans. A difficult task was before him which needed a special man, specially trained, and, as the old proverb says, "Not to Palladius, but to Patrick, God gave the conversion of Ireland."

CHAPTER IV.

THE SOURCE AND DATE OF ST. PATRICK'S MISSION.

WHEN the Celtic Churches finally conformed to the Roman Easter and abandoned their struggle for independence, everything Roman became fashionable. Even before Ulster had yielded, and while it was still anti-papal, as it is at the present day, Munster had led the way in adherence to Rome. For men poured forth from the southern ports of Ireland and flocked to "the Apostolic See," and were there impressed by a gorgeousness of ritual and architecture to which they had hitherto been strangers, and when they came back they infected others with their enthusiasm.[1] Pilgrimages had always been popular with the Celts; even in the fifth century Britons were found at Jerusalem and beneath the pillar of the Christian fakir, Simeon Stylites. But the fashion had changed; Jerusalem was still respected, but it did not hold the first place in the mind of the Celt of the eighth century, as it had held it with Columbanus in the sixth. Rome had first awed and then subdued the Celtic churches, and they regarded their new mistress with a respect blended with a certain amount

[1] See the interesting narrative of the growth of this feeling in Professor G. T. Stokes' "Ireland and the Celtic Church," 157, &c

of wholesome fear, and did their best to imitate her. And so in recording the histories of their saints, the legend-writers are not content unless they bring their heroes to Rome and obtain for them the sanction of Roman authority, without which they would scarcely appear respectable in the eyes of the men of later times. Thus Cadoc, Beuno, Brynach, Oudoceus, Cadwaladr, Kentigern, and Aedh are all taken to Rome by their biographers, and St. Patrick must similarly be honoured by receiving a commission from Pope Celestine.

Nothing is said of any mission by Celestine, either in Patrick's own writings or in the greater part of the earlier Patrician literature.[1] Muirchu indeed gives a narrative which implicitly denies such a mission. The earliest authority in its favour is a passage among several supplementary notes at the end of Tirechan's life. It runs thus: "In the thirteenth year of the Emperor Theodosius, Patrick is sent as bishop to teach the Scots[2] by Bishop Celestine, Pope of Rome; which Celestine was the forty-fifth bishop in the city of Rome from the apostle Peter. Palladius is first sent as bishop, who was called Patrick by another name, who suffered martyrdom among the Scots, as ancient saints relate. Then Patrick the second is sent by the angel of God, named Victor, and by Pope Celestine, whom the whole of Hibernia believed, who baptised nearly the whole of it." Later stories im-

---

[1] It is not mentioned in the Hymn of Secundinus, in the Hymn of Fiacc, or by Muirchu. Neither does Tirechan mention it in the main narrative.

[2] Before the tenth century Scot means Irishman.

prove upon this simple statement, and tell the tale with much enlargement and much mutual contradiction. They generally agree in making St. German send Patrick to Celestine, and sometimes mention Segitius as his companion; but they differ as to whether Celestine gave Patrick his commission at his first or at his second application, and also whether Pope Celestine or Bishop Amatorex performed the consecration.

Those who defend this story have a difficult task to explain away the silence of Patrick on the subject of this commission. Had such been given, Patrick would surely have mentioned it in a work, one object of which seems to have been to defend himself against any suspicion of presumption in undertaking the evangelization of Ireland. The glowing picture of the saint's emotions at the sight of the aged Celestine, which is presented to us in one modern life written with much ability and grace of style,[1] receives no justification from Patrick's own words. He had been called by an angel, he had been vouchsafed visions, he had even seen the Lord Himself on Mount Hermon: so this writer assures us; but when he knelt before the shrine of Peter he felt that the angel's voice was not to be obeyed without the commission of Rome, and that the Lord required that he should obtain from the Pope the right to undertake the mission to which He Himself had condescended to call him. "Thou art Peter" was the thought in Patrick's heart. But if this be indeed so, how mar-

---

[1] Miss Cusack, "Life of St. Patrick" (Kenmare Series), 197.

vellous that Patrick has said nothing at all about Peter, about Celestine, or about Rome! His silence is almost as great a miracle as any of those with which he has been credited by legends.

What finally condemns this story, and puts it quite beyond the pale of credibility, is the ignorance of Prosper of Aquitaine. He relates the earlier mission of Palladius, who was sent out by Pope Celestine as bishop for the "Scots" in A.D. 431, but he knows nothing of Patrick. Had Patrick been commissioned by Celestine, he must have known it, and had he known, he would certainly have mentioned it. The whole idea seems to rest upon an anachronism,[1] whereby the opinions of a later age were imputed to St. Patrick, who, it was supposed, would not have ventured upon undertaking his mission without papal authority. Possibly, too, the story may have partly arisen from a confusion of Patrick with Palladius, who was also called Patrick. The romancers were not satisfied with Patrick's own statement that he was sent by God himself; they thought that so illustrious a saint must have derived his authority from the Holy See. The consecration by Amathorex, or Amatorex, which is probably historical, had accordingly to be put directly under the authority of Celestine, and finally Amathorex is politely super-

[1] "Before the sixth century Roman claims were not opposed [by the Celtic Churches], partly because such claims were not yet in existence in the form which they assumed after St. Augustine's mission, partly because, so far as they may have existed potentially, there was an entire unconsciousness of them on the part of the Christian Church in these islands."—Warren. "Liturgy and Ritual of the Celtic Church."

seded, and changed into "Amatho rex Romanorum" (Amatho, king of the Romans), who is a spectator of the consecration, and the Pope himself honours the saint by performing the act. It is rather curious to note the eagerness of Roman controversialists in supporting the story of this mission by Celestine, for whether it be a fact or not, it cannot in any way benefit their position. It would indeed be rather better for them to oppose it, for if Patrick were so commissioned, he must have thought very lightly of it indeed, as he deemed it quite unworthy of mention when he was defending himself against objectors.

With the collapse of this story of the mission from Celestine, the traditional date of Patrick's arrival in Ireland also falls to the ground, and therewith the traditional scheme of chronology of his life, so far as one prevails amid the various contradictions and inconsistencies of his biographers. For the date (A.D. 432) was chosen for Patrick's arrival because in that year Pope Celestine died, and it was therefore the latest year in which he could have given a commission to Patrick. An earlier date would not have suited, because the mission of Palladius took place in 431.[1] The confusion between Patrick and his unsuccessful namesake, which helped the story, accounts for the circumstance that no other pope was selected than Celestine. But to enable Patrick to reach Ireland the very next year to Palladius, it is necessary to crowd within the narrow compass of one year, or a little more, the landing of Palladius in Ireland, his

[1] Yet Joceline and others place Patrick's mission in A.D. 425. See Usher, "Antiq." 878-80.

preaching and rejection by the people, possibly his departure to the country of the Picts in Northern Britain, his death, and the return of some of his disciples with the news to the Continent. It is not probable that in those days of slow transit all these events could have occurred in so small a space of time, especially if, as some late legends assert, Palladius stayed in Ireland long enough to found three churches.

Early Irish chronological records are so exceedingly inexact that it is unsafe to found any argument upon them, especially to support a variation of but a few years from the prevalent tradition. There is, however, a curious passage in Nennius,[1] in which two dates are assigned for Patrick's arrival in Ireland. It runs thus:—" From the nativity of the Lord to the coming of Patrick to the Scots is four hundred and five years. From the death of Patrick to the death of Saint Brigid sixty years. From the birth of Columba to the death of Saint Brigid four years. The beginning of the calculation, twenty-three cycles of nineteen years from the Incarnation of the Lord to the coming of Patrick into Ireland, and they make four hundred and thirty-eight years in number. And from the coming of Patrick to the cycle of nineteen years in which we are, there are twenty-two cycles, that is four hundred and twenty-one, two years in the period of eight years up to this year in which we are." These are two opposite calculations, unless the first refer to Patrick's first arrival as captive. But

---

[1] "Nennius" in W.S., 498.

both differ from A.D. 432, and the latter agrees fairly with what we might regard as a probable date, which would allow for all the circumstances of Palladius' mission and death.

Further, Tirechan counts 436 years from the Passion of Christ to the death of Patrick, and states that " Loiguire reigned either two or five years after Patrick's death, but, as we think," he says, "all the time of his reign was 36 years."[1] This would make the beginning of Laoghaire's reign to be in 435 or 438, but Laoghaire was already king at the time of Patrick's arrival, as stated by Muirchu and generally received, and Patrick is said[2] to have come in the fourth year of Laoghaire's reign, which would consequently be about 439 or 442.

Again, in a tract called "The Synchronizing of the Kings of Ireland and of the Kings of the provinces after the faith here," we read: " Forty-three years from Patrick's arrival in Ireland to the battle of Ocha." Now the accepted date of the battle of Ocha is 482 or 483, and therefore the date of Patrick's arrival, according to this authority, would be 439 or 440.[3]

---

[1] "Book of Armagh." W.S., 302.
[2] "Chronological Tract in Lebar Brecc." W.S., 550.
[3] W.S. cxxiv. See further Todd (393-399), who also refers to a statement in the Irish Nennius that Patrick was a captive with Miliuc when Palladius came to Ireland. He also infers a later date for Patrick's arrival from a statement in the Book of Lecan, but Mr. Whitley Stokes (cxxii.) states that his translation of the passage is contrary to the Irish idiom, and himself gives a translation which is in harmony with the earlier date. I may add that Dr. Todd's quotation from the chronological poem of Gilla Coemain does not

Without laying too much stress upon these statements, it may be concluded from the probabilities of the case, that the mission of Palladius and the return of his companions must have occupied some years, so that it was probably about 439 when Patrick arrived in Ireland. This furnishes us with a date whereby to reckon the early events of his life. We know from his "Confession" that his consecration took place thirty years after his boyish sin, which was committed when he was about fifteen, and thus we can find the approximate dates of his birth, of his captivity, and of his escape from Miliuc. Greater exactness it is impossible to attain, as the chronological scheme of the majority of Patrick's biographers is manifestly fictitious, and of the other biographers some are mutually contradictory.

help matters much, for though Gilla Coemain counts 162 years from the coming of Patrick to the death of Gregory, he is so inexact as to count the same number of years to the death of Columba. Now Gregory died in 604 and Columba in 597, or, as some Irish authorities say, in 595 or, in 592.

CHAPTER V.

THE RELIGIONS OF IRELAND.

THE history of the Irish Church begins with St. Patrick. Its historian is not beset, at the outset of his task, by the difficulties which the historians of many other churches have to encounter ; he has not to discuss and dismiss the claims of various apostles, and of other saints of the apostolic age, to be its founder; for the fame of Patrick has predominated in the traditions of the Irish people, so as to obscure completely whatever pretensions might have been advanced on behalf of others. Ireland has no part in the legends of the Holy Grail, and a story that St. James preached on her soil has been altogether neglected by Irish patriotism, which has clung, instead, with singular fidelity to the memory of the unlearned and rustic saint, who loved the Irish people, and whom they still love. The stories of early bishops in Ireland do not invalidate the claim of Patrick to be the founder of its church, and his only rival in Irish legend is the soldier Altus.[1] He, according to the poetical story, had served in the Roman army, and, as one of the guard at Our Lord's crucifixion, had been converted

---

[1] "Ireland and the Celtic Church," by Prof. G. H. Stokes, 18, 19.

by the miracles which he witnessed, and when he returned to Ireland he preached the Christian religion, and

> "Told that half the world barbarian thrills already with the faith
> Taught them by the god-like Syrian Cæsar lately put to death."

Without doubt, there were Irish Christians before Patrick landed in Ireland. Tradition relates that Mansuetus, the first bishop of Toul, who lived probably in the fourth century, " was sprung from a noble race of the Scots "[1] (and at that time Scots always meant Irish); and one tenth-century poet rhetorically states that " Hibernia then boasted of races that worshipped Christ."[2] But it is not certain that Mansuetus received the faith in his own country; he appears to have been sent to Toul from Rome.[3] In St. Jerome's day there was a Christian Irishman among the Pelagian leaders, whom the saint abused, with more vigour than dignity, as "an unlearned calumniator," "a most stupid fellow overloaded with the porridge of the Scots,"[4] and "a huge and corpulent Alpine dog."[5] Probably the unfortunate Irishman who was thus designated was Cælestius, the coadjutor of the Briton Pelagius.[6]

There is no certain historical proof of a Christian church, or even of Christian dwellers in Ireland, in

---

[1] Haddan and Stubbs, ii. 289. "Acta Tullens. Episc."
[2] Adso. H. and S., ii. 289.
[3] Usher. "Antiq." 747.
[4] *Comment in Jerem. Prolog.* H. and S., ii. 289.
[5] Ib. iii. "Præf." H. and S., ii. 290.
[6] Concerning Cælestius, see Stokes' "Ireland and the Celtic Church," 21-23.

the fourth century. Most of the stories in the legends of the Irish saints, about bishops and missionaries before Patrick, seem to have originated in a desire to establish a claim for archiepiscopal jurisdiction, in opposition to Armagh.[1] Chrysostom about A.D. 387 makes a general statement that the " Britannic islands " had felt the power of the Word, and had churches and altars,[2] but this is too vague to be pressed as an argument in favour of an Irish Church. It is not till 431 that any certain evidence can be found of the existence of any body of Christians in the country, and then " Palladius was consecrated by Pope Celestine, and sent as first bishop to the Scots believing in Christ."[3] The most natural interpretation of the statement that Palladius was "the first bishop" is that there were no bishops in Ireland before him,[4]

---

[1] Todd, 198-221. The four Munster Bishops, Kieran, Ailbe, Declan, and Ibar, who are said to have been in Ireland before Patrick, are proved by other evidence to have been posterior in date. See also H. and S., ii. 291.
[2] " Cont. Judæos." H. and S., i. 10.
[3] Prosper of Aquitaine, "Chron." H. and S., ii. 290.
[4] Todd, 285. For another interpretation, see Usher; also compare Warren, " Liturgy and Ritual of the Celtic Church," 30, 31. John of Fordun (*Chronica Gentis Scotorum*, iii. 8), interpreting " Scots " of the people of Scotland, states that Palladius was sent into Scotland as first bishop thereof, and that before his arrival, from the time of Pope Victor (A.D. 203), " the Scots had as teachers of the faith and administrators of the Sacraments, priests only, or monks, following the rite of the primitive Church." The blunder and the conjecture contained in this passage are the main foundation of the figment of a primitive Presbyterian Culdee Church in Scotland, which has been refuted by Innes in his essay, " Of the Ancient Inhabitants of Scotland" ("Historians of Scotland," vii. 391-394. See also i. 94, iv. 395.) Fordun, believing that the people of Scotland were converted in A.D. 203, and that they only

and the incidental references in the "Book of Armagh" to a bishop who met Patrick in Mag Tochuir,[1] and to another named Colman, who offered his church to Patrick,[2] would not be by themselves very decisive evidence to the contrary. But as it was known at Rome that there were Christians in the country, it is not improbable that missionaries had previously laboured there, and one passage in Patrick's "Confession" may very possibly imply that some of these missionaries were bishops; for Patrick says that he had travelled to remote parts, "where no one had ever come to baptize, or ordain clergy, or to confirm the people"[3]—an idle boast, had not some missionary bishops performed these offices in the less remote parts before his landing. The words can hardly be merely a reference to the work of Palladius, unless that bishop were very much more successful than ancient records admit. Tirechan's narrative occasionally presupposes the existence of Christians in various districts before Patrick passed through them in his missionary journeys, and the tradition of a subterranean stone altar, which he says that Patrick showed to a disciple in County Sligo,[4] may suggest that the early Irish Christians met secretly to worship in caves.[5]

received their first bishop in A.D. 431, had to adopt his hypothesis in order to account for the constitution of the church in the interval.

[1] By Tirechan, W.S. 329.
[2] In the later addition in "Book of Armagh," 337.
[3] "Confession," H. and S., ii. 311.
[4] W.S. 313.
[5] The evidence in favour of a pre-existing Christianity is summarised by Dr. Whitley Stokes, clx.

But if we make full allowance for the scanty evidence that we find of the prosecution of missionary labours in Ireland before Patrick and his party landed, and even are led to the conclusion that there were already the beginnings of an organised church, we have no ground for supposing that very much impression had been made as yet upon the national paganism, or for questioning the claim of Patrick to be the Apostle of Ireland and the true founder of her church. Patrick came not so much to take charge of Christian believers as to preach to the heathen. Here and there he might find Christian congregations, worshipping in caves, or in churches, where such were permitted; and some scattered families in other places may have kept the light of truth burning, though deprived wholly of sympathy from their neighbours, and surrounded by the deepest pagan darkness. Nor must we forget the presence of Christian slaves in Ireland, British captives, among whom sometimes may have been women, who were promoted to be the wives of their masters, and whose influence in persuading their husbands to accept the new teaching would be considerable. But though the missionary might receive some sympathy, he had reason to expect much more hostility. The druids were a mighty army, whose reputation as "soothsayers, priests, medicine-men and magicians,"[1] kept the people in subjection to their control through sheer fear, and their influence was sure to be exerted in every way against the new religion. They claimed to be able to summon to their aid the spirits of wells

---

[1] Rhys, "Celtic Britain," 70.

and mountains; they were priests of "the power of the air," and could, so they said, cause snow to fall and fogs to arise.[1] The people feared them, but perhaps the princes and the aristocracy had already a conviction that the religion of Britain was a more civilised religion than their own, and so were not altogether unwilling for the most part to tolerate its practice in their territories.

Patrick mentions that the Irish at his arrival worshipped idols and impure things,[2] and alludes to their adoration of the sun.[3] The "Hymn of Fiacc" says: "On Ireland's folk lay darkness; the tribes worshipped *side*."[4] Muirchu mentions the worship of idols.[5]

When Patrick set foot in Cashel all the idols of the city fell flat on their faces, and when the king arose in the morning he saw them thus overthrown.[6] This story, though literally untrue, is symbolically accurate, and pictures the rapid decline of the worship of the greater gods at the advance of Christianity, not only in Ireland, but also all over Europe. It was not these that the people most fondly che-

---

[1] See the stories told by Muirchu and Tirechan. W. S., 284, 312. Broichan the druid told Columba that he could make the winds unfavourable to his voyage, and cause a great darkness to envelope him when he was about to sail on Loch Ness. "Nor should we wonder," says Adamnan, "that God sometimes allows them, with the aid of evil spirits, to raise tempests and agitate the sea." Adamnan. *Vita S. Columbae*, ii. 35.
[2] "Confession," H. and S., ii. 308.
[3] Ib. 313.
[4] W. S. 409.
[5] W. S. 275.
[6] "Tripartite Life," W.S., 195.

rished; in Ireland they were probably the imported gods of the Celts, and had never taken hold of the affections of the earlier non-Aryan race. So we hear little of their names, and as for their temples, it may be that they had none, except perhaps in the chief towns. Fiacc's hymn speaks of the Irish as sons of Erem,[1] where Erem may be the name of a divinity identical with Aryaman, "one of the Indian Adityas," and we hear also of Cenn Cruaich, and a few more, but for records of many of the personal gods of the Aryan mythology we have to seek in the mysterious regions of Irish romance. The great God Cenn Cruaich, "the Chief of the Mound," dwelt in what is now county Cavan, in a plain called Mag Slecht, "the plain of Kneeling." He was an image covered with gold and silver, and around him stood twelve subordinate idols, covered with brass. To him in the days of his greatness the Irish used to sacrifice the firstborn of their children and of their flocks, to secure power and peace in their tribes, and milk and corn in their families.[2] In later days his glory had departed, but he was still to be seen, battered and leaning as if about to fall, and his attendants buried up to their heads in the ground. Men told a story how Patrick had stricken the cruel god with the Staff of Jesu, so that he had bowed westwards, and the demon had fled from the stone to hell, and the earth had swallowed up the smaller idols as far as their heads.[3] The Chief of the Mound was now

[1] W.S., 275 cf. clviii.
[2] Rhys, "Hibbert Lectures," 200-204; W.S. clviii.
[3] "Tripartite Life," W.S., 91.

called "the Crooked one of the Mound" (Cromm Cruaich), and perhaps, also, Cromduff,[1] "the Crooked Black One." His festival, which once was held on the eve of the solar feast of Samhain, that is on November 1st, was abolished, and the previous Sunday became known in Ireland as Cromduff Sunday.[2]

The name "Chief of the Mound" suggests the connection of this god with an artificial mound or gorsedd, such as is found in many places in various countries. Even now, when the Welsh have their National Eisteddfod, they hold a gorsedd for the granting of degrees and other purposes, and for this a circle of stones is formed with a large one in the centre, just as Cenn Cruaich stood in the open air with his gods in a ring around him.[3] The date of one of the god's festivals, the eve of November 1st, shows that he was in some way connected with the sun-worship, which Patrick found prevalent. The three great Celtic solar feasts, Beltaine, the Lugnassad, and Samhain, were held respectively on the 1st of May, the 1st of August, and the 1st of November. Even now in Celtic countries these festivals are more or less observed, for when the old gods passed away, the sun, the mountains, stones, wells, and rivers, still remained, and throughout all subsequent ages have had their votaries. The winter festival occupied in all seven days, of which Samhain was the middle; the trophies of the heroes were

---

[1] Or Cromdubh.
[2] Todd, 128.
[3] See further, Rhys, "Hibbert Lectures," 204 *et seq.*

viewed that had been won during the year, and games and banquets were held. It was the time of the sun's subjection to the powers of darkness, and human victims were probably sacrificed: fire also was lighted at Tlachtga, in Meath, and from thence was supplied to every Irish home. Samhain would seem to have been the New Year's-day of Ireland, and was considered the proper time for prophecy.[1] Burns's poem of "Hallowe'en" will recur to the mind of everyone, and those who are familiar with Wales will recall many a custom practised there on that day.[2] Beltaine, or the 1st of May, when the sun began again his career of victory, was also, like Samhain, celebrated by the sacrifice of human victims. Two great fires were made by the druids, and cattle were driven between them to guard them against evils through the year. On the Lugnassad, or 1st of August, great fairs were held at various places. The fair at Tailltin [3] was held with sports and horse-racing, marriages were solemnized, and princes were always bound to be present on the last day if they would avoid disaster in the future.[4]

A strange contrast to these ceremonies, in which cruelty and revelling went hand in hand, was the austere and yet gentle religion of Patrick. "That sun," he says, "which we see, rises daily for our sake at God's command, but will never reign, nor will its

---

[1] Rhys, "Hibbert Lectures," 514, 515.
[2] Called by the Welsh *Nos Galan-gaeaf*, the "Night of the Winter Calends."
[3] Now Teltown.
[4] "Hibbert Lectures," 409-419.

brightness abide; but they also who adore it, miserable ones, will wretchedly be punished. But we believe and adore the true sun, Jesus Christ, who never will perish, neither will he perish who has done His will, but he will abide for ever, as Christ abideth for ever, who reigneth with God the Father Almighty and with the Holy Ghost before the ages, and now, and for ever and ever. Amen."[1]

The Side, whom the "Hymn of Fiacc" mentions, lived in mounds, and seem to be identified with "gods of the earth,"[2] in which case they may have been the spirits of ancestors. Ancestor-worship is one of the most widely spread cults, and even seduced God's ancient people at times from their worship of Jehovah.[3] In the seventh century, when Tirechan and Muirchu wrote, the Irish still believed that the pagan dead dwelt in their sepulchres. Patrick on one occasion, as these writers state,[4] found a cross on a grave, and stopped his chariot and asked the dead man who he was. And the man answered from his grave that he was a pagan, and in reply to the question, "Why is the Holy Cross erected near you?" he explained that it had been placed there by mistake.

---

[1] *Conf.*, H. and S., ii. 313.

[2] Tirechan; W.S., 315; "Trip. Life," 101; also W.S., clviii.

[3] Ps. cvi., 28: "They joined themselves unto Baal-peor, and ate the sacrifices of the dead." Isaiah, viii. 19; "Are not the people wont to speak unto their gods (Elohim), unto the dead instead of to the living" (Cheyne's translation). The Teraphim were probably ancestral gods, like the Lares and Penates of Rome and Greece.

[4] W.S., 325, 294.

In this story the Christian cross has taken the place of the pagan pillar-stone. So, too, the earliest Christian burial-grounds in Ireland copied the fashion of the Pagan cemeteries, except that each one of the circle of pillar-stones in Christian times was marked by a cross.[1] These pillar-stones were originally associated with the worship of the dead. Very probably, as has been suggested, they "in a certain sense actually stood as the visible presence of the departed," and "were spirits in stony shape."[2] A pagan cemetery was, therefore, in some respects a pagan temple, wherein the worship of the dead was practised.

The worship of stones was forbidden by a canon of the reign of Edgar, together with "well-worshippings and necromancies and divinations," and also by the Council of Tours in 567 A.D. The Irish in Patrick's time undoubtedly worshipped stones; "from Heremon's reign to the coming of good Patrick of Armagh there was adoration of stones."[3] A notable fetish-stone was the Lia Fail, which at Tara had the power of screaming when sat upon by a lawful sovereign, and which is supposed by some to be the stone in the coronation chair at Westminster Abbey. The pillar-stone of Cleghile, near Tipperary, was another fetish; it was said to be part of a wheel which was

---

[1] Miss Stokes, " Early Christian Art in Ireland," 154.
[2] See a valuable paper on Stonehenge, by Mr. Arthur J. Evans, "Archæological Review," ii. 326. The stone circles and dolmens of the Khasis of north-east Bengal are not sepulchral, but are based on a sepulchral worship, being erected to spirits of ancestors or friends.
[3] " Book of Leinster," quoted W.S., clv.

made by Simon Magus in conjunction with the Irish druid, Mog Ruith. This wheel was accidentally broken, and the druid's daughter brought pieces of it to Ireland. That at Cleghile produced blindness if looked at, and death if touched. Patrick, according to a story told by Tirechan, seems to have attempted to purify certain stones at Mag Selce by inscribing Christian symbols upon them,[1] and at Uisnech, where there possibly was a sacred circle, he is represented by later writers as cursing the stones, so that afterwards they were of no good. "Not even washing-stones were made of them,"[2] we are told, and if a bad stone were used in a building it was proverbially called a stone of Uisnech. Possibly the legend may symbolically represent the overthrow by Patrick of some pagan worship with which the stones were associated, for long afterwards there was a stone there which was supposed to be placed in the exact centre of the island. The old superstition died hard, and in the time of Tirechan one of the stones was called "the stone of Cothraige,"[3] that is, of Patrick, as if then the place had not lost its sanctity, but the pagan reverence was disguised by the use of the name of Ireland's great Apostle. This was a favourite device among the Celts, and several stones in Ireland bore Patrick's name.[4] One tradition relates that he sailed from Ireland

---

[1] Tirechan; W.S., 319. Compare "Tripartite Life;" W.S., 107.
[2] "Trip. Life;" W.S., 81.
[3] W.S., 310.
[4] *E.g.*, at Drummurraghille, Cashel, and Dunseverick (see Tirechan; W.S., 331, 329.; "Trip. Life," 197).

to Cornwall on a stone altar,[1] a method of journeying quite customary with Celtic saints, if we may believe their legends. Such ridiculous stories show how hard the people sought to combine their new creed with their old superstitions. At Clogher a stone, dedicated to an idol called Cermand Celstach, was kept in the porch of the cathedral, at least as late as the fifteenth century—a curious instance of the preservation of a pagan symbol under the shelter of a Christian sanctuary.[2] The same attempt to retain pagan customs under Christian disguises is seen in the transference of the sacred wells of Paganism to Christian saints. Patrick did not countenance such a compromise, for he did his best utterly to overthrow the reverence paid by the people to the well Slan, which the druids honoured as a god and called the king of waters,[3] but Columba, with different policy on one occasion, drove the demon out of a well and made it henceforth a Christian holy-well.[4] In Patrick's age sacrifices were offered to wells, and coins were thrown into them as offerings. Roman coins have been discovered in the English well of Chollerford, and as late as the seventeenth century bulls were still occasionally offered to "the god Mourie," who had his well on an island in the beautiful Scottish Loch Maree.[5] So also horses

[1] Usher, "Antiq.," 877. Compare Borlase, "Age of the Saints," in *Journal of the Royal Institution of Cornwall*, xx. 53-56.
[2] Todd, 129.
[3] Tirechan, W.S., 323.
[4] Adamnan, *Vita S. Columbæ*, ii. 10.
[5] Mitchell, "The Past in the Present." "The god Mourie" was St. Maelrubha. Bulls were sacrificed to him as late as 1678.

used to be sacrificed at St. George's Well, near Abergeleu, in Wales,[1] and the unholy rites of the cursing well of St. Elian, in the same principality, at which money was offered for a curse to be laid on an enemy, are still fresh in memory. This pagan reverence is not yet extinct in Celtic districts, and where the Roman Church has power receives a measure of ecclesiastical sanction. The Bretons still go in procession with their priests in time of drought to the enchanted Fountain of Baranton, and the Rector of the Canton dips the foot of the Cross into the waters, and, we are told, "it is sure to rain before a week elapses."[2] But sacrifices are no longer offered to wells, and even gifts of money are rare; yet rags at times are hung on neighbouring trees or bushes, and bent pins are thrown into the water, as at St. Madron's Well, in Cornwall, where love-sick girls augur the date of their wedding-day by the bubbles which are formed. The olden worship now survives in the form of an interesting and generally a pretty harmless superstition,[3] but in Patrick's day it had the hard

[1] "St. George had in this parish his Holy Well, at which the British Mars had his offering of horses; for the rich were wont to offer one to secure his blessing on all the rest. He was the tutelar saint of those animals; all that were distempered were brought, sprinkled with the water, and this blessing bestowed: *Rhad Duw a saint Sior amat*), "The blessing of God and St. George be on thee."—Pennant, "Tour in Wales," iii. 149 (Rhys' ed.).

[2] Lady Charlotte Guest, *Mabinogion* (2nd ed.), 75. She further quotes Villemarqué, who says of this fountain, "Les enfans s'amusent a y jeter des épingles, et disent par commun proverbe: 'Ris donc, fontaine de Berendon, et je te donnerai une épingle.'"

[3] See further, Roberts' "Cambrian Popular Antiquities," 234-267. Wirt Sikes, "British Goblins," iv. 2. Blight's "Churches of West

cruel features of debased and relentless paganism. It is probable that even human sacrifices were offered beside a spring of uncommon fame,[1] just as they were offered to Cenn Cruaich, and at the festivals of Samhain and Beltaine. In famine, pestilence, or defeat in war, there would be special recourse to this dread means of propitiation.

> "Help us from famine,
> And plague and strife!
> What would you have of us?
> Human life?
> Were it our nearest,
> Were it our dearest,
> (Answer, O answer),
> We give you his life."

We may with the help of a poetic imagination clothe paganism in a garb of attractive beauty, but

---

Cornwall," 230-232. Borlase, "Natural History of Cornwall" (1758), 31. W.C. Borlase "Age of the Saints," 56-60. Halliwell's "Rambles in Western Cornwall," 78-81. "Journal of British Archaeological Association," 34, 476-479. Pennant's "Tours in Wales." Brand's "Popular Antiquities." The whole literature of Welsh and Cornish well customs is most interesting and instructive, as showing how paganism survived and still survives in remote districts. At least as late as 1856 money was still thrown into Ffynon Tegla, in Denbighshire, a well which was famed for the cure of epilepsy. At the Cornish well of Chapel Uny children "were dipped three times *against the sun*, and dragged three times round the margin of the grass in the same direction." At Madron Well rags are still hung on the surrounding bushes, just as ribbons and pieces of cloth might have been seen quite lately fastened to the stump of the tree at Loch Maree. This custom is still observed among the Shintoists of Japan, and seems to be "a part and parcel of the most primitive and widely extended worship of the Sun."

[1] Rhys' "Hibbert Lectures," 186.

really it was a religion of dread, not of love; it sprang from fear, and also inspired it, demanding its human victims even in cultured Athens and imperial Rome. It was no love of nature that led the Celts to worship wells and streams, mountains and hills, which, as Gildas says, were "an abomination and destruction to them," when "the blind people paid them divine honour." To early man nature was an enemy. The struggle for existence was for him a very hard struggle indeed, and nature at times did her best for his extermination. He divinised the powers of nature because he feared them, and paid them reverence in order to avert their wrath. There was scarcely anything in external nature from which the Celts of Ireland did not apprehend some evil, and which they did not seek to propitiate, and their religious condition at Patrick's arrival was one of the grossest darkness. Gildas mentions rivers as worshipped by the Celts, and Deva's "wizard stream" recurs to our memory: one of the best known parallels to which in Ireland is the Boyne, the divinity of which was wife of the sea-god Nodens.[1] We find that hills were still honoured by a Celtic parish in Scotland as late as the seventeenth century, for the Presbytery Records of Dingwall record "pouring of milk upon hills as oblationes" among the superstitions laid at that date to the charge of the people of Applecross.[2] Fire-worship was kept up in Ireland under the sanction of St. Bridget's name, in the time of Giraldus Cambrensis. There were an innumerable number of

---

[1] Rhys' "Celtic Britain," 67, 68.
[2] Mitchell, "The Past in the Present."

minor superstitions in the time of St. Patrick, and of many the impression still remains on the minds of the lower and uneducated classes of the Irish people. Patrick in the "Deer's Cry" mentions the "spells of women, and smiths, and druids," against which he beseeches protection. An ancient poem, which is ascribed to Columba, enumerates certain signs, which in the minds of the credulous people were fraught with the utmost importance :

> "Our fate depends not on sneezing ;
> Nor on a bird perched on a twig ;
> Nor on the root of a knotted tree ;
> Nor on the noise of clapping hands;
> Better is He in whom we trust,
> The Father, the One, and the Son.
>
> * * * *
>
> I adore not the voice of birds,
> Nor sneezing, nor lots in this world;
> Nor a boy, nor chance, nor woman ;
> My Druid is Christ, the Son of God."[1]

It is not difficult to perceive what use the "druids, pythonesses, and augurs"[2] would make of these superstitions, and how their "chants of wizardry and arts of devilry"[3] would be required by the terrified people, over whom they would have a dominion as absolute as that of the medicine-men of Africa. It is not wonderful that the early Christians retained a dread of the evil deities and influences which they had formerly sought to propitiate, and regarded the pagan gods as terrible realities, wicked demons, the army of

---

[1] Todd, "St. Patrick," 122.
[2] "Irish Canons," in W.S., 507.
[3] "Tripartite Life," W.S., 55.

the apostate angels. The air, they thought, was full of the stormy flock of the devil's followers, who yet were unseen, "lest men should be so polluted by their evil examples and foul acts as to defile themselves openly before the eyes of all, unhidden by screen or wall."[1] Before Christianity came to Ireland, the prevalent dread was unrelieved by any gleam of supernatural hope. Life would not have been worth living in a world which was filled with evil powers, had not the sweet and sacred ties of the family, the love of husband and wife, of parent and child, kept alive some idea of the existence of goodness and love.

There was much in this picture to make Patrick despair, but there were also some grounds for hope. He had to break down the power of the druids over the common people, but the aristocracy were doubtless not blind to the revolution which was at work in the world, and had recognised the superior civilisation of Christianity. Even when old prejudices were strong enough to prevent them from embracing a new

---

[1] Hic sublatus e medio
Dejectus est a Domino ;
Cujus aeris spatium
Constipatur satellitum
Globo invisibilium
Turbido perduellium
Ne malis exemplaribus
Imbuti ac sceleribus,
Nullis unquam tegentibus
Septis ac parietibus
Fornicarentur homines
Palam omnium oculis.

—"The Altus" of St. Columba, p. 16 (ed. by Marquess of Bute).

religion, they were prepared to tolerate it, if its preacher were personally acceptable to them. Patrick's long and arduous training had taught him the necessary lesson of patience and self-restraint, his natural impetuosity of nature had been curbed and humbled by suffering and disappointment, and he was not likely to imperil success by haughtiness or headstrong rashness. The Roman missionary, Palladius, had failed with the Celtic Irish, just as Augustine failed afterwards with the Celtic Welsh, perhaps for the same reason ; for the Celtic nature will never brook aught that savours of an arrogant assumption of superiority. Patrick came as a Celt to Celts, and with that Celtic charm of manner which goes straight to the Celtic heart and clears away mountains of difficulty, which a man of a different bearing can never pass. By winning the aristocracy he gained access to the common people, who regarded their princes with religious reverence. Stranger still, he won over to his side here and there a druid, and as the friend of the princes and converter of druids, he became a formidable person to encounter. The prestige of the druids waned before the growing reputation of this new teacher, whom popular rumour accounted a still greater magician than they. Success then was easy ; he had to deal with a people of strong virtues, though of grievous faults, impressionable, impulsive, and affectionate. He came to them with a message of love, strangely at variance with their prevalent conceptions of the supernatural, but supported by the gentle influences of home and family life. There was hope for half-civilised Ireland with its savage virtues and vices, more than there is for a highly-civilised Christian country where faith is dwindling and the morality of the home corrupted and dying.

CHAPTER VI.

LANDING IN IRELAND AND EARLY SUCCESSES.

THE mission party, as we have seen, set sail from Gaul somewhere about the year 439, and came to Ireland without any delay. There is no hint in the early narratives of any preliminary sojourn in Wales, such as Welsh legends relate. With Patrick there were Auxilius and Iserninus, and others of inferior rank;[1] and Tirechan speaks, with some exaggeration, of "a multitude of holy bishops and presbyters and deacons and exorcists, ostiarii and readers, as also sons, whom Patrick ordained."[2] The party appears to have been composed of natives of Gaul and of the Roman provinces of Britain. "Romans," "Franks," and Britons are mentioned among Patrick's bishops,[3] and Tirechan

---

[1] Muirchu, W.S. 273.

[2] W.S., 303.

[3] "Catalogue of the Saints of Ireland," II. and S. 292. Dr. Skene ("Celtic Scotland,") ii. 14-26, treats of the constitution of Patrick's Church, the nationality of his missionaries, &c., and refers to the writings of Angus the Culdee, who mentions the ten sons of Bracean, King of Britain, among early Irish saints, and invokes "the Romans in Achadh Galma, in Hy Echach; the Romans in Leter Erca; the Romans and Cairsech, daughter of Brocan, in Cill Achadh Dallrach; Cuan, a Roman, in Achill; the Romans in Cluan Caincumni; and the Romans with Aedan in Cluan Dartada;

gives a list of Patrick's "Franks," which includes three bishops.[1] Some of these missionaries must have come afterwards, when Patrick needed more help in consequence of his successes, but from the outset probably his party was a composite one.

Patrick appears to have landed first at the mouth of the Vartry, where the town of Wicklow now stands. It bore in ancient times the name of Inbher Dea, and was in the territory of the Coolenni, the tribe of Cualann. The harbour is described as "convenient and renowned,"[2] and for the ships of that time—shallow and almost flat-bottomed as they were—it was, doubtless, excellently adapted, for they could be easily drawn up on shore.[3] It was there that Palladius had landed on his unsuccessful mission.[4] Patrick did not stay long at this place, but sailed away northwards with the view of visiting his old master Miliuc.[5] On the way he came to the island now called after him, Inis Patrick, or St. Patrick's Island, which lies off Skerries, on the coast of county Dublin.[6] Thence he sailed until

the Gauls in Saillidu; the Gauls in Magh Salach; and the Gauls in Achadh Ginain; the Saxons in Rigar; and the Saxons in Cluan Muicceda; fifty men of the Britons with Monan in Lann Leire." Mochta, abbot of Louth, who is called Patrick's presbyter, was a Briton. See Todd, "St. Patrick," 29.

[1] W.S. 305.
[2] Muirchu's Life, W.S. 275.
[3] Professor G. T. Stokes, "Ireland and the Celtic Church," 52.
[4] Some stories in late lives about hostility manifested to Patrick at Inbher Dea may possibly have been borrowed from traditions about the elder Patrick, viz., Palladius. Todd, 338-9.
[5] Muirchu's Life, W.S., 275.
[6] Ib. 275. Tirechan mentions also the islands Maccu-Chor, which may be the Skerries group. W.S., 303. Miss Cusack says (218),

he came to a strait called Brene, and landed at the mouth of the river Slain, at the south-west extremity of Strangford Lough. He and his companions hid their boat and walked on through the country. They were met before long by a swineherd, who, supposing them to be robbers, ran away and told his master, a chieftain named Dichu. Dichu came out to slay them, but was so struck by Patrick's appearance that he became friendly, and gave ear to his preaching, and finally believed, and the saint and his company stayed with him many days. Dichu dwelt at the place, afterwards called Sabhall Padhrig, or Patrick's Barn, now Saul, in County Down,[1] and there, probably, the saint built his first church.

From Saul Patrick went to see Miliuc, and came to the old familiar hill of Slemish. As he looked thence over the woods and hills among which he had lived and toiled as a slave, and where the chastening love of his Lord had brought him to repentance, he was

"The word Macchucor signifies the islands of the sons or descendants of Corr, and the appellation belongs properly to the islands of Arran."

[1] All this is related by Muirchu, W.S., 275-6. The "Tripartite Life," W.S., 37, says that Dichu gave Sabhall to Patrick; and the "Lebar Brecc Homily," W.S., 451, states that Patrick built a church there. The latter adds to the first simple story a statement that Dichu came with a drawn sword, but Patrick made the sign of the cross, so that Dichu could not stir hand or foot. Both the "Tripartite Life" and the "Homily" state that Dichu set his dog at Patrick's party, but Patrick chanted a verse against it. The story, as given by Muirchu, contains nothing marvellous or improbable. It is said that the church of Sabhall was built north and south, and as there was a church at Armagh, called Sabhall, and built in the same manner, it has been conjectured that Sabhall was the name given to such churches. Todd, 410-2.

astonished by beholding his master's house in flames. Miliuc, we are told, fearing that he should be made a convert and subject to his former slave, and, probably, like Ethelbert with Augustine, fearing that Patrick possessed magical powers, had gathered all his substance into his house, and, setting it on fire, burned himself with his property. Patrick, astonished at the sight, stood a long time on the right side of the hill at a spot which in Muirchu's time was marked by a cross.[1]

This strange story of self-cremation is not necessarily a fable. Parallels have been adduced from the Hindoo custom of dharna. In one kind of dharna a circular enclosure, called a kurh, is constructed, in which a pile is raised and a victim placed, who is to be sacrificed on the approach of the objectionable person. It has been suggested that the superstitious Miliuc, who is said to have been a wizard, constructed a kurh to prevail on Patrick to desist, and when Patrick came on, notwithstanding his precaution, he burned himself alive, either expecting that Patrick would do the same, "according to the rigour of the etiquette," or that he would fear the displeasure of some god, and cease his missionary efforts, and so the ancient heathenism would not be overthrown.[2]

[1] Muirchu adds a prophecy (which he says was uttered by Patrick after his long silence) that Miliuc's posterity should never reign, but always be subjects. His son, Guasacht, nevertheless, is said to have become a bishop. Todd, 408 *note*.

[2] This is Mr. Whitley Stokes' suggestion, clxxviii. "Or," he adds, "Miliuc may have been a devotee, like the Mexican, Nanahuatzin, who leapt into a fire to propitiate the gods."

Baffled by this strange device Patrick returned, after "praying and arming himself with the sign of the cross," probably to avert any evil from the malevolent power which Miliuc served, and from which Patrick may have anticipated some attempt at revenge for the death of its devotee. He stayed many days with Dichu, and went about the whole plain; and, we are told, the faith began to increase there.

But Patrick was not content with the evangelisation of a corner of Ireland: he was anxious to overthrow paganism at the great central capital of Tara, and by winning over the king to influence the whole nation. This policy was a necessity of his position; he might otherwise gain a few converts among the more enlightened members of the aristocracy and their immediate followers, but his mission would have no effect upon the bulk of the people. He knew well the Celtic nature, and he saw that a bold stroke was required, whereby he might awaken general interest in his claims and in the message he brought. It was first necessary for him to impress and astonish the Irish, and then he would be able to teach and convert them. If he hesitated from fear of danger, or showed lack of courage in the crisis, he would never break down the prestige of the druids, upon which their dominion over the people was based; but if he succeeded in his enterprise, his personality henceforth would overshadow theirs, and his religion would in the end destroy their superstition. Thus he probably argued, and the result justified his anticipations. The victory at Tara was the salvation of Ireland. It was not a complete victory, but it was so far decisive that from the day on which Patrick conquered at Tara the dominion of paganism in Ireland ceased. Henceforth it had to take a lower place and abate somewhat of its claims.

There was of course a defect in this policy of Patrick, of which the saint may have been as conscious as his modern critics. What " a breath has made " a breath can also unmake, and the missionary who puts his "trust in princes" overmuch is apt to find, as Augustine's successors in England found for a time, that the succession of a pagan king may undo much of the work that seemed so prosperous during the lifetime of his Christian predecessor. The nation that throws off paganism at the bidding of its chief does not become Christian at heart, and is ready to relapse at the first invitation. But in the case of Patrick's mission, as with Augustine's, the higher and more cultivated classes of the country were the most susceptible to Christian influences; the common people of Ireland were too rigidly held in spiritual bondage to venture of their own accord to listen to a new creed, unless first their druids were discomfited. Patrick took the best course open to him in the circumstances in which he was placed, and his action is not to be censured because after his death there was, as might have been expected, a falling away from the faith. Such alternations of progress and decline are common in the records of missionary work in all ages. It is a popular mistake to suppose that in ancient times nations were converted in one day: the work of missions has ever been a slow work, needing persistent effort and the sacrifice of many lives.

There is sowing as well as reaping to be done ; "Not to Palladius, but to Patrick, God gave the conversion of Ireland," and Patrick and his coadjutors left much imperfect and ready to perish in the fabric they erected.

In pursuance of his design of visiting Tara, Patrick bade farewell to Dichu, and left Mag Inis (the island plain), afterwards called Lecale, and sailed away to Inbher Colpthi, or the mouth of the Boyne, and landed in what is now Drogheda Bay. It is perhaps to this point in Patrick's mission-work that we may refer the story of Benignus,[1] which is the sweetest of all the traditions connected with the great apostle of Ireland, and, wet with "the dropping of warm tears," atones for many a page of monotonous marvels. Such stories as this show a new feeling in literature ; the old Roman hardness has gone, and a new era of gentleness and love has commenced. There is much in this story of Benen, or Benignus, and its early date and the absence of any improbabilities favour its authenticity.

The River Boyne is near its mouth the northern boundary of the present County of Meath. A few miles to the south is the little river Delvin, which divides Meath from County Dublin. Patrick, we are told, came to Inbher Ailbine, or the mouth of the

[1] Tirechan first mentions this story, "Book of Armagh," W.S., 303. Muirchu does not mention it. Tirechan's narrative is disjointed ; he omits the conversion of Dichu and the death of Miliuc altogether, and it is difficult to infer from his narration whether the adoption of Benignus occurred before the visit to Dichu or after. The "Tripartite Life,"W.S., 37, inserts it before: the" Lebar Brecc,"W.S., 455, after. It is more in accordance with Muirchu's Life to adopt the latter alternative.

Delvin,[1] and there found a certain good man, whom he baptised. He took a fancy to his little son, and called him Benignus (the kindly one), for the child would take Patrick's feet and clasp them to his bosom, and when Patrick was asleep, he gathered sweet-scented flowers and placed them in the saint's bosom, though they said to him, "Do not so, lest Patrick should awake."[2] Neither would the little one sleep with his father and mother, but wept unless they let him sleep with Patrick. On the morrow when the saint was departing, and had now one foot on the chariot and the other on the ground, the child held Patrick's foot with both his hands, and cried out "Let me go with Patrick, my true father." And Patrick said, "Baptize him, and lift him up in the chariot, for he is the heir of my kingdom." So he became Patrick's gillie; the same was Benignus, or Benen, the Bishop who succeeded Patrick in the Church of Armagh.

> "If of such be the kingdom of heaven,
> It must be heaven indeed."

There is an ancient tradition (not recorded by either Muirchu or Tirechan, but preserved together with their biographies in the ninth century "Book of Armagh"),[3] which mentions that when Patrick arrived at the mouth of the Boyne he left there Lomman, his sister's son, in charge of the ship, while he himself went on to Tara, and that this was by God's grace the cause of the foundation of the Church of Trim.

---

[1] Reeves' *Columba* in "Historians of Scotland," vi. 267.
[2] This story of the flowers is not in Tirechan, but is given in the "Tripartite Life," W.S., 37.
[3] W.S, 334-336.

For Patrick bade Lomman to wait forty days, and Lomman waited twice that period, and yet Patrick did not return ; so thereupon Lomman sailed up the stream[1] as far as the Ford of Trim, to the door of the house of Phelim,[2] son of Laoghaire. In the morning Phelim's son, Foirtchernn, found Lomman reciting the Gospel and was converted by him. He stayed listening to Lomman's instruction, until at last his mother came to seek him, and when she saw him with Lomman, she was glad, for she was a Briton, and possibly therefore a Christian at heart. She also, we are told, believed in like manner, and went and told her husband, Phelim, who also was glad, for his mother too was of the Britons, a daughter of the king of the Britons, and her name was Scothnoe, or Fresh-flower. This may suggest that the Irish princes preferred British wives on account of their superior culture and refinement, just as afterwards Ethelbert and other English kings about his time preferred wives who had the graces of Christianity, rather than to wed pagans like themselves. In the Welsh romance of Branwen, Matholwch, an Irish king, marries the gentle British princess, Branwen.[3] Such marriages must have prepared the way for Christianity in Ireland, as they afterwards did in England, for even if the British wife was not permitted to hold her faith, she would be glad to re-

---

[1] Usher,"Antiq.," 853, says that the river is too narrow and rocky to allow a little boat to come up as far as Trim. Todd, 258, replies that " the light boats of the period might easily have been carried over the shoals and rapids."

[2] Feidilmid in the old spelling, and also Feidlimidh.

[3] Lady Charlotte Guest's "Mabinogion," 365, 84, 2nd edition.

turn to it, when the British missionaries came to her husband's house, and would use her influence to get her husband to accept it too.

Phelim, who probably knew something of Christianity from his British mother, came out to meet Lomman, and saluted him in the British tongue, and questioned him concerning his faith and family. And Lomman answered him, "I am Lomman, a Briton, a Christian, a disciple of Bishop Patrick, who has been sent by the Lord [1] to baptize the tribes of the Irish, and convert them to the faith of Christ, who sent me hither according to the will of God." Phelim and all his family believed, and he devoted to Lomman and Patrick his territory, with his possessions and all his substance and all his race.[2] And Phelim went across the river Boyne, and remained at Cloin Lagen, and Lomman stayed with Foirtchernn at the Ford of Trim, until Patrick came to them and founded a church with them, twenty-two years before the church of Armagh was founded. Lomman became the first bishop of Trim, and when his time came to die, he went on a visit to his brother, and Foirtchernn went with him. Now before his death he insisted that Foirtchernn should succeed him as bishop, but Foirtchernn at first refused, for he said that his father had given the land to God and Patrick, and he ought not to take it back even as bishop. But Lomman said, "Thou shalt not have my blessing unless thou receive the chieftainship of my church." So Foirtchernn

---

[1] Not by Pope Celestine, as a later invention might add.

[2] *i.e.*, His patriarchal rights, as a chieftain, over his followers or clan.—Todd, 152.

yielded, but on his return to the Ford of Trim, he gave up the "chieftainship" to Cathlaid the pilgrim, three days after Lomman's death. The bishopric of Trim remained for generations in Foirtchernn's family, as the narrator tells us; he mentions eight bishops, including Foirtchernn, as the ecclesiastical race of Phelim, viz.—Foirtchernn, Aodh the Great, Aodh the Little, Conall, Baitan, Ossan, Cummene, and Saran. "These all," says the narrator, "were bishops and chiefs, venerating holy Patrick and his successor," that is, in other words, acknowledging the primacy of Armagh. Then follows a list of the "lay race" of Phelim.

This story, though acknowledged by its narrator to be one of those discovered at later times by the bishops of Armagh, is very ancient, and probably authentic. It contains no element of the marvellous; suggests one cause of Patrick's success with the higher classes, many among whom must have had British and Christian relations; and throws a light upon one of the curious customs of the ancient Irish Church, which apparently had its origin, as Dr. Todd remarks, "in the laws which regulated the tenure of land, and the relation between chieftain and clansman, or vassal, in ancient Ireland. The land granted in fee to St. Patrick, or any other ecclesiastic, by its original owner, conveyed to the clerical society of which it became the endowment all the rights of a chieftain or head of a clan; and these rights, like the rights of the secular chieftains, descended in hereditary succession. The com-arb, or co-arb, that is to say, the heir or successor of the original sain.

who was the founder of the religious society, whether
bishop or abbat, became the inheritor of his spiritual
and official influence in religious matters. The
descendants in blood, or 'founder's kin,' were in-
heritors of the temporal rights of property and
chieftainship, although bound to exercise those rights
in subjection or subordination to the ecclesiastical
co-arb." [1]

[1] Todd, 149. See also Skene's "Celtic Scotland," ii. 67 *et seq.*

CHAPTER VII.

ST. PATRICK AT TARA.

THE hill of Tara, whither Patrick turned after leaving Lomman and blessing Benignus, is situated in the county of Meath, about twenty-five miles from Dublin. Irish tradition assigns it pre-eminence from the earliest antiquity, and one hundred and thirty-six kings are said to have reigned there before the coming of Patrick. Without discussing this somewhat extravagant statement, it may suffice to know that there still exist traces of "Tara's halls," which are supposed to date from Cormac MacArt, who flourished in the third century. Some of these buildings were large; the great Hall of Assembly was 759 feet in length and 90 feet in breadth, and had 14 distinct entrances. But there is no trace at Tara of stone houses; all were of wood and clay, and the magnificence of the Irish capital, it may therefore be concluded, was of a rather barbaric and primitive description. Yet it must not be altogether despised; the wooden buildings may have been made very showy in their way; and the heroes, clad in purple mantles with collars of gold about their necks, and the noble maidens, also in purple mantles, with their golden-yellow hair flowing over their shoulders, decked out with ornaments on their necks, arms, wrists, and ankles, may have lived as gay a life as if the "halls" had been of costly marble. The wine went round at the feast, and jugglers performed before the company, with buffoonery that was not always seemly. The harp and the timpan [1] "the soul of music shed," and courtly bards chanted the praises of heroes and of kings.

The glory of Tara must have presented strange contrasts, such as are seen in a state of imperfect culture, where magnificence and meanness go hand in hand. In the wilder districts of Ireland Patrick may have occasionally met with families which had not yet emerged from a savage state. Cannibalism was laid to the charge of the Irish by classical writers,[2] and even as late as the fourth century, Jerome, as a youth, saw Irishmen eating human flesh, and skilled in the selection of the daintiest morsels.[3] There is no reference to this abomination in any documents referring to Patrick, but it is said that, two hundred years after Patrick, about 693, there was a relapse in time of grievous famine, when "man ate man."[4] The savage customs and scanty clothing of Irish invaders are referred to by Gildas, and even in the reign of Henry II. some sailors, who had been

---

[1] A kind of stringed instrument.
[2] Diodorus and Strabo. Solinus states that conquerors drank the blood of their enemies.
[3] So he states in his second book against Jovinian. Perhaps he was mistaken.
[4] "Book of Leinster," W.S., 519.

driven out of their course, were visited by two Connaught savages, who rowed towards them in a small boat, narrow and oblong, made of wattles, and covered with the hides of animals. The men were naked except for belts of skin around their loins, and they had long yellow hair, which fell below their shoulders and covered the greater part of their bodies. They wondered at the sight of ships, as such marvels were quite unknown to them.[1] Hasty generalisations from such isolated instances are to be avoided, but it is necessary at the same time to take note of savage survivals and traces of imperfect culture, if only as a corrective to the ideas gathered from the pretty pictures of Thomas Moore.[2]

Tara was the residence of the Ard-ri, or Supreme King. The Irish nation consisted of a number of tribes, each of which had a certain measure of Home Rule, for each had its own petty king or chieftain, who received tribute, held councils, and made edicts. But the tribes were held together by a loose bond of union, and at times the supreme king, who governed himself the kingdom of Meath, held at Tara a great assembly of the subordinate chiefs. At the time of Patrick's visit, the reigning king was Laoghaire.[3]

After journeying along the valley of the Boyne, Patrick came at nightfall to the "graves of the men of Fiacc," now Slane, a few miles from Tara, and

---

[1] Giraldus Cambrensis, "Topography of Ireland," iii. 26.
[2] For startling survivals in the seventeenth century, see "Conditions for the Survival of Archaic Custom," by Mr. G. L. Gomme, in *Archæological Review*, iv. 428-420.
[3] Pronounced "Leary."

there pitched his tent, close to that extraordinary series of raised mounds, raths, pillar-stones, circles, and caves which is now the wonder of antiquarians. The "Fairy Mound" of the Brugh,

> "The royal Brugh,
> By the dark-rolling waters of the Boyne,
> Where Angus Og magnificently dwells,"

is renowned in many a romantic story of ancient Erin. What Patrick did that night, or what happened subsequently, is, unfortunately, very obscure, owing to the fact that Muirchu, who hitherto has been our chief authority, has at length succumbed to the temptation of fine writing. Hitherto it has been possible to accept his guidance without much distrust, but he seems to have considered all the previous narration to be merely preparatory to the great conflict between Christianity and paganism at the capital. His style now rises to the height of the subject; he introduces Scriptural parallels, and compares King Laoghaire to Nebuchadnezzar and to Herod, while Patrick overthrows the magi or druids, just as Peter overthrew Simon Magus, or as Moses overthrew the magicians of Egypt. A druid has his brains dashed out miraculously for blasphemy, and those who attempt to seize Patrick at the king's command are confounded by darkness and an earthquake. Afterwards Patrick and his companions, one of whom was a boy, seem to those who would slay them to be eight deer and a fawn. The druid Lucetmael and Patrick work miracles in opposition to one another, till at length the druid is burned alive. Such is the narrative upon which Muirchu has lavished all his powers of eloquence, and of which undoubtedly he was proud as a monument of his rhetorical skill, likely to make the age that was to come his own. It is difficult to deal with such a story; it has no elements of beauty which warrant its narration as a legend, and, if purged of the miraculous, it can still lay no claim to the rank of genuine history. But, when thus purged, it may be summarised as follows:—

The Pagan festival, then being celebrated by Laoghaire at Tara, commenced by extinguishing every fire in the country, and whosoever violated the order was to be put to death. But Patrick lighted his Paschal fire on the hill of Slane. This was seen from Tara, and led to a conflict between Patrick and Laoghaire's magi, and finally the king was persuaded to be a Christian. Dubthach Maccu-Lugil,[1] the chief of the bards, was converted at the same time.[2]

There is little doubt that Patrick visited Laoghaire and brought Christianity before him with sufficient success to secure its toleration. It is also not improbable that Patrick, with that politic boldness which is not rashness, and with that contempt of peril which leads him in his "Confession" to express his ambition for a martyr's death, adopted some striking

[1] Or Maccu-Lugair.
[2] Tirechan gives little help here. He mentions that Kannan was consecrated bishop by Patrick at this time, and carried with him the first blessed fire. He also mentions the destruction of the magi, but very briefly, and leaves out many of the wonderful incidents recorded by Muirchu. But he throws little light upon the event which really happened at Tara.

method of publicly defying the evil powers of paganism, as in a later age Coifi of Northumbria set at nought the pagan customs of his country, and threw his lance within the enclosure of the heathen temple, or as Boniface cut down Thor's oak. The subsequent history of Patrick's mission and his remarkable success seem to prove that paganism and the druids were routed in some very striking way at the national capital. The news passed over Ireland that a wonderful stranger had come with a new creed, and rumour magnified his fame as it carried it along. Two centuries afterwards the story had reached the dimensions which it has in the narrative of Muirchu. Tirechan gives a modified version of it, but the main features are the same. Attempts have been made to identify Laoghaire's feast with the Beltaine, which, however, was held on the 1st of May, and some legends state that it was the Feast of Tara, which was held on Samhain, the first of November. If either of these theories be true, the story of Patrick's Paschal Fire must be an invention. Another statement of the legends is that Laoghaire was holding the feast on his birthday. It is quite impossible to determine what the truth is,[1] but the very exaggerations of the legends may testify to the greatness of the impression pro-

---

[1] It is, on the whole, more probable that the coincidence of the Pagan festival with Easter Eve, the opposition between the Paschal fire of St. Patrick and the idolatrous fire of the druids, together with the other manifestly fabulous stories introduced into the legend, are all circumstances created by the imagination of the biographers, which cannot be dealt with as history. — Todd, "St. Patrick," 417.

duced in Ireland by Patrick's visit to Tara, and the importance of the advantage he gained through it.

In one important point Tirechan corrects the narrative of Muirchu. He makes it clear that Patrick did not succeed in converting King Laoghaire, although he won his confidence and friendship.[1] For he tells us that not long afterwards Patrick "came a second time to the city of Tara, to Laoghaire, son of Niall, because he had made a covenant with him that he should not be killed in his kingdom. But he could not believe, saying, 'For Niall my father did not permit me to believe but that I should be buried on the ramparts of Tara, as men who stand in battle'; for the heathen are wont to be buried in their sepulchres armed with weapons ready face to face until the day of Erdathe, as the magi call it, that is the Day of the Judgment of the Lord. 'I the son of Niall must thus be buried as the son of Dunlaing in Maistiu in the plain of Liffey, on account of the hardness with which I have hated.'"

There is more of a true ring about this pathetic story than in Muirchu's plagiarisms from the Book of Daniel. The grim pagan sees dimly the truth of the new gospel of love and gentleness, and he respects its teacher; but his soul must be gathered to the souls of his fathers and share their doom, whether it be good or bad, and, faithful to the traditions of his clan, he scorns to do otherwise than face his hereditary foemen after death, as his hereditary foeman is already placed to face him. Yet he is willing enough that

---

[1] "Book of Armagh," W. S., 308; Todd, 438.

others, on whom no such obligation is laid, should hear the new creed and embrace it, if they so please. As for himself he cannot change; and so, as an old manuscript tells us, " the body of Laoghaire was brought afterwards from the South, and interred with his armour of valour, in the south-east of the outer rampart of the royal Rath of Laoghaire at Tara, with his face turned southwards upon the men of Leinster, as fighting with them, for he was the enemy of the Leinster-men in his lifetime."[1]

It was at the time of his visit to Tara, according to tradition, that Patrick composed the wonderful Irish hymn which is known as the " Deer's Cry,"[2] one of the most powerful expressions of faith in the protection of God against all evils, ghostly and bodily, which has been ever written. There are several translations of this hymn in existence,[3] but the ablest is the verse translation of James Clarence Mangan, the greatest and most unfortunate of Ireland's poets. It is inaccurate in a few particulars, but it compensates for these defects by an energy and spirit which distinguishes it as the work of an original genius. Dr.

[1] "Leabhar na huidhre" in Todd, 439.
[2] *Faed Fiada* (Stokes), *Feth-fiadha* (Colgan), interpreted as "The Deer's Cry" by Stokes in "Trip. Life," and as "The Instruction of the Deer," by Petrie, who first published it; also interpreted as "The Guard's Cry." *Faed*, later *faodh*, is the same word as the Welsh *gwaedd*, a cry.
[3] Probably the most accurate is contained in Dr. Whitley Stokes' "Tripartite Life," &c., 49-53. There is another literal translation by Dr. Todd in his "St. Patrick," 426-429, which is also contained in H. & S. ii. 320-323. A third is in Miss Cusack's "St. Patrick," 252-255 (Kenmare Series). A verse translation by Mrs. Alexander is included in Wright's " Writings of St. Patrick," 99-102.

Todd has said that "it preserves in a wonderful manner the *tone* and spirit of the original." As I believe that there is no other which so thoroughly brings St. Patrick's words home to the modern reader, I subjoin it:—

> At Tarah[1] to-day, in this awful hour,
>   I call on the Holy Trinity!
> Glory to Him Who reigneth in power,
> The God of the elements, Father and Son,
> And Paraclete Spirit, Which Three are the One,
>   The ever-existing Divinity!
>
> At Tarah to-day I call on the Lord,
> On Christ the Omnipotent Word,
> Who came to redeem from Death and Sin
>   Our fallen race;
>   And I put and I place
> The virtue that lieth and liveth in
>   His Incarnation lowly,
>   His Baptism pure and holy,
> His life of toil, and tears, and affliction,
> His dolorous death—His Crucifixion,
> His Burial, sacred and sad and lone,
>   His Resurrection to life again,
> His glorious Ascension to Heaven's high Throne,
> And, lastly, His future dread
>   And terrible coming to judge all men—
> Both the Living and Dead.
>
> At Tarah to-day I put and I place
> The virtue that dwells in the Seraphim's love,
> And the virtue and grace
>   That are in the obedience
>   And unshaken allegiance
> Of all the Archangels and Angels above,

---

[1] This poem of Clarence Mangan is founded on Dr. Petrie's translation, and retains his error of translating the first word of the poem, which really means "I bind myself." See Todd, 426 *note*, 429 *note*.

And in the hope of the Resurrection
To everlasting reward and election,
And in the prayers of the Fathers of old,
And in the truths the Prophets foretold,
And in the Apostles' manifold preachings,
And in the Confessors' faith and teachings,
And in the purity ever dwelling
    Within the Immaculate Virgin's breast,[1]
And in the actions bright and excelling
    Of all good men, the just and the blest.

At Tarah to-day, in this fateful hour,
I place all Heaven within its power,
And the sun with its brightness,
And the snow with its whiteness,
And fire with all the strength it hath,
And lightning with its rapid wrath,
And the winds with their swiftness along their path,
And the sea with its deepness,
And the rocks with their steepness,
And the earth with its starkness :[2]
    All these I place,
    By God's almighty help and grace,
Between myself and the Powers of Darkness.

    At Tarah to-day.
    May God be my stay !
May the strength of God now nerve me !
May the power of God preserve me !
May God the Almighty be near me !
    May God the Almighty espy me !
May God the Almighty hear me !

---

[1] There is no reference to the Virgin in the original. Todd has, "In the purity of the Holy Virgins"; the version in Miss Cusack's life has, "In purity of holy Virgins"; Dr. Whitley Stokes, "In innocence of holy Virgins."

[2] "Stability of Earth, Compactness of Rock."

Dr. W. Stokes.

ST. PATRICK AT TARA.

May God give me eloquent speech!
May the arm of God protect me!
May the wisdom of God direct me!
May God give me power to teach and to preach.
May the shield of God defend me!
May the host of God attend me!
    And ward me,
    And guard me,
Against the wiles of demons and devils,
Against the temptations of vices and evils,
Against the bad passions and wrathful will
Of the reckless mind and the wicked heart,
Against every man who designs me ill,
Whether leagued with others or plotting apart.

    In this hour of hours,
    I place all those powers
Between myself and every foe,
    Who threaten my body and soul
    With danger or dole,
To protect me against the evils that flow
From lying soothsayers' incantations,
From the gloomy laws of the Gentile nations,
From Heresy's hateful innovations,
From Idolatry's rites and invocations,
Be those my defenders,
My guards against every ban—
And spell of smiths,[1] and Druids, and women:
In fine, against every knowledge that renders
The light Heaven sends us dim in
The spirit and soul of Man!

---

[1] "Workers in metals were held in the highest estimation; the smith especially was regarded as invested with superhuman attributes of intelligence and power. . . . The ordinary smith of common life is to this day regarded by the peasantry as endowed with magical power and influence. In ancient times he was looked on as a sorcerer and an adept in necromancy."—*Ulster Journal of Archæology*, No. xxxv., pp. 219-20.

May Christ, I pray,
Protect me to-day
    Against poison and fire,
Against drowning and wounding,
That so, in his grace abounding,
    I may earn the Preacher's hire.[1]

    Christ, as a light,
    Illumine and guide me!
Christ, as a shield, o'ershadow and cover me!
Christ be under me! Christ be over me!
    Christ be beside me
    On left hand and right!
Christ be before me, behind me, about me!
Christ this day be within and without me!

Christ the lowly and meek,
Christ the all-powerful, be
In the heart of each to whom I speak,
In the mouth of each who speaks to me!
    In all who draw near me,
    Or see or hear me.

At Tarah to-day, in this awful hour,
    I call on the Holy Trinity!
Glory to Him Who reigneth in power,
The God of the Elements, Father and Son,
And Paraclete Spirit, which Three are the One,
    The ever-existing Divinity!

Salvation dwells with the Lord,
With Christ, the Omnipotent Word.
From generation to generation,
Grant us, O Lord, Thy grace and salvation.[2]

---

[1] "Christ to protect me to-day against every poison,
    Against burning, against drowning, against death-wound,
    So that I may have a multitude of rewards."
                                  Dr. Whitley Stokes.

[2] This last verse is in Latin in the original.

CHAPTER VIII.

WORK IN MEATH AND JOURNEY TO TIRAWLEY.

PATRICK went from Tara to Tailte, now Teltown, between Navan and Kells, to Coirpriticus,[1] or Coirpre, a brother of Laoghaire. Tirechan incidentally refers to the great Fair,[2] which was held there in August, and which seems to have been connected with pagan sun-worship. This fair lasted down to living memory, and in its later days is said to have closely resembled the celebrated Fair of Donnybrook.[3] Patrick in this visit pursued his usual bold policy of striking at paganism in its greatest strongholds, for Teltown is notable in Irish legend for its connection with the mythology of heathenism. There the Tuatha De Danaan, the fairies of Ireland, fought a great battle against the intrusive human race of the Sons of Mile, and were defeated, so that they took refuge in

---

[1] This is the form of his name in Tirechan's biography.

[2] " Where is held a royal contest" (*agon regale*). Tirechan, W.S. 307, Todd (439) and Professor Stokes' "Ireland and the Celtic Church," 79 assume, that Patrick visited Tailltin at the time of the fair, which happened in July and August. But Tirechan implies that it was during the festival of Easter. Miss Cusack (260) infers from the statement that Patrick came *prima feria*, that he went there on Easter Monday.

[3] Stokes' "Ireland and the Celtic Church," 79.

mounds, especially in burial-mounds and cemeteries. Teltown itself was the place of one of the greatest cemeteries of the island. The fair of Teltown was held "a fortnight before Lammas, and a fortnight after," and is mythically said to have been founded by a king of Ireland, named Lug, in honour of her who nurtured and brought him up, namely, Tailltiu, daughter of Maghmor, the King of Spain, who was wife to the last king of the Fir Bolg, and afterwards to the chief of the Tuatha De Danaan. From this commemoration by Lug, the name Lugnassad is said to have been given to the first of August.[1]

It is not surprising that at a centre of paganism such as Teltown was, Patrick was not left wholly unmolested. Coirpriticus, the brother of Laoghaire, "desired to slay him, and caused his followers to be scourged in the river Sele (or Blackwater) in order that they might point out Patrick to Coirpriticus."

Patrick next went to Conall, another brother of Laoghaire, who was converted, and gave the God of Patrick the site of a church, measuring it with his feet to the length of sixty feet. It was called in Tirechan's day "the Great Church of Patrick," or Domnach[2] Mor Patraic, now Donagh Patrick. Not long after this success he was reminded by a chance conversation of his dream concerning the voices of the wood of Fochlut, and was led in consequence thereof to journey towards Connaught.

---

[1] Keating, quoted by Rhys, "Hibbert Lectures," 409. Professor Rhys further gives his interpretation of the statement.

[2] Domnach = Church, from Latin *dominicum*, the Lord's house. "Donnybrook" is for Domnach Broc, "the church of Broc."

He had returned to Tara, and was baptising there at the fountain Loigles, and on that day he baptised Erc mac Dego[1] and many thousand others. There were some scoffers who were laughing at the ceremony, and others were talking close to Patrick about their private concerns. And one said to another, " Tell me your name, and that of your father and of your farm, and of your plain, and where your home is." The other answered, " I am Endeus, son of Awley,[2] son of Fechrach, son of Echach, from the western regions, from the plain Domnon, and from the wood of Fochlut." When Patrick heard the name Fochlut, he was exceeding glad, for he remembered the dream which he had had long before concerning the voices coming from the wood of Fochlut, which had prayed him to come to their help. So he turned round and said to Endeus or Enna, " I also will go with you, if I shall be alive, because the Lord has told me to go." Enna was unwilling that he should go with him, for he feared that they might both be slain upon the way. He asked Patrick to baptize his son Conall, but as for himself and his brethren, he said they could not believe until they came to their own people, as otherwise they would be laughed at. A dispute about their inheritance had brought the sons of Awley to

---

[1] He was afterwards made bishop of Slane. "A small chapel, called St. Erc's Hermitage, still exists in the Marquis of Conyngham's demesne on the banks of the Boyne." (" Ireland and the Celtic Church," 76 *note*.) The well Loigles, according to Professor Stokes, has been filled up, but the ground is still marshy just beneath it, p. 81.

[2] Written by Tirechan, *Amolngad;* also written Amalgaidh in old Irish, but pronounced Awley.

the court of Laoghaire, in order that it might be decided by the king. Laoghaire and Patrick acted together as arbitrators, and they divided the inheritance into seven parts, one for each son. And Enna said: "I devote my son and the part of my inheritance to the God of Patrick and to Patrick." "Wherefore," adds Tirechan, who is the authority for the story, "some say that we are servants of Patrick up to the present day," a note which indicates that he is here relating a piece of his own family or tribal history, which is therefore likely to be perfectly authentic.[1]

Patrick made a league with the sons of Awley for a safe-conduct to their country. "He paid," says Tirechan, "the price of fifteen souls of men, as he affirms in his own writing, that no wicked men might hinder them as they went straight across the whole of Ireland." The passage referred to occurs in the "Confession," where Patrick says that he gave presents to the kings, besides the cost of keeping their sons, who were his companions, and yet at one time they were eager to kill him, and the party was plundered and himself bound in irons, but on the fourteenth day the Lord delivered him from their power. "You," he adds, "know how much I expended on those who were judges through all the districts which I used more frequently to visit; for I think I distributed to them no less than the price of fifteen men."[2]

---

[1] Tirechan, W.S. 308, 309.
[2] "Confession," H. and S. 311.

Tirechan after this story gives a list of churches founded by Patrick, and further illustrates the perils to which the saint and his party were exposed by relating how at Uisnech of Meath, a notable centre of pagan worship (where, as we have already seen, was probably a celebrated circle of stones), Patrick stayed by the Stone of Cothraige, but some foreigners (or pilgrims) were slain around him by Fechach, son of Neill. He crossed the river Ethne, now the Inny, in county Longford, as he travelled north-west towards Connaught, and next consecrated Bishop Mel, who, later authors say, was brother of Bishop Lomman of Trim, and son of Patrick's sister, Darerca. He also ordained Bishop Gosacht of Guasacht, the son of his old master Miliuc.

Patrick afterwards entered Mag Slecht, "the plain of kneeling," a plain of counties Cavan and Leitrim. There he stationed Methbrain, or Mabran, and there, according to the "Tripartite Life," he saw Cenn Cruaich with "his sub-gods twelve." The mark of a blow from Patrick's staff was long pointed out on the left side of Cenn Cruaich, and the condition of the other idols buried in earth up to their heads was popularly ascribed to a miracle wrought on the occasion of his visit.[1] After this Patrick crossed the Shannon at Snam da En, "the Swimming of two Birds," the ancient name, as is said, of that part of the Shannon lying between Clonmacnois and Clonburren, in the parish of Moore, and barony of Moycarnen, county Roscommon.[2] The name of a

[1] "Tripartite Life," W.S., 93.
[2] "Tripartite Life," W.S., 93. Tirechan, W.S., 312.

neighbouring spot, Cell Buadmoil, was said to commemorate the death of Patrick's charioteer.

It was during Patrick's stay in Connaught, before he had yet reached Tirawley, that he met the daughters of king Laoghaire. The story is ancient, being related by Tirechan, and it has a strange, weird beauty, which Mr. Aubrey de Vere has caught and infused into his poem on the subject. It is related in considerable detail, and contains one mythical statement for which it is hard to account. Tirechan was an honest chronicler and did his best to gather facts, but he was not critical; he has given the story as he found it, for to him it presented no difficulties. To modern criticism it appears to be more than mere legend, and yet the facts are so mixed with legend that it is difficult to separate them. It is an echo from a far distant time, with other habits and ways of thought than our own, and will throw light upon the condition of the society in which Patrick laboured, and perhaps also upon his own modes of instruction and his own ideas of Christianity.[1]

The two daughters of King Laoghaire, Ethne the fair and Fedelm the Ruddy, were staying in Connaught, under the care of two Druids named Mael and Caplit. Now Patrick came one morning before sunrise to the fountain Clebach, on the east side of Crochan, which Crochan, now Rath-Croghan, near Belanagare, in county Roscommon, was an old residence of the kings of Connaught. Patrick and his company sat down near the spring. And lo (says

---

[1] Dr. Whitley Stokes says it "bears internal evidence of antiquity and genuineness," cxlii., cxliii.

Tirechan) the two girls came to the fountain "early,[1] to wash, after the manner of women, and they found near the fountain a holy synod of bishops with Patrick. And whence they were, or of what form, or of what people, or of what district, they knew not; but they supposed them to be men of the Side, or of the terrene gods, or a phantasm.[2]

"And the girls said to them : ' Where are ye and whence have ye come ? ' and Patrick said to them, ' It were better for you to confess to our true God than to ask us concerning our race.'

" The first girl said, ' Who is God ? And where is God ? And of what is God ? And where is His dwelling ? Hath He sons and daughters, gold and silver, this God of yours ? Is He ever-living ? Is He beautiful ? Have many fostered His Son ? Are His daughters dear and fair to the men of the world ? Is He in heaven or in earth ?

" ' In the sea ?
" ' In rivers ?
" ' In mountains ?
" ' In valleys ?
" ' Tell us the knowledge of Him ?
" ' How shall He be seen ?
" ' How is He loved ?
" ' How is He found ?
" ' In youth,
" ' In age,
" ' Is he found ? '

---

[1] From this point I translate the " Book of Armagh."
[2] This whole sentence is broken up into eight lines in the Book of Armagh, as being somewhat rhythmical.

"But Saint Patrick, full of the Holy Ghost, answering, said : ' Our God, the God of all men, God of heaven and earth, sea and streams, God of sun and moon, of all stars, God of mountains high and valleys low, God above heaven and in heaven and under heaven, hath his dwelling in heaven and earth and sea and all things that are therein.

" ' He inspireth all things,
" ' Quickeneth all things,
" ' Is over all things,
" ' Sustaineth all things.

' He lights the light of the sun, and the light of the moon. . . . .[1] and hath made springs in the dry ground and dry islands in the sea, and stars hath He placed for the service of the greater lights. He hath a Son co-eternal with Himself and like Himself. The Son is not younger than the Father, nor the Father older than the Son. And the Holy Ghost breatheth in Them. The Father and the Son and the Holy Ghost are not divided. I verily wish to unite you to the King celestial, seeing ye are daughters of a king terrestrial. Believe.'

" And the girls said, as if with one mouth and one heart : ' Teach us most carefully how we can believe the King celestial. Show us how we may see Him face to face, and as thou shalt say to us, let us do.'

" And Patrick said, ' Believe ye that by baptism ye put off the sin of your father and mother ? '

" They answered, ' We believe.'

" ' Believe ye in repentance after sin ? '

---

[1] Here the Latin text is obscure and corrupt.

"'We believe.'

"'Believe ye in the life after death? Believe ye in the resurrection in the day of judgment?'

"'We believe.'

"'Believe ye in the unity of the Church?'

"'We believe.'

"And they were baptized, and Patrick blessed the white garment on their heads. And they asked to see the face of Christ. And the saint said to them: 'Ye cannot see the face of Christ unless ye shall taste death, and unless ye receive the sacrifice.'

"And they answered, 'Give us the sacrifice that we may be able to see the Son, our spouse.'

"And they received the eucharist of God, and they slept in death.[1] And they placed them on a bed, covered by one mantle, and their friends made great lamentation and mourning. And the druid Caplit, who had fostered the second girl,[2] came and wept; and Patrick preached to him, and he believed, and the hairs of his head were taken off.

"And his brother Mael came and he said: 'My brother has believed Patrick, and it shall not be so;

---

[1] " Give us the Sacrifice !" Each bright head
  Bent towards it as sunflowers bend to the sun.
  They ate; and the blood from the warm cheek fled;
  The exile was over; the home was won.
  A starry darkness o'erflowed their brain;
  Far waters beat on some heavenly shore;
  Like the dying away of a low, sweet strain,
  The young life ebbed, and they breathed no more.
      Aubrey de Vere, "Legends of St. Patrick."

[2] Or "one of them," but see "Tripartite Life," W.S., 103. The Latin is *alteram*.

but I will bring him back to heathenism and to magic.'¹ And he spake rough words unto Patrick, and Patrick spake to him and preached, and converted him to the repentance of God, and the hairs of his head were taken off, that is, the magical rule which before was seen on his head, *airbacc giunnæ* ("as a band of hell"),² as is said.

"Concerning him is the proverb which is more celebrated than all Scotic proverbs, 'Mael is like to Caplit.'

"And they believed in God. And the days of mourning for the daughters of the king were accomplished, and they buried them near the well Clebach, and they made a round ditch like a Ferta (a Pagan mound), because thus the Scotic men and heathen used to do, but with us it is called Relic, that is, remains, and Feurt. And it was granted with the bones of the holy maidens to God and to Patrick, and to his heirs after him for ever, and he made a church of earth in that place."³

> Such were the ways of those ancient days —
> To Patrick for aye that grave was given;
> And above it he built a church in their praise,
> For in them had Eire been spoused to heaven.⁴

---

¹ *Ad mathoum* perhaps means "to Mathu." Dr. Whitley Stokes suggests perhaps we should read "*et te ad Milchoum.*" I will bring thee back to thy old master, Milchu or Miliuc. This is also suggested by Dr. Todd, 454.

² This is the interpretation of Dr. Todd, 455 *note*; but Dr. W. Stokes says that *airbacc giunnae* seems to mean a tonsure or cutting off of the hair of the forepart of the head.

³ Tirechan, W.S. 314-317.

⁴ Aubrey de Vere.

The clergy "in their white garments with their books before them,"[1] seated beside the well; the young princesses with the light of the rising sun shining full on their faces[2]—one, fair and white, questioning with impulsive Celtic features and eager hands; the other, dark and ruddy, as interested, but more retiring and loveable, standing a little in the rear of her sister;[3] and Patrick, with that countenance of gentleness and calm which quieted the passion of Dichu and won the love of little Benen—these form a picture such as none but a great artist could fittingly reproduce. There are few things in literature to equal, in simplicity and power, Tirechan's story of Ethne the Fair and Fedelm the Ruddy.

[1] This touch is found in the "Tripartite Life." W.S. 101.
[2] They were coming eastward from Crochan to the well.
[3] It was Ethne who took the lead in questioning— "The first maiden said," etc., says Tirechan before the longest question. It is allowable to suppose that Fedelm was the best beloved, for the druid Caplit, who fostered her, wept, whereas Mael is not said to have wept at all.

CHAPTER IX.

TRAINING OF PUPILS AND FOUNDING OF CHURCHES.

For seven years Patrick remained in Connaught, and taught and baptised the people; he erected many churches and trained pupils for holy orders. On several occasions, both in Connaught and elsewhere, Patrick is said to have written alphabets[1] for his pupils. It has been supposed from these statements that Patrick was the first to introduce an alphabet into Ireland, or at least that he introduced the Roman alphabet, which eventually superseded the Ogmic letters.[2] It is very clear that the instruction in the

---

[1] The word sometimes used is *abgitorium*, an Irish corruption of *abecedarium*. Sometimes the phrase is *elementa scripsit*. Patrick wrote an alphabet for Locharnach, son of Ernaisc (Tirechan, W.S. 320); for Oengus, son of Bishop Senach (ib. 322); for the boy Mac Ercae, whom he blessed with a father's blessing (ib. 326); for Macc Rime and Muirethach, who afterwards became bishops (ib. 327); for Cerpan (ib. 308); for a tender boy named Hinu, whom he baptized and blessed with a bishop's blessing; and, the "Tripartite Life" adds, for the bard Fiacc, when he made him a bishop (W.S. 191). Nennius says that Patrick wrote 365 alphabets or more; and the Chronological Tract in the Lebar Brecc mentions 300.

[2] On this subject there has been a brisk controversy. See, among others, Innes, "Of the Ancient Inhabitants of Scotland." ("Historians of Scotland," vii. 246-259.)

alphabet was given by Patrick to prepare his pupils for holy orders. Tirechan says that he could not give the number of Patrick's priests, "because he was daily baptising men, and was reading letters to them and¹ alphabets, and of some he was making bishops and priests, because they had received baptism in mature age." It is possible, therefore, that the expressions used simply mean that Patrick gave instruction in the A B C of Christian doctrine, and that the "letters" and "alphabets" which he used to read to his converts were religious epistles and primers. But it is perhaps more natural to suppose that something more than this is intended.² One curious story in the "Book of Armagh" represents a pagan mob as mistaking the writing-tablets in the hands of Patrick and his disciples for swords, which argues rather a low state of knowledge at the time. "When they saw him," the writer says, "with eight or nine men with tablets in their hands, written after the manner of Moses, the pagans cried out upon them that they should kill the holy men, and said: 'They have swords in their hands to slay men. They seem to be wooden,³ but we think them swords of iron to shed blood.'" The party was saved from the fury of the mob by the interposition of "a merciful man" named

---

¹ Here Dr. Whitley Stokes inserts conjecturally "was writing" (*scribebat*). 304; see also cliii.

² There is an Abecedarium stone at Kilmalchedar, County Kerry, with the Roman alphabet upon it in minuscules, together with DNI and a cross. It is supposed to date from the seventh century.

³ *Lignei in die apud illos.*

Hercaith, for whose son Patrick wrote a Book of Psalms, "which," adds the narrator, "I have seen." From this story it would appear that the tablets were wooden staves, like in form to the short straight swords of the Irish.[1] In some places we read of books given by Patrick to his disciples. He gave Bishop Mune, says Tirechan, "seven books of the law."[2] A note in the "Book of Armagh" states that "Patrick carried through the Shannon with him 50 bells, 50 patens, 50 chalices, altars, books of the law, books of the gospel, and left them in new places."[3] There may be a certain amount of exaggeration in this note, which is not of very high authority, but from this and other passages it may be inferred that various churches in Ireland had books, bells, and other articles, which were supposed to have been originally bestowed by Patrick. The scribe who wrote the "Book of Armagh" copied Patrick's "Confession" from a manuscript which he supposed to be in the saint's handwriting, and we have just noted the mention of a book of Psalms, concerning which there was the same tradition. The books of the law were evidently copies either of the whole, or, more probably, of portions, of the Old Testament; the book

---

[1] This story is found in the "Book of Armagh" placed between Muirchu's Life and the "Sayings of Patrick." There are features which it contains in its complete form which indicate that it is of late date and of doubtful value, but the very fact that such a story could arise throws a curious light upon matters in Patrick's time, and the existence of a Book of Psalms supposed to be in Patrick's handwriting is notable. See W.S. 300, 301.

[2] W.S. 326.

[3] Ib. 300.

of Psalms given to Hercaith's son would perhaps be classed among them. Tirechan states that Patrick gave "books of baptism" to deacon Justus, whom he left in the territory of the Hui-Maine, which was in the modern counties of Galway and Roscommon. From one of these books Justus afterwards baptized "Ciaran son of the wright." "Patrick's liturgy" is mentioned by the same author, who states that it was received by the church of Aghagower.[1] The "Tripartite Life" says that Patrick gave to Mochae of Noendruim a gospel, a credence-table, and a crozier, which fell from heaven with its head in Patrick's bosom and its foot in Mochae's bosom, and which was known in later days as the Etech or Winged Thing of Mochae.[2] In another passage it states that Patrick left with Presbyter Columb his book of ritual and a bell.[3] One story attempts to enhance the value of some of Patrick's books by making them originally gifts from Pope Sixtus.[4] In later days many such relics may have been falsely ascribed to Ireland's great missionary, but Tirechan's testimony is sufficient to prove the existence in his time of books which had come down from Patrick; and it is inherently probable that he would provide the churches which he built with books of ritual and with portions of the Scriptures.

These churches were exceedingly numerous. It would be somewhat dreary reading, except for an

[1] W.S. 322.
[2] Ib. 41.
[3] Ib. 171.
[4] Scholiast on "Fiacc." W.S. 421.

Irish antiquary, were a complete list to be given of those which are recorded in the pages of Tirechan, who mentions some thirty churches and cells which Patrick built in Connaught alone. They were generally of wood, according to the ancient custom of the Celts. In the towns of Roman Britain there were churches of more solid construction, but in the country places it was more usual to build by setting upright stakes in the ground and weaving wattles between. Most of the early churches in Wales were built in this way; thus Gundleus, according to his legend, "marked out a cemetery and founded a church in the midst with planks and wattles";[1] thus Cadoc built his monastery at Llancarvan,[2] and thus the followers of Kentigern built the cathedral of St. Asaph. "Some cleared and levelled the ground; others began to lay the foundations in the ground thus levelled; some also cutting down trees, others carrying them, and others fitting them together, began, as the father had arranged by measuring, to build a church and its offices of polished wood, after the manner of the Britons, since they were not yet able to build of stone, nor were so accustomed."[3] This fashion, introduced into Ireland from Britain by St. Patrick, became known in the time of Bede as the Scotic or Irish fashion, and was practised by Columba, and afterwards by the Columban missionaries in

---

[1] *Vita Sancti Gundlei,* § v. Rees' "Cambro-British Saints," 148.
[2] *Vita Sancti Cadoci,* § v. Rees' C.B.S. p. 34.
[3] *Vita Kentegerni, auctore Jocelino,* § xxiv. "Hist. of Scotland," v. 203.

England.[1] It was practised in Ireland as late as the twelfth century, when Malachy, Archbishop of Armagh, built such a church, "a rather pretty piece of Irish workmanship."[2] But Patrick's churches were not invariably built of wood. At Foirrgea, in the territory of the sons of Awley, Patrick, according to Tirechan, "made a quadrangular church of earth, because there was no forest near at hand."[3] At Clebach also, where Ethne the Fair and Fedelm the Ruddy were buried, he made a church of earth. The special record of quadrangular or square churches[4] at Foirrgea, and in the region of Conmaicne, has been held to imply that Patrick's churches were usually round. We are told by the "Tripartite Life" that Patrick measured seven feet for the oratory or church of the Ferta, which was first built at Armagh before the church on the hill was built. As one dimension only is given for this and the other buildings of the Ferta, they were probably circular.[5] The whole passage may give some idea of the construction of a primitive Irish monastery.

"In this wise, then, Patrick measured the Ferta, namely, seven score feet in the enclosure, and seven-and-twenty feet in the great-house, and seventeen

---

[1] Thus Finan built his cathedral at Lindisfarne of planks covered with reeds, "after the Scotic fashion" (*more Scottorum*). For other instances see Warren's "Liturgy and Ritual of the Celtic Church," 85-88.
[2] *Opus Scoticum pulchrum satis.* St. Bernard's "Life of Malachy," quoted by Mr. Warren, p. 86.
[3] W.S. 327.
[4] "Aecclesiae quadratae."
[5] So Todd, 478.

feet in the kitchen; seven feet in the oratory; and in that wise it was that he used to found the cloisters always." [1]

There is little doubt that some churches in or about Patrick's time were built of stone,[2] but these were comparatively few in number. Tirechan mentions Cennanus[3] in his list of Patrick's bishops, and afterwards alludes to the stone church of this bishop, evidently as an example of an uncommon style of building. So in Britain Ninian's church at Candida Casa, now Whithorn, in Wigtonshire, was built of stone about A.D. 397, "in a manner unusual among the Britons," as the historian Bede says.[4] At a later date the Irish missionary Piran built a stone church in Cornwall, if the rude building disinterred in 1835 at Perranzabuloe be, indeed, the original church. Its external length and breadth are respectively 29 ft. and 16½ ft., the height of its gables 19 ft., the height of the north and south walls 13 ft., and the thickness of its walls 2ft.[5] In construction this little church, so long concealed beneath the sand, is similar to early Irish examples, and its window[6] has been said to be identical in structure with that of the oratory of St. Nessan, in Limerick, which is reputed to have been

[1] Translation of Dr. W. Stokes, 237. Dr. Guest, "Origines Celticæ," ii. 70, suggests that the "great house" of Durrow was a large bee-hive house. See also his remarks on Celtic churches, p. 73.

W.S. 304.

Ib. 3, 18, "juxta domum (sancti) episcopi Cennani, id est lapidum."

[4] H.E. iii. 4.

[5] Haslam's "Perranzabuloe," 67.

[6] Figured by Haslam, p. 72.

founded in the time of St. Patrick.[1] Similar stone churches are those of Gwithian and Porth Curnow, in Cornwall, and the chapel of St. Medan, at Kirkmaiden, Wigtonshire. St. Gwithian's oratory, when discovered, was totally buried beneath the sand in a turf-clad mound. Its length internally is 48 ft. 11 in., of which the chancel occupies 17 ft. 1 in. The chancel is 12 ft. 2 in. wide internally; the nave 14 ft. 4 in. at the eastern end, and 13 ft. 10 in. at the western. Gwithian was one of the Irish missionaries to Cornwall. The oratory at Porth Curnow seems to have been built on an artificial mound, and a sepulchral urn has been discovered in digging, about two or three yards from its western wall; facts which have given rise to the suggestion that the spot may have been greatly venerated originally as the grave of some noted personage during the age of urn-burial. There are ruins of other ancient stone oratories in Cornwall, which are smaller than St. Piran's and St. Gwithian's, and are especially to be found in the Land's End district. Nearly all these oratories are built close to a small stream.[2]

It is, of course, impossible to assign exact dates to existing remains of early Irish ecclesiastical buildings, but it is possible that some may date from the age of St. Patrick. The quaint oratory of Gallarus[3] has been assigned to a still earlier date. It would appear from these remains that the settlements of the Christian

[1] See Borlase, "Age of the Saints," *Journal R.I.C.*, xx. 62.
[2] See further, Blight, "Churches of West Cornwall," 137-142.
[3] Figured in Miss Stokes's "Early Christian Art in Ireland," 155.

missionaries were arranged after the manner of the Irish dun or fortress. In some cases, doubtless, they were built within the old fortress itself, which had been handed over by the chief. Tirechan states that the "Great Church of Patrick" was built on the spot where formerly was the house of Conall, brother of king Laoghaire. Conall[1] measured it with his feet to the length of 60 ft., so that it was called the Great Church,[2] because most of the churches were much smaller, like the oratory at Armagh.

All round these early settlements ran an enclosure of earth or stone. The great house spoken of in the description of the Ferta at Armagh was the dwelling-place of the ecclesiastics. The stone oratories, which are still in existence, measure on an average 14 ft. long, by 9 ft. wide, and 12 ft. high. They are " angular, oblong structures, with walls either sloping in a curve towards the roof, or built in steps, and often formed like upturned boats." They have projections in front of the door at each side, apparently intended for shelter, and projecting stones in their corners and roofs, which were originally supports for scaffolding: " Over the doorway, five or seven quartz stones, rounded and waterworn, whose whiteness tells in strong contrast to the dark slate, of which the walls are often built, are set in the form of a cross."[3] Within the enclosures are often found remains of round beehive huts, and there also were the burial-grounds, "the

---

[1] Or Patrick, if the reading suggested by Dr. Whitley Stokes be accepted.
[2] Tirechan, W.S. 307.
[3] Miss Stokes ' Early Christian Art in Ireland," 153-156.

beds of the dead," as they were called, and the wells and gardens of the ecclesiastics.

In Inchaguile, in Lough Corrib, there exists a curious old church, which has been considered a memorial of Patrick's missionary labours in Connaught, and a survival from the very age of the saint. It is called Tempull Phaidrig, and is 34 ft. 7 in. in length; the thickness of its walls is nine feet, and the height of its doorway is six feet. It is evidently a relic of a very early age of Irish Christianity, and its appearance seems to justify the tradition that it was one of Patrick's original churches. There has been much discussion about a rough monolith, at Tempull Phaidrig, on which may be seen a very ancient inscription, which has been variously interpreted to mean "The Stone of Lugnæd, the son of Limania," and "The Stone of Lugnædon, son of Menuch." As some stories relate that Lugnath, a priest, was son of Patrick's sister Liamain, or Limania, considerable interest attaches to the reading of this inscription, but unfortunately the stone cannot with any certainty be ascribed to this Lugnath, as some of the best authorities favour the other interpretation.

Some of Patrick's churches appear to have been built north and south. Some lives of Patrick[1] have a story to account for this position of Patrick's first church, that of Sabhall, or Saul, near Downpatrick, and attribute it to the special request of Dichu. The original cathedral of Armagh, on the hill, is described

[1] Colgan's "Third Life" and Jocelinc. See Todd, 410.

by Muirchu as a "northern church,"[1] a term which may imply the same deviation from usage. It must have been rare, as otherwise the old lines, which are translated in Muirchu's Life,[2] and which are said there to be a Druidical prophecy of Patrick's coming, would never have been invented:

> Adze-head will come over a furious sea;
> His mantle head-holed, his staff crook-headed,
> His dish in the east of his house.
> All his household shall answer
> Amen, Amen!"[3]

As both the church at Saul and that at Armagh were called by the same name, Sabhall or Barn, it has been supposed that that was a generic name for

---

[1] *Sinistralis ecclesia.* In Celtic Latin, *dextralis* means southern, and *sinistralis* northern. See Professor Rhys' "Welsh Philology," p. 10. "Whether he (viz., our Aryan forefather) worshipped light or not, as such, he seems, in the performance of his religious rites, to have been in the habit of standing with his face turned to the rising of the sun and his right hand to the south. [Welsh, *dchau*, 'right (hand), south;' O. Ir. *dess*; Mod. Ir. *deas*, *Deheu-dir*, 'the south land—*i.e.*, South Wales,' also called *Deheu-barth*; O. Ir. *descert*, words which account for the Brit-Latin adjectives *dextralis* and *sinistralis*, 'southern' and 'northern' respectively.]" Compare the Irish proverb, "Aghaidh gach nidh fa dheas"—"The front of everything to the south." A ploughman in Ireland always turns his horses' heads to the south when yoking or unyoking them.

[2] W. S. 274.

[3] Translated by Dr. W. Stokes from the Irish verses in the "Tripartite Life," W.S. 35. The name Adze-head is given to Patrick because of his tonsure. See Reeves' "Columba." "Hist. of Scot." vi. 237. "If *Tailcenn* (adze-head) denote the coronal tonsure, it will be open to the suspicion of having been coined in the seventh ceutnry if ,but *lævigatum caput*, it will suit any date."

churches built north and south. The "Black Church" of Columba, at Derry, was built in the same way.[1]

It is said that Patrick founded in all seven hundred churches, and wrote three hundred alphabets.[2] There is no necessity to accept this estimate, for seven and three were sacred numbers in the early Irish church. This very sanctity, however, probably influenced Patrick in the founding of his little churches, for we read in Tirechan's Life that he built seven churches in Dulo Ocheni,[3] and three at the fountain Sini. The "Tripartite Life" ascribes to him seven churches at the river Fochaine,[4] now the Faughan, which flows into Lough Neagh; seven at Cianacht;[5] and seven among the Hui Tuirtri,[6] who lived near the river Bann. It has been supposed[7] that towards the end of his life Patrick founded a large number of Collegiate Churches of seven bishops, and the Litany of Angus the Culdee invokes one hundred and fifty three groups of seven bishops. The practice of building small churches in groups of seven prevailed largely after Patrick's age. "Increase of magnificence was sought more by extending the number than by augmenting the size. The favourite number for a complete ecclesiastical establishment was seven, as in Greece, this number being identical

[1] Dr. Reeves' "Introduction to Life of Columba." "Hist. of Scotland," vi. 50.
[2] Chronological Tract in "Lebar Brecc," W.S. 553.
[3] W.S. 329.
[4] Ib. 154.
[5] Ib. 160.
[6] 168.
[7] Skene's "Celtic Scotland," ii. 24-26.

with that of the seven Apocalyptic Churches of Asia. Thus, there are seven at Glendalough, seven at Cashel, and the same number is found at several other places, and generally two or three at least are grouped together. . . It is not only at Mount Athos, and other places in Europe, but also in Asia Minor, that we find the method of grouping a large number of small churches together, seven being the favourite number, and one often attained."[1] There are a few indications of similar usages in Wales, at a later age than that of Patrick. One tradition says, concerning the famous Glamorganshire College of Llantwit Major, that "Illtyd founded seven churches, and appointed seven companies for each church, and seven halls, or colleges, in each company, and seven saints in each hall, or college."[2] The Triads state that the number of the students at Llantwit was 2,400, whereas this computation makes the number 2,401, a difference which is more curiously suggestive than exact agreement would be. At Bangor Iscoed, according to Bede, there were seven companies, each of three hundred monks, an arrangement evidently based upon the two sacred numbers, and possibly implying a group of seven oratories. The Welsh fondness for triads is universally known. The Laws of Howel the Good mention seven Bishop-Houses in Dyfed,[3] which may suggest the existence at some period of seven

---

[1] Fergusson, J., "Illustrated Handbook of Architecture," ii. 915.
[2] Iolo MSS. 555. See also "Ancient British Church" (S.P.C.K.) 119.
[3] H. and S., i. 281.

bishops for that Principality. The selection of seven British bishops to meet Augustine was probably determined by the same principle.

Of the interior of Patrick's churches and their furniture it is difficult to speak with any certainty. Even if we accept Cogitosus' description of St. Bridget's Church at Kildare as an accurate picture, we cannot transfer it to the churches of Patrick's age. When we read in so late a document as the "Tripartite Life" that Cochmaiss and Tigris and Lupait and Darerca were the nuns who made altar-cloths, or that Patrick left 50 bells and 50 chalices and 50 altar-cloths in the land of Connaught, we cannot venture from these statements either to affirm or deny the use of altar-cloths in the earliest Irish churches. The latter statement seems to be borrowed, with some change, from the passage already quoted from the "Book of Armagh" regarding the bells, patens, chalices, altars and books which Patrick carried into Connaught, but nothing is said there about altar-cloths. Tirechan twice mentions stone altars, one in a church of Patrick's and the other in a pre-existing cave-church in a mountain of the sons of Ailello, the latter being called a "wonderful stone altar."[1] Probably these passages rather indicate that altars were not usually of stone, but of wood, as in the case of the altar which St. Bridget is said to have touched when she received the veil at the hands of Bishop Mel, of Ardagh. It is scarcely probable that Patrick would carry many stone altars across the Shannon, unless they were like his portable

[1] There were stone altars at Perranzabuloe and St. Gwithian's.

stone-altar, which a foolish legend relates swam across from Brittany to Ireland.[1] The statement in the "Book of Armagh," that he carried altars across the Shannon for his churches must imply that they were comparatively light, for no miracle is hinted. Tirechan gives further information about Patrick's altars. "Saint Assicus, the Bishop," he says, "was Patrick's coppersmith, and used to make altars and square bookcases. He used to make also patens of our saint for the honour of Bishop Patrick; and of these I have seen three square patens, that is, a paten in Patrick's church in Armagh, and a second in the church of Elphin, and a third in the great church of Saeoli on the altar of the holy Bishop Felart."[2] Tirechan is as fully to be believed concerning things which he had seen as any author, for his honesty is unimpeachable, and his testimony in this matter is decisive as to the patens. It would also seem to be implied in this passage that Assicus made altars of copper or bronze.[3] Tirechan

[1] "Lebar Brecc Homily," W.S. 447.
[2] W.S. 313.
[3] Assicus is not mentioned in Tirechan's list of Patrick's bishops, unless Asacus be the same. Asacus is identified by Dr. W. Stokes with Tassach, *i.e.*, t'Assach, "thy Asacus." Bishop Tassach is a notable person in later stories. He was the first to make a case for "Jesu's staff." The "Tripartite Life," W.S. 251, says that "the artisans making the patens and the credence-tables and the altar chalices" were "Tassach and Essu and Bitiu." The same Life does not identify Assicus with any of these, but borrows Tirechan's account of him elsewhere (p. 97) without altering the form of his name. Bitiu or Bite was a nephew of Assicus. Assicus was Bishop of Elphin, and was buried at Racoon in Donegal. Tassach is said to have been buried at Raholph, near Downpatrick, and was commemorated on April 14. According to Muirchu he administered the Sacrament to Patrick when he was dying.

also mentions a paten and chalice as existing in his time in the cell of a nun Adrochta, who took the veil from Patrick's hand, and seems to have received the paten and chalice from him.[1] The "Tripartite Life" adds to the story of the wonderful altar in the mountain of the Sons of Ailello that there were four chalices of glass at the four corners of the altar, which may point to an early use of glass chalices in Ireland, as in Gaul. The use of bronze altar vessels, which Tirechan ascribes to Assicus, is illustrated by a story in the Life of the Irish missionary in Switzerland, St. Gall, who refused to use silver vessels for the altar, saying that his teacher, the Blessed Columbanus, was wont to offer the sacrifice of salvation in vessels of bronze, in memory of the fact that his Saviour was fastened to the cross with bronze nails.

The only existing specimen of the workmanship of St. Patrick's artificers does not justify any high encomiums upon their skill. This is the rude iron bell of St. Patrick, of which so many legends are told by later writers, but which is altogether ignored by Muirchu and Tirechan. It is said to be "at once the most authentic and the oldest Irish relic of Christian metal-work that has descended to us," having an unbroken history through fourteen hundred years. It has been enshrined in a richly-ornamented cover since the end of the eleventh century, and is now preserved in the Museum of the Royal Irish Academy. "This bell is quadrilateral, and is formed of two plates of

---

[1] W.S. 319. "There are a paten and chalice in the cell of Adrochta, daughter of Talain, and she received the veil from Patrick's hand."

sheet iron, which are bent over so as to meet, and are fastened together by large-headed iron rivets. The corners are rounded by a gentle inclination of the parts which join. One of the plates constitutes the face, the crown, and upper third of the back, as well as the adjacent portion of each side, being doubled over at the top, and descending to meet the smaller plate, which overlaps it at the junction. Subsequently to the securing the joints by rivets, the iron frame was consolidated by the fusion of bronze into the joints and over the surface, giving to the whole a metallic solidity, which very much enhanced its resonance, as well as contributed to its preservation. The inside also was coated with bronze, though more irregularly than the outside, owing to the unevenness of the surface; and the coating seems to have been effected by the dipping of the iron shell into a vessel of the fused metallic compound, a process which has been employed to a recent date in the manufacture of the Wiltshire sheep-bells. The handle is of iron, let in by projecting spikes to perforations on the ridge of the bell, and further secured on the outside by bronze attachments of its straps."[1]

Such was the primitive Irish bell, a small bell of iron, which the missionary could carry in his hand. St. Patrick's bell is only 6 inches high, 5 inches broad and 4 deep. The "Book of Armagh," as we have seen, states that Patrick carried fifty such bells with him into Connaught; and in the same manuscript, in some additions to Tirechan's Life, we are told that Patrick

[1] Miss Stokes' "Early Christian Art in Ireland," 59, where the subject of early Irish bells is ably treated.

gave Fiacc, the Bishop of Sletty, a bell and a credence-table and a crozier and a polaire or writing tablet.[1] Curiously, neither Muirchu nor Tirechan mention bells, though late legends, both Irish and Welsh, are full of marvellous stories about them. There are between fifty and sixty bells of the primitive type in Ireland; there are others in Scotland and Wales, and a few on the Continent. Giraldus states that such bells were in use in the time of German and Lupus. One most interesting specimen of a British bell of this class has been recently presented to University College, Cardiff. It was dug up originally upon the site of an oratory of St. Ceneu, at Llangeneu, near Crickhowel, Brecknockshire. It is four inches taller than Patrick's bell, and weighs a little over six pounds fifteen ounces.[2] The Irish bells in later times were enshrined in beautiful and most elaborate metal covers, which are triumphs of Celtic art, and of which six are still in existence.

The few English tourists who go to Killarney by the Waterford route stay awhile, if they are well advised, in the middle of the beautiful scenery of wood and water at Lismore. The old castle of

[1] W.S. 344. On the subject of *Polaires* see Miss Stokes, 50, 51. Dr. W. Stokes translates *poolire* by "writing-tablet." Books, according to Miss Stokes, were carried or hung up on the walls of the monasteries in these *polaires*, which she considers to be "book-satchels." See further, W.S. 655, 195, on *polaire*. "Polaire," he says, "is either *pugillaris*, one of the names of the tube through which the sacramental wine was imbibed, or (as I think) *pugillares*, 'writing tablets.'"

[2] For list of Welsh bells, see *Archæologia Cambrensis*. iv. Ser. ii. 271 *et seq*. See also "Cymru Fu," 365. Stories of Welsh bells are to be found in *Vita S. Cadoci*, sec. 23, *Vita S. Illuti*, sec. 19, etc.

Lismore is notable not only for its picturesque position and the magnificent view to be gained from the tower, but also for containing a relic of early Irish Christianity in the Pastoral Staff or Crosier of the Bishops of Lismore. It measures 3 feet 4 inches in length, and is a beautiful specimen of bronze work. But this bronze case holds something more precious still: an old oak stick, which is probably the staff of Mochuda the founder of Lismore. The short walking-stick of yew and oak of the early teacher received superstitious veneration in later days. Patrick's was said to have been given him by the Lord Himself, from which circumstance it was called the Staff of Jesus. In later times this was covered with gold and adorned with precious stones, but in Patrick's day it was undoubtedly a plain walking-stick, and the "Book of Armagh," in strange contrast with the romance of the later lives, does not even mention it.[1]

Staff in hand, clothed down to the feet in a long rough, hairy chasuble,[2] shod with sandals, carrying on his back the gospels, or a book of ritual slung in a leathern satchel, the early missionary moved from

---

[1] It is said to have been adorned by Bishop Tassach, Patrick's disciple. This story of itself testifies that it was originally unadorned, but it is very probable that its ornamentation was later; for the statements respecting Tassach's enrichment of it are quite late. For further particulars of Celtic pastoral staves, see Miss Stokes, 96-112; Warren, 115-117.

[2] The Chasuble is mentioned as Patrick's usual garment in the "Tripartite Life," W.S. 114, 119, &c. Tirechan speaks of the chasuble of the boy Benignus, W.S. 306. The primitive chasuble was circular, with a hole in the middle for the head: "a head-holed mantle." It covered its wearer from the neck to the feet. See Du Cange, *sub voce*.

place to place with his clergy, and as they went through the forests they would beguile the labours of the way by chanting psalms.¹ Patrick and his numerous company of attendant bishops and clergy with their brazen bells and altars, probably travelled along the main roads in two-horsed chariots when they were taking long journeys, as that from Tara to Connaught, and only went on foot in their shorter excursions, or among the wilder districts. A rough company they might seem to us, for each was disfigured by the ugly Celtic tonsure, all the hair of the forepart of the head being shaved off in front of a line drawn from ear to ear, and the rest hanging untrimmed along the back.² But they suited the people well enough among whom they laboured. When they approached the great duns or fortresses of the native chiefs, they were often welcomed within the massive stone walls that encircled those large amphitheatres, were treated with all hospitality, and listened to with respect. The

---

¹ S. Mochuda, when keeping his father's swine, heard a bishop and his clergy chanting psalms as they passed through the woods, and followed them to hear the melody, and thenceforth resolved to become a monk. Montalembert, "Monks of the West," viii. 3.

² The first order of Irish saints, of which Patrick was head, had this tonsure: *Catalogus Sanctorum Hiberniæ*, II. and S. ii. 292. Patrick's tonsure is frequently alluded to. This Celtic tonsure has been supposed to be Druidical (Rhys' "Celtic Britain," 72-74), and was sneered at by the Roman party as the tonsure of Simon Magus. Tirechan, in his account of Mael's conversion, seems to indicate a difference between the priestly tonsure and the *airbacc giunnæ* of the Druids, W.S. 317. See further, Reeves' *Columba*, "Hist. of Scotland," vi. cxiv., 237, 238. Adamnan confessed that his tonsure was that of Simon Magus, but he was then in a fair way to be converted to the Roman side. Bede, H.E. v. 21.

chief would at times offer his fortress to them and to their God; the nobles honoured them by walking "righthandwise" towards them;[1] and all alike, chief and nobles, freemen and slaves, flocked from their round huts of wood[2] towards the stream or well where the missionary performed the rite of baptism. Noble women too came and gave their "necklaces, wristbands, anklets, and bracelets"[3] as offerings, and prayed that they might receive the veil at the hands of the saint. The fathers would bring their sons to the stream, and ask that they might be baptized, and the missionary, as he looked with benevolent affection and wise discrimination upon the eager faces of the boyish converts, would now and then choose one as his especial pupil, for whom he would forthwith write an alphabet, and whom he would take with him, to train henceforth for the sacred work of the Christian ministry. In vain did the Druids scowl upon the saint and his company, and mutter their incantations; in the general enthusiasm for the new teachers the people had for awhile forgotten their old superstitions; and as the baffled wizards stood on one side, conspicuous by their white garments[4] and tonsure, they felt that their power had waned before the adze-head with his head-holed mantle and his crook-headed staff.

[1] *i.e.*, With the right hand towards the person or thing to be honoured, a custom still observed in India. See Dr. Whitley Stokes, clxxii.

[2] W.S. cxlviii.

[3] So did Senmeda, daughter of Endæ. Tirechan, W.S. 321. See also *Confession*, H. and S. ii. 310.

[4] Tirechan, W.S. 325.

CHAPTER X.

WORK IN CONNAUGHT.

TIRECHAN gives a lengthy account of Patrick's missionary labours in Connaught, with details which seem to indicate an intimate personal knowledge of the district, due, probably, to the fact which he suggests, that he himself was a member or a connection of the family of Enna the son of Awley. Shortly after the conversion of Ethne and Fedelm, according to his narrative, Patrick's Frankish companions, who were fifteen brethren and one sister, quitted him while he was still in Roscommon. The two leading Franks were named Bernicius and Hernicius, and the sister was named Nitria, and "many places were given to them," says Tirechan; "but I am ignorant of all save one wherein is the Basilica of the saints, because St. Patrick pointed out to them the likeness of the place, and pointed it out to them with his finger from the rampart of Garad, when they came to him that he should choose for them from the places which they found." This place appears to be the modern Baslick in the barony of Castlerea, in county Roscommon. Garad is supposed to be the modern Oran.

Not far from these places, in Mag Selce, " the plain of the chase," Patrick halted with many bishops and other clergy, whose names are recorded; and in memory of the visit, or rather, perhaps, with the idea of destroying pagan stone-worship by consecrating the stones by the inscription of Christian sacred words, the party inscribed letters on certain stones among which they sat. Tirechan[1] had seen the inscriptions himself, but does not record their purport; but the "Tripartite Life" states that there were three words on three stones—Jesus, Soter, Salvator.[2]

At Loch Selce Patrick founded a church, and baptized the Hui-Briuin, or "Sons of Brian."

After this Patrick entered what is now the county of Sligo, and is next found in Mayo, at Cruachan Aigle, "the Mount of the Eagle," now Croagh Patrick or "Patrick's Mount," which looks over Westport Bay—

> "Huge Cruachan, that o'er the western deep
> Hung through sea-mist, with shadowing crag on crag,
> High-ridged, and dateless forest long since dead."

There, as Tirechan believed, he fasted for forty days and forty nights, and had a vision. "The birds were troublesome to him, and he could not see the face of the sky and earth and sea, because God had said to all the saints of Ireland, past, present, and future: 'Ascend, O ye saints, to the mountain which rises higher than all the mountains of the west, to bless the tribes of Ireland,' so that Patrick might see the fruit of his labour, because the company of all the Irish saints came to visit their father. And he founded a church in the plain of Humail."

There is nothing inherently improbable in the keeping of such a fast by Patrick alone in retirement on a mountain. The Celtic hermits loved such retreats by the sea. Thus Gwynllyw retired to the hill overlooking the Bristol Channel, where his church still stands;[1] thus Tudno lived on the Great Orme's Head, and left his name to Llandudno; thus Columba ascended for solitary meditation to a cairn in Iona above the "thunder of the crowding waves upon the rock;"[2] and thus Finán founded his monastery on the perpendicular rock of the Skelligs, twelve miles away from the nearest land, out in the broad Atlantic. Solitary fasts of forty days may have been common among the Celtic saints. Cedd, bishop of the East Saxons, consecrated the monastery of Laestingaeu in a way which attracted the notice of Bede, who relates it as a curious instance of Columban usages. He first sanctified the site by fasting and prayer during the season of Lent, prolonging his fast each day, except the Lord's day, till the evening. Even then he took nothing save a little bread, one egg, and a little milk and water. This, he said, was the custom of those Lindisfarne clergy of the Columban Church from whom he had learned a rule of regular discipline, first to consecrate to the Lord by fasting and prayer those places which they had newly received for building a monastery or a church.[3] The legend of St. Cadoc records or invents a fast similar

---

[1] St. Woolos, Newport, Monmouthshire.
[2] Skene, "Celtic Scotland," ii. 92, where a translation of the poem ascribed to him is given.
[3] Bede, H.E. iii. 23.

to that of Patrick. This saint used to retire for forty days in Lent to the lonely islands of Barry and the Flat Holme, in the Bristol Channel, and return to Llancarvan on Palm Sunday.[1] There are curious statements in the Legends of Cybi [2] and Beuno [3] of the stay of each for forty days and forty nights in a place where a church was founded, which suggests that the legend-writers were unwittingly recording instances of Celtic consecration similar to that practised by Cedd and the Columban Christians. Fiacc of Sletty used to retire to a cave in the hill of Druim Coblai from Shrove Saturday to Easter Saturday, and live in the meanwhile, according to the story, on the exceedingly scanty rations of five cakes; and, adds our authority, with a finishing touch of hyperbole characteristic of the later Irish legends, "there always remained with him a bit of the five cakes" when he went back to Sletty.[4] Kentigern retired to desert places during Lent, afflicting his body, and oftentimes abiding in caves.[5]

The Celtic saints were noted for the rigour of their personal austerities, which rivalled those of the Egyptian monks.[6] It is not improbable that Patrick led the way, and that his fast on Cruachan Aigle is a historical fact. Doubtless it attracted the attention of

[1] *Vita S. Cadoci.* Rees, C.B.S. 45.
[2] *Vita S. Kebii.* Rees, C.B.S. 185.
[3] *Buchedd Beuno Sant.* Rees, C.B.S. 15.
[4] "Tripartite Life," W.S. 242.
[5] *Vita Kentigerni*, sec. 17.
[6] "The personal austerities which are attributed to some of the Irish saints are almost incredible. Reeves' *Columba*, "Historians of Scotland," 233.

his followers as well as of the pagans, and legends, such as that recorded by Tirechan, would be the natural product of the excitement of the popular imagination. In later times these legends attained a prodigious development, in which profanity was blended with marvel. The most harmless story is that of Joceline, who relates that the saint compelled all the noisome reptiles of Ireland to muster on the top of the mountain, and drove them thence into the sea with the wonderful staff of Jesu. On the northern face of the mountain looking down on Clew Bay is a deep hollow, called Lugnademon, the Hollow of the Demons, into which it is said they all retreated on their way.[1]

The next incident recorded of Patrick's stay in Connaught is a great baptism of many thousand men at the well Sini, where he founded three churches. After this he came to the well Findmag or Slan, which was worshipped by the people. The druids used to offer gifts to it as a god. Patrick here, as always when he came in conflict with heathen superstition, acted with characteristic boldness. "The well," we are told, "was four-cornered, and there was a four-cornered stone above it. Now the foolish people believed that a certain dead prophet had made a coffin for himself under the stone in the water, that it might wash his bones always, because he feared the fire. And Patrick was jealous for the living God, and said, 'Ye say untruly that this fountain was King of Waters.' . . . And Patrick bade them lift up the

---

[1] Professor G. T. Stokes ("Ireland and the Celtic Church," 90, 91,) discusses the legends that cluster round Croagh Patrick.

stone, and they were unable to do so. But Patrick along with Cainnech, whom he baptized, lifted it.[1] And they found nothing in the spring save water only, and they believed in God most High." [2]

There are curious features in this story, which may be due to confusion and corruption in the tradition; and Tirechan at this part of his narrative manifests a tendency towards the marvellous, which leads him immediately afterwards to tell two exceedingly curious, but perfectly mythical, stories, the origin of which is not plain. They are not, however, more extravagant than some which are recorded in the pages of Bede, and have none of the faults of the late Irish romances, so that they do not seriously detract from the general value of his biography. Tirechan shared the superstitions of his age, but he was honest, and according to his lights a careful chronicler.

At length, after a long and curious delay, the cause of which we do not know, Patrick came across the Moy to what is now the barony of Tirawley, and there met with the sons of that Awley after whom the place is still called. It will be remembered that he had previously met these princes at Tara, and had bought a safe-conduct from them. Tirechan states that Patrick baptized many in this district, and the "Tripartite Life" records that twelve thousand were baptized in one day, in the well of Oen-adare, with

---

[1] "Tripartite Life," 123. Dr. W. Stokes' translation. Tirechan gives a longer account, rather diffuse in style, and he represents the raising of the stone by Patrick as a miracle. The "Tripartite Life" is shorter, and introduces no idea of the miraculous.

[2] Tirechan, W.S. 324.

the seven sons of Awley. This great baptism is said to have taken place at Forrach or Foirrgea, now Mullaghfarry, near Killala. Enna seems to have been a firm friend to Patrick, and the adhesion of the chief and his brothers secured the conversion of the clan to the new religion, so that the tradition of a great baptism is probably correct in its general purport. Such a baptism had previously taken place at Tara, on the day when Erc mac Dego was baptized; and Patrick himself in his "Confession" mentions that he baptized many thousands. Possibly one of these great baptisms was celebrated by the ancient festival of Patrick's Baptism, which was kept on April 5th, as it seems fairly certain that this did not refer to the day on which Patrick was himself baptized, but to a baptism which he performed. The "Calendar of Angus" states that on that day "the Baptism of noble Patrick was ignited in Erin," and a commentator adds that on that day Sinell, his first convert, was baptized. But Dichu is the first convert mentioned in the "Book of Armagh," and the story of Sinell's conversion at Wexford is late.[1] The great baptisms at Tara, at the spring Sini, and at the Well of Oen-adare would strike the popular imagination and be very likely to lead to a festival in commemoration of one or other of them.[2]

Patrick appointed Mune over the district of Tirawley. Two maidens came to the saint and

[1] "Tripartite Life," W.S. 33.
[2] See Todd, 450. Compare Miss Cusack, 262, who following Lanigan, places it on the Easter Wednesday after Patrick's triumph over the Druids at the court of Laoghaire.

received the veil from his hand, and he blessed a place for them over the wood of Fochlut.

Tirechan relates that at the river Moy Patrick erected a stone in sign of the cross of Christ. He and Muirchu also tell a story of a cross erected before Patrick's arrival to mark a grave. Perhaps these statements, taken in connection with the inscription of Christian words on the stones at Mag Selce, may indicate that Patrick introduced the custom of erecting stone crosses, which afterwards became so widely prevalent in Ireland. Possibly Patrick may have seen that strange unhewn monolith at Whithorn, with its curious incised Maltese cross within a double circle, and its inscription, which may belong to the time of St. Ninian. There are several other of these rude pillar stones at Kirkmadrine, in Wigtonshire, and elsewhere in Britain, which may be as old as the time of Patrick, and it is fairly certain that they belong to a period of transition between Christianity and paganism. The pagan menhir developed into the Christian cross, and the Christian missionary preferred to consecrate the old fashion by associating it with new emblems, rather than abolish it altogether. None of the Irish crosses have the Chi-Rho monogram,[1] which is found on eight of the earliest British crosses, but there are three rude pillar stones with the Maltese cross within a circle, and with Ogham inscriptions. Altogether there are existing at the present time in Ireland one hundred and twenty-one rude

---

[1] *I.e.*, the monogram formed from XP, the two first letters of the Greek for "Christ."

pillar stones with incised crosses, the date of which is supposed to be between A.D. 402 and 700.[1]

[1] See further, Romilly Allen, "Christian Symbolism of Great Britain and Ireland," 82-105. See also *Notes on Interlaced Crosses*, by the same writer, in *Journal of the Archæological Association*, xxxiv., 352-359.

CHAPTER XI.

COMPLETION OF THE GREAT JOURNEY. — FOUNDING OF ARMAGH, AND DEATH OF ST. PATRICK.

AFTER spending in all seven years in Connaught, Patrick came to Ulster, travelling from west to east and founding churches, especially in Tirconnell, or Donegal. He crossed the Banda or Bann and came into Dalaradia and Dalriada, the two divisions of the modern Antrim, and at Dunseverick, near the Rock of Patrick, is said to have ordained Olcan as bishop. He revisited the place where he had dwelt as a slave, and from which at his first missionary visit he had retired in horror at the sight of Miliuc's funeral pyre, and beheld again those mountains of Skerry and Slemish which had been the silent witnesses of his many prayers and vigils. Then passing on and founding churches as he went, he consecrated Victoricus bishop at Mugdoirn, the present barony of Cremorne, and finally returned to Meath, to Laoghaire and his brother Conall.

Tirechan, who in the total silence of Muirchu, has been our sole authority of any value for the great missionary journey of Patrick through Connaught and

Ulster, gives very few details of the subsequent labours of the saint, and Muirchu's few stories are not trustworthy. Tirechan mentions that Patrick founded a church near Bile Torten, or Torten's Tree, for the presbyter Justan. After this Patrick left Meath and entered Leinster, and there placed a House of Martyrs at Drummurraghille, in county Kildare. " Here," says Tirechan, " is Patrick's Stone in the way." Patrick then passed into the plain of the Liffey and ordained the boy Auxilius, Patrick's exorcist, and also Iserninus and Mactaleus, in Cellola Cuilinn. He also baptized the sons of Dunling. From later sources we hear that this baptism took place at Naas. " The site of Patrick's tent is in the green of the fort, to the east of the road ; and to the north of the fort is his well, wherein he baptized Dunling's two sons, Ailill and Illan, and wherein he baptized Ailill's two daughters, Mogain and Fedelm ; and their father offered to God and to Patrick their consecrated virginity, and Patrick blessed the veil on their heads."[1]

In Sletty, Patrick consecrated the bard Fiacc the White as bishop.[2] The story of his consecration is curious, and although too late to be quite certain, is perhaps not altogether out of keeping with the primitive ideas of an early age and a remote people. While Patrick was in Leinster he visited the house of the chief poet, Dubthach, who had been his first convert at Tara. And Patrick asked him " for the material of a bishop " from among his bardic disciples in Leinster, a man freeborn, of good lineage,

---

[1] " Trip. Life," W.S. 185.
[2] Tirechan. W.S. 331.

without defect or blemish, without too little or too much wealth, a man of one wife, unto whom had been born but one child. Dubthach knew only one such paragon. "Of my household," quoth he, "I know not such a man, save Fiacc the White, of Leinster, who hath gone from me into Connaught." As they were thus talking, Dubthach saw Fiacc coming, and "his circle" of bards with him. "Here," he said, "stands he of whom we were thinking." "How will it be," said Patrick, "if what we have been saying is not pleasing to him?" Then Dubthach answered, "Come to tonsure me, for the man will succour me to my consolation by being tonsured in my stead, for great is his dutifulness." Fiacc was astonished when he saw the preparations, and asked Patrick's disciples what they were for. "To tonsure Dubthach," said they. Fiacc began to remonstrate, but was told that if he liked, he could be tonsured instead. "The loss of me," he answered, "is less to Ireland than Dubthach's loss would be." So Patrick tonsured Fiacc, and baptized him, and ordained him bishop; the same was the first bishop consecrated in Leinster.[1]

After this, Patrick entered Munster, and baptized the sons of Natfraich on the Rock of Cothraige (or Patrick) in "Cashel of the kings." Later writers add that all the idols fell on their faces at Patrick's coming.

---

[1] This curious story is found in Ferdomnach's additions in the "Book of Armagh," W.S. 345, from which I have taken it, with some graphic touches from the preface to Fiacc's Hymn in the Franciscan "Liber Hymnorum," W.S. 403.

> " Aengus, in his father's absence lord,
> Rising from happy sleep and heaven-sent dreams,
> Went forth on duteous tasks. With sudden start
> The prince stept back ; for o'er the fortress court,
> Like grove storm-levelled, lay the idols huge,
> False gods and foul, that long had awed the land,
> Prone, without hand of man. O'erawed he gazed
> Then on the air there rang a sound of hymns,
> And by the eastern gate Saint Patrick stood,
> The brethren round him." [1]

Patrick is stated by the "Tripartite Life" to have stayed seven years in Munster, but we have no trustworthy account of the details of this period of his labours. The men of North Munster are said to have gone to him in fleets, and he baptized them in Tirglass, but he did not enter Thomond or West Munster.

The only other incident in St. Patrick's missionary life which may be regarded as certain is his foundation of churches at Armagh, one of which stood on the top of the hill on which the present town is situated, and on the site of the present cathedral. This has been always regarded as the seat of Patrick's own bishopric. According to the legend related by Muirchu, the land in Patrick's time was in the possession of a rich and honourable man, named Daire. Him Patrick besought to give him a place for the practice of religion. And he answered the saint, "What place dost thou request?" "I ask," he replied, "that thou give me that height of land which is called 'The Hill of the Willow,' and there will I build a place." But he would not give the saint the

---

[1] Aubrey de Vere, " Legends of Saint Patrick."

high ground, but gave him a place lower down, where afterwards was Fertae Martyrum, the Graves of Relics, and there Patrick and his companions dwelt.

This first settlement of Patrick at Armagh was in a spot in the present Scotch Street. At the time of the Reformation there was a nunnery there, which bore the name of Temple-fertagh, and which was then suppressed.

Muirchu relates certain wonders by which Daire's stubborn heart was subdued, but which are more akin to the savage spirit of Irish paganism than to the mild and gentle spirit of Christianity. Finally Daire gave Patrick the high ground also, and the two went up to view the spot, and found lying there a roe with her little fawn. The companions of Patrick wished to catch the fawn and kill it, but the saint would not have it so, and himself took up the fawn and carried it on his shoulders, the roe following him, until he came to a field on the north side of Armagh, where he laid the fawn down. On the height thus granted him Patrick built a Sabhall, or barn-church.

Armagh was founded, according to the story preserved in the Supplementary Notes of the "Book of Armagh," twenty-two years after the foundation of the Church of Trim, which would be about 462 A.D. But Bishop Usher[1] claims an earlier date, in accordance with the "Annals of Ulster," which give 444 as the date. However, some long time must have been occupied by those missionary journeys which Tirechan relates, and 444 certainly seems to be too

[1] "Antiq.," 854.

early. It is by no means certain how the latter years of Patrick's useful life were spent; probably age prevented him from continuing his long and arduous journeys, and he confined himself to work around Armagh, of which he is always reckoned first bishop. Some foolish stories [1] relate that he returned to Britain, sailing upon his stone altar to Cornwall, and that he lived as a monk at Glastonbury for thirty-nine years.[2] But these were invented for the sake of glorifying Glastonbury, and are repugnant to Irish tradition.

Patrick in his "Confession" mentions several interesting points respecting his missionary life, in addition to his baptism of thousands, and to the perils he had undergone, which have been already alluded to. He had travelled, he says, to remote parts of the island, " where there was no one beyond, and where no one had ever reached, in order to baptize, or ordain clergy, or confirm the people in the faith."[3] Even when he wrote he was in daily expectation of death or slavery,[4] and was not anxious to escape, if the Lord willed, for he had cast himself into the hands of the Omnipotent God, who reigned everywhere, and had cast his thought on the Lord, as the prophet said,

---

[1] Ib. 877-9.
[2] Sailing upon stone altars was customary with Celtic saints. Kea, Piran, Crantock or Carannog, and Nimanaue did the like. These legends are doubtless inspired by paganism, which reverenced and worshipped stones. See above, chapter v., also *Vita S. Paterni* and *Vita S. Carantoci*, in Rees' "Cambro-British Saints," 191, 99. —also, Borlase's "Age of the Saints," 53, 54.
[3] H. and S. 311.
[4] B. 312.

L.

knowing that he would sustain him. Nay, he was even desirous of martyrdom. "If," he says, "I have ever imitated any good thing for the sake of my God whom I love, I pray Him to grant me that with these proselytes and captives I may pour out my blood for His Name's Sake, even though I may even lack burial and my corse most miserably be torn in pieces, and be cast out to birds, to dogs, or wild beasts, that they may devour it. For I most surely believe, if this be a care to me, that I have gained my soul in my body; because without doubt we shall rise again in that day in the brightness of the sun; that is, we all shall be redeemed in the glory of Jesus Christ as sons of God and joint heirs with Christ, and creatures conformable to His image; since from Him, and through Him, and in Him are all things; to Him be glory for ever and ever. Amen. For in Him we shall reign."[1]

Those who before had worshipped idols and unclean things had through his preaching become a people of the Lord and were called sons of God. Sons of the Scots and daughters of chieftains were seen to be monks and virgins of Christ. One case especially the kind-hearted saint mentions, as one which had greatly touched him.

"Also," he says,[2] "there was one blessed Scotic lady, nobly born, very beautiful, of adult age, whom I baptized. And after a few days she came to us for a reason, and told us that she had received an answer from a messenger of God, who admonished her to remain a

---

[1] H. and S. 312, 313.
[2] H. and S. ii. 2. 208.

virgin of Christ and so draw near to God. Thanks be to God! on the sixth day after that she most excellently and eagerly seized on that, which also all the virgins of God do in like manner; not with the will of their own fathers;—nay, they suffer persecutions and false reproaches from their parents, and nevertheless the number grows the more: and of our race who have been born there to Christ, we know not their number, besides widows and those who are continent. But those also especially suffer, who are held in slavery; in spite of terrors and threats, they have assiduously persevered;[1] but the Lord has given grace to many of His handmaidens; for though they are forbidden, they nevertheless boldly imitate Him."

At last the saint died at Saul, the scene of his first successes, after having received the sacrament at the hands of Bishop Tassach,[2] and was probably buried at Downpatrick. Tradition unanimously states that March 17 was the day of the saint's death, and it is sometimes said to have been a Wednesday.[3] The year is doubtful, but the following lines fix it in A.D. 493:

---

[1] This is Wright's translation, p. 57. There are other readings.

[2] Muirchu's "Life" W.S. 297. Fiacc's "Hymn," W.S. 411. "Calendar of Oengus," W.S. 504. "The royal bishop Tassach gave, when he came, the Body of Christ the truly strong king, at the Communion, to Patrick." Also "Lebar Brecc Homily," W.S. 487, and "Tripartite Life," W.S. 261. Tassach is called "Patrick's artisan," W.S. 425, 504.

[3] "Chronological Tract in Lebar Brecc," W.S. 553. Usher, "Antiq.," 882.

> "From Christ's Nativity a joyful step,
> Four hundred upon dear ninety,
> Three noble years after that
> To the death of Patrick the chief apostle."[1]

There are however traces of an earlier date in the "Annals of Innisfallen," which gives 465 as the date.[2] John of Teignmouth gives 472; others would place it in 491 or 492; and Giraldus Cambrensis in 458. The curious chronicle of Welsh origin, which is known as "Annales Cambriæ," and which contains numerous references to Irish affairs, places the death of St. Patrick in the thirteenth year of its arbitrary chronology, which is supposed by its editor to be equivalent to A.D. 457.[3] Tirechan, the earliest authority—whose statement therefore is of some importance—states that there were 436 years from the passion of Christ to the death of Patrick, and that King Laoghaire reigned either two or five years after Patrick's death. This would put Patrick's death in A.D. 469.

The date 493 has been preferred by some authorities, notably by Bishop Usher[4] and by Dr. Todd,[5] and it has in its favour the fact that in that year the 17th of March fell on a Wednesday, though, as Patrick's death on Wednesday is only a late tradition, this is not of much importance. The fact that in the Epistle to the Subjects of Coroticus Patrick mentions that he

---

[1] Tigernach, W.S. 573.
[2] See Todd, 495.
[3] See Rolls edition, p. 3. See also Preface, pages xv., xvi.
[4] See Usher "Antiq.," 879-884.
[5] Todd, 494-497.

DEATH OF ST. PATRICK.

had sent a holy[1] presbyter, whom he had taught from infancy, at the head of his mission to the British King, has been held to justify the opinion that Patrick's labours in Ireland lasted very many years, as the Hymn of Fiacc says:

"He preached for three-score years Christ's cross to the tribes of the Feni."

As to the age at which Patrick died there is even more discrepancy among authors. Usher's summary of the various opinions illustrates so curiously the contradictions of Patrick's late biographers, and ponderous learning of the worthy bishop himself, that it is worth quoting.[2]

---

[1] "Sanctus": Todd renders this "venerable," which is rather begging the question, as "venerable" is frequently used to indicate age. Todd, 391.

[2] "Antiq.," 885.

"The reasons of our Stanihurst attribute 97 years to him; the *Annales Buelliani*, 110; William of Malmesbury, with the monks of Glastonbury, 111; Nennius, Tirechan, the Author of the 'Tripartite' Work, Giraldus, Vincentius, Antoninus, an old book of Chromellia, the *Officium Patricii*, together with the Annals of Ulster and Dublin, and the 'Acts of Patrick,' composed in the Irish language, 120; Marianus, Sigebert, Wendover, the Cottonian author of the 'Life of Patrick,' and others before mentioned, 122; Joceline, 123; John of Teignmouth, 130; the 'Anglo-Saxon Martyrology of the Church of Exeter,' 131; Probus, 132; not to mention the old tract concerning the origin of the Church Liturgies, in which Patrick is related to have lived 153 years. The more common and more generally received opinion is that he lived 120 years; to which age Asclepiades is our authority that old men were wont to arrive in Britain, and in which Nennius and Tirechan, the most ancient writers of his Life, have observed that our Patrick was equal to Moses: concerning which that statement of Trebellius Pollio in 'Claudius' is known. 'The most learned of the mathematicians judge that 120 years are given to man to live, and they

There is really not the slightest reason for putting the date of Patrick's death so late as 493. If 469, the date given by Tirechan, be accepted, there is abundant space in the 30 years this assigns for his mission, for all the incidents that are recorded of his work by any biographers worthy of attention. It is certainly strange that Secundinus, his nephew, Benignus, his pupil, and Jarlath, who are all said to have succeeded him in the Bishopric of Armagh, should all have died before him, as they must, if he really died in 493. It is plain that the whole chronology of Patrick's life, as given in later authors, is fictitious. The year 432 was taken as a starting point, because that was the only year to which they could assign a mission from Celestine. It was necessary to place so many years of Patrick's life before that date, and so many after, and, with a love of uniformity, several placed an equal number, 60. Thus he was born in 373 or 372, reached Ireland in 432, and died in 493 or 492. The number of 120 years was assigned because a parallel was established between him and Moses. This is found in those curious notes at the end of Tirechan's Life, which seem suspiciously different from the Life itself. They say that his age was 120 years, like Moses, and divide his life into periods—30 years of his early life, 30 of

---

repeat that no more is granted to anyone; adding this also, that Moses alone, the friend of God, as the books of the Jews say, lived 125 years, and when he complained that he died a young man, they relate that it was answered to him, by an uncertain power, that no one would live longer' ": which story Usher forthwith proceeds to refute.

study, and 60 of missionary work. In four things he was like Moses: he heard an angel from a bush, he fasted 40 days and 40 nights, he lived 120 years, and no one knew where his bones were laid. The same artificiality is found in other writers; sometimes the life is divided into three periods of 40 years, sometimes into four periods of 30 years. Moses, we are told, was 40 years in Pharaoh's house and in captivity, 40 in exile, 40 in preaching and leadership; so Patrick was 40 years of age when he ended his captivity, for 40 years he studied, and for 40 he taught. Extreme longevity is a common attribute of the Celtic saints: St. Kentigern is said to have lived 185 years, St. David 147, St. Cadoc 120; but, although the great temperance of their lives would contribute to this end, the imagination of their biographers has no doubt played a more important part.

CHAPTER XII.

THE WRITINGS OF ST. PATRICK.

IN the library of Trinity College, Dublin, is a small and beautifully illuminated [1] vellum quarto of two hundred and twenty-one leaves, which is one of the greatest literary curiosities in the kingdom. It was written at Armagh by a scribe named Ferdomnach, who begs, as ancient scribes were wont to do, for the prayers of his pious readers, and who occasionally makes remarks of his own concerning the progress and difficulty of his work. From one of these we learn that he finished copying the Gospel of St. Matthew on St. Matthew's day, and another, now half erased, has been interpreted to mean that he

---

[1] Miss Stokes, "Early Christian Art in Ireland," 21, says that "no scribe surpassed Ferdomnach, the scribe of the 'Book of Armagh.' . . . We may instance, as one remarkable specimen of this writer's skill, the folio 103, where the central portion of the text is written in semi-cursive letters, in the shape of a diamond. The volume contains four uncoloured drawings of the Evangelical symbols. After folio 104 the capital letters are slightly coloured—yellow, red, green, and black. In design and execution these ornamental portions equal, if they do not in some points surpass, the grace and delicate execution of the letters in the 'Book of Kells.'" In the "Annals of the Four Masters" the death of the scribe is thus noted: "A.D. 844, Ferdomnach, a sage and choice scribe of the Church of Armagh, died."

wrote from the dictation of Bishop Torbach of Armagh. As Bishop Torbach only held the see for a year, and died in the July of 808, it is clear that the Gospel of St. Matthew must have been finished on the 21st of September, 807. Not only does this little book contain the whole New Testament in Latin; it also has a life, dialogues, and epistles of St. Martin; and, what is of much greater importance, a long and valuable series of documents concerning St. Patrick. These include the two earliest known lives of the saint, those by Muirchu and Tirechan, and a copy of his "Confession," the last taken from an ancient and obscure manuscript, which Ferdomnach supposed to have been written by Patrick himself.

This little volume, which is usually known by the name of the "Book of Armagh," is our chief source of trustworthy information respecting the life and deeds of the great Apostle of Ireland. Muirchu's Life is found also in a late twelfth century manuscript, and Patrick's "Confession" exists in later copies; but the lateness of these manuscripts would have told heavily against the claims of both works to antiquity and genuineness, had not the older copy of the "Book of Armagh" existed. For there is no dearth of documents about St. Patrick, but the majority are so full of fable and invention that their existence would only serve to discredit the older works, unless these had a claim to antiquity otherwise established. "There is no saint of whom more Lives have been written, or fables told, than of St. Patrick, the Apostle of Ireland."[1]

[1] T. Duffus Hardy, " Descriptive Catalogue,' i. 63.

The "Confession" of St. Patrick is the most important of his writings. Its genuineness is now admitted by all competent scholars.[1] Muirchu borrowed from it, and in one place where he uses it, he adds the words, "as he himself says," thereby acknowledging the source of his information. Tirechan refers to it as "his own (viz., Patrick's) writing," and the scribe of the "Book of Armagh" believed that he was copying from Patrick's own manuscript. "Thus far," he says at the end, "the volume which Patrick wrote with his own hand; on the seventeenth day of March, Patrick was translated to the skies." The internal evidence to the genuineness of the work is strong; no writer of the seventh or eighth century had the wit to perpetrate so skilful a forgery. Defoe himself could not have introduced such *vraisemblance* into a work. The writer is animated by a conviction of the truth of his mission; the zeal for the Lord's work hath eaten him up. An honest man, who reads the book, will easily recognise in it the voice of another honest man speaking to him, and will regard all further evidence of its genuineness as superfluous. But if such be wanted, it is ready to hand; the style is not such as a forger would adopt, the Latin is exceedingly bad, but is said to correspond to that of Gregory of Tours. Again, the author speaks of

[1] It was doubted by Mr. T. Duffus Hardy ("Descriptive Catalogue," i. 71), who calls it "this pretended Confession"; but he knew nothing, it would appear, of the "Book of Armagh." "St. Patrick," says Dr. Guest ("*Origines Celticæ*," ii. 21), "has left two works behind him, the Confessio and his Epistle to Coroticus. Ussher, and every other competent scholar who has examined the subject, admit their genuineness."

Britain as one who was familiar with its organisation in the closing years of Roman rule; he calls it by the name of "the Britains" (Britanniæ), the natural term for a man to use who knew it as it was divided into provinces. The quotations from an old Latin version of the Bible also show that the work must have been composed at an early date. Besides, forgeries are usually directed to some end, to the inculcation of some particular doctrine, or to the advantage of some church or monastery; and, as has been acutely remarked, if the "Confession" "be a forgery, it is not easy to imagine with what purpose it could have been forged."[1] The copy in the "Book of Armagh" seems to be an abridgement of the original, and contains from time to time certain notes of the transcriber, which are supposed to indicate this. The full text, however, has been supplied from later manuscripts, which contain long additional passages, the genuineness of which there is no reason to question.

It is a beautiful tractate, this "Confession" of St. Patrick, and ought to be familiar to every Briton, as well as to every Irishman. It breathes throughout a genuine and fervent piety, animated by a genuine enthusiasm for the service of the Divine Master and for "the service of man." It is perfectly free from the miraculous element which mars, in some respects, even the work of the good and honest Tirechan, but at the same time it is full of the recognition of the invisible world and of the guidance of supernatural power. Perhaps the author gives an undue weight to

[1] Todd, "St. Patrick," 347.

the visions which he records, but only a very harsh and crabbed opinionativeness could venture to censure him as superstitious; there is a wonderful freshness, energy, and virility in every page he writes, which sharply contrasts with the intellectual and moral feebleness of the majority of the legendary lives which profess to recount his labours. Muirchu is restrained by the more powerful spirit of Patrick, when he writes with Patrick's "Confession" before him, and does not venture to let his flighty imagination and his rhetorical powers have full play until he has advanced somewhat farther in his narrative. There is more revelation of the real Patrick in a few words of this epistle than in all the lives written by Muirchu and his kin. The Apostle of Ireland was no vulgar wonder-worker, but a true man, filled with apostolic zeal and a burning desire to be to the tribes among whom he laboured what St. Paul was to his converts. St. Paul is evidently his ideal next to the Divine Master himself.

I have already quoted so freely from the "Confession" in my earlier chapters, that it would be mere repetition to give here any detailed account of its contents. It is not intended as a narrative of the saint's life and labours, but as a defence of himself against those who cavilled at his mission. He is Patrick "the sinner," "unlearned," and "most rustic," but God has sent him. To prove this he relates his early life and his visions, which called him and strengthened him for his work; and therein he acts from a sense of duty, for he feels that he must exalt and confess the wonderful works of God before every nation under the whole heaven. In the beginning of his "Confession," after mentioning his parentage and captivity, he sets down his creed, declaring his belief in God the Father, God the Son, and God the Holy Ghost, "one God in the Holy Trinity of the sacred Name," and throughout to the last page he ascribes all the glory of his great work to God alone. He is anxious to clear himself of any suspicion of presumption or self-seeking. When the virgins of Christ and religious women gave him small voluntary gifts, and cast off some of their ornaments upon the altar, he always returned them, although they were offended with him because he did so. Though he had baptized so many thousand men, he had never taken half a screpall[1] from them; he had ordained clergy without taking aught at their hands, but had rather spent money for the good of others.

"I pray," he says, in conclusion, "of those who believe and fear God, whoever shall deign to look into or receive this writing which Patrick, the sinner, unlearned indeed, has written in Ireland, that no one may ever say if I have done or shown anything according to the will of God, however little, that it was my ignorance which did it. But judge ye, and let it be most truly believed, that it has been the gift of God. And this is my confession before I die."

Patrick's "Epistle to the Subjects of Coroticus" is not found in the "Book of Armagh," but exists in later manuscripts. Coroticus, called in the heading of a chapter in Muirchu's Life, Coirthech, King of Aloo.

---

[1] A screpall weighed 24 grains, and was worth about threepence.

that is, possibly, king of Alclud or Dumbarton, was a British king,[1] who had made an incursion on the coast of Ireland, in which certain of the Irish had been slain on the day after their baptism, "while the faith was shining on their foreheads," and others had been carried off as slaves, some of whom had been sold to the apostate Picts. Patrick's embassy of a priest whom he had taught from infancy, and other clergy, was dismissed with scorn and laughter, and they returned without any of the captives and spoil; whereupon Patrick wrote this " Epistle," in which he most sternly rebukes and excommunicates the prince and his followers. It is referred to in the Life of Patrick by Muirchu,[2] where it is said that Coroticus was "a very great persecutor and slayer of the

[1] Joceline calls the prince Cereticus, and places him "in certain territories of Britain which now are called Vallia," *i.e.*, Wales. Cereticus is the old Welsh Ceretic, or later Ceredig. There was a Welsh Ceredig, the son of Cunedda, who gave his name to Ceredigion, or Cardiganshire. According to Welsh stories his father came to Wales from North Britain on account of Pictish irruptions, and afterwards Ceredig and his brethren drove out the Irish who had settled in North Wales. These stories, however, are not universally accepted. See Rees' "Welsh Saints," 108-110, 135-136; Todd, "St. Patrick," 352. The Triads give a different account of this Ceredig and his brethren than Patrick does of Coroticus. "'The three Holy Families of the Isle of Britain . . . . . The second was the family of Cunedda Wledig, who first gave lands and privileges to God and his saints in the Isle of Britain." Triad 18, quoted in "Ecclesiastical History of the Cymry," 53.

[2] The passage is not found in the "Book of Armagh," but the heading of the chapter is given in a list of the headings. The missing chapter itself is preserved in the Brussels manuscript (W. S. 498; compare 271).

Christians, but Patrick attempted by a letter to recall him to the way of truth." Muirchu adds a wonderful story that when he despised this letter, Patrick cursed him, and he was turned into a fox, which ran away from the midst of the assembled court, and was never seen afterwards. The scribe of the " Book of Armagh " seems to have originally intended to include this " Epistle" in his volume, for he places at the head of the " Confession " the words, " Here begin the books of St. Patrick, Bishop," whereas only one book, the " Confession," is really given. The internal evidence to its genuineness is strong; its Latin and its general style are like those of the " Confession "; there is the same vigorous personality making itself apparent through the language; and a Latin Bible, older than the Vulgate text, is used here as in the other work. It contains an interesting statement that Patrick's father was a decurion, an incidental reference to the customary government of a Roman provincial town, which a forger would scarcely have had sufficient knowledge to make. " Even a century later the forger would have known nothing of decurions."[1] The " Epistle " also mentions "apostate Picts," which implies a knowledge on the writer's part of Ninian's work among the southern Picts. Now Ninian founded Candida Casa, or Whitherne, somewhere about A.D. 397,[2] and the relapse of the Picts, whom he converted, into idolatry, cannot consequently have happened until some time in the fifth century. In another

---

[1] Professor G. T. Stokes, in note to Wright's " Writings of Patrick," 125 (R.T.S.).
[2] Skene's " Celtic Scotland," ii. 3.

passage the author says, " There is a custom of the Roman and Gallican Christians; they send holy and suitable men to the Franks and foreign nations with many thousand solidi to ransom baptized captives." This must have been written at a time when Frankish raids upon Gaul were frequent, and certainly before A.D. 496, when the Franks became Christians. All these little indications show a familiarity on the part of the writer of this " Epistle " with the events of Patrick's own age, such as a forger would not have mastered, or in that unskilful age have thought it necessary to master, for it is quite a modern device to impart probability to an historical novel, or to an ingenious imitation of the ancients, by carefully reproducing as far as possible the manners, customs, and modes of thought prevalent at the supposed date of the work. Ancient forgeries were less artistic, and yet were equally well adapted to uncritical ages, which readily gave credence to the grossest anachronisms if they harmonised with their own opinions. There are several coincidences of thought and expression between the "Confession" and the "Epistle," which give further support to the claims of the latter. In both the writer speaks of himself as sent by God to be one of the hunters and fishers which He had promised to commission, and he uses identical words in both concerning "the sons of Scots and daughters of princes" who had become "monks and virgins of Christ."

The " Book of Armagh " contains a few sayings which are there ascribed to Patrick. Their antiquity is vouched for by the manuscript in which they are contained, and they are couched in very bad Latin; but I cannot think that all of them are really sayings of Patrick.[1] They are as follows:—

(1.) "I had the fear of God as the guide of my journey through the Gauls and Italy, even in the islands which are in the Tyrrhenian Sea."

(2.) "From the world ye have departed to Paradise. Thanks be to God."

(3.) "The Church of the Scots, nay, of the Romans, as Christians, so that ye may be Romans, chant, as it ought to be chanted with you at every hour of prayer, this praiseworthy sentence. '*Curie lession, Christe lession.*'[2] Let every church which follows me chant, '*Curie lession, Christe lession.*' Thanks be to God."[3]

The first of these sayings has something like the true Patrician ring about it; but there is little on the whole to recommend them save the rusticity of their Latin, and the last seems to have a slight Roman flavour, more pronounced than is natural to a Christian of Patrick's age.

There are some canons of a later date ascribed to St. Patrick,[4] and there is a story[5] that he, with two other bishops, Benen and Cairnech the Just, took

---

[1] Mr. Whitley Stokes, however, classes them as genuine, cxxix.

[2] This, of course, is a corruption of the Greek words for "Lord, have mercy upon us; Christ, have mercy upon us." The whole saying seems to be imperfectly recorded.

[3] Wright, "Writings of Patrick," 76-80, divides the sayings into five.

[4] Haddan and Stubbs' "Councils," ii. 2, 328-338.

[5] Ib. 341. W.S., 571.

part with three kings and three sages in reforming the pagan laws of Ireland, and drawing up the code which is generally known by the title of Senchus Mor, or "Great Antiquity."[1] But the only remaining work which can with any probability be assigned to the authorship of Patrick is the Irish Hymn, called sometimes Patrick's Lorica or Corslet, or Faed Fiada, "the Deer's Cry."[2] It was called Patrick's Corslet, because it was one of those prayers which were repeated by the early Irish Christians, half as prayer, half as charm, to ensure the divine protection. Another of these "Corslets" was ascribed to the British saint Gildas, and Adamnan in his "Life of Columba" tells how by the recitation of certain Irish poems in honour of that saint some men, "though wicked men of lewd conversation and men of blood," escaped from their enemies, who by night had surrounded their house, and only a few who had failed to join in the hymns perished in that assault.[3] Patrick's Corslet, we are told, is "a corslet of faith for the protection of body and soul against devils and human beings and vices. Whosoever shall sing it every day, with pious meditation on God, devils shall not stay before him. It will be a safeguard to him against every poison and envy. It will be a defence to him against sudden death. It will be a corslet to his soul after dying."[4] Such was the veneration with

---

[1] Also called Cain Patrick, or "Patrick's Law," and Noi-fis, or "Knowledge of Nine."—Todd, 483.
[2] W. S., "Tripartite Life," 48. H. & S. ii. 2, 320
[3] Reeve's Adamnan in "Historians of Scotland," vi. 113.
[4] Preface in the *Liber Hymnorum*. W. S., 381.

which the early Irish regarded this poem, a veneration wherein paganism may be detected blended with Christianity. The Irish name for the hymn, "the Deer's Cry," might very suitably be applied by an Irish poet to a hymn wherein the author regards himself as one compassed about by all kinds of enemies, ghostly and bodily, and solemnly in the name of God claims the protection of all things visible and invisible which are not in their nature evil and malign. No more suitable or more beautiful title could be devised for this magnificent poem than one which paralleled the case of the persecuted saint with that of the hunted deer. But the old legend-writers explain the title to mean that Patrick uttered this hymn when he fled from King Laoghaire, and appeared to those who sought his life as a wild deer passing over the plain.

The Hymn is found in a manuscript book of hymns belonging to Trinity College, Dublin, and ascribed to the eleventh or twelfth century. It is, however, mentioned at an earlier date in the "Book of Armagh," in the supplementary section of Tirechan's Life. It is there stated that Patrick ought to receive four honours from the churches and monasteries of Ireland; first, his festival was to be honoured for three days and nights with all good cheer except flesh meat, that exception being due to the fact that March the 17th is in Lent; secondly, his proper preface was to be used on the same day at the celebration of Holy Communion; thirdly, his Hymn was to be chanted for the whole time;[1] and fourthly, they were "ever to

---

[1] Viz., of his festival, says Todd, 430.

sing his Irish Hymn." The "Irish Hymn" is undoubtedly the "Deer's Cry." It is acknowledged to be a very ancient composition, being written in a very archaic dialect, and it was evidently composed when pagan practices were common in Ireland. It moreover contains nothing incompatible with the supposed authorship of St. Patrick.

The other Hymn referred to by Tirechan, and also contained in the Book of Hymns, is an early Latin hymn on St. Patrick, said to have been written by Secundinus, or Sechnall. This Sechnall is said by tradition to have been a nephew of Patrick, being "a son of Restitutus, from the Lombards of Letha (*i.e.*, Brittany), and of Darerca, Patrick's sister,"[1] or, as another tradition says, of another sister of Patrick, named Liamain.[2] The poem is evidently a very early one, as it contains no mention of miracles, and it may quite possibly belong to the date which is claimed for it. It speaks of Patrick throughout in the present tense, and is supposed to have been written during his life; but it is unfortunately singularly destitute of incident, being simply the description of a good missionary.

This also was used by the Irish as a corslet, and according to a curious, but rather ridiculous, story, Patrick promised that whosoever should repeat its last three stanzas on lying down and on rising up should go to heaven. This story is much later than the Hymn itself, and in no wise invalidates its genuineness or authenticity.

[1] Preface to Secundinus Hymn in Franciscan *Liber Hymnorum*, W.S., 383.
[2] "Lebar Brecc." W.S., 506.

CHAPTER XIII.

THE TWO PATRICKS, HISTORICAL AND LEGENDARY.

THE writings of St. Patrick contain in some measure his spiritual biography, and reveal what manner of man he was. But for the details of his mission it is necessary to refer to the early lives by Tirechan and Muirchu, which are contained in the "Book of Armagh," and upon these I have based my narrative of his missionary labours, as recorded in the foregoing chapters.

Some comment has been caused by the silence of Bede and some other early authors with regard to the mission of St. Patrick. But Bede's knowledge of Celtic Christianity was exceedingly small, and much of his information regarding early times was gathered from authorities of Roman tendencies,[1] who knew nothing of the missionary who was sent by God, and not by the Pope. It is perhaps more noteworthy that Columbanus never mentions Patrick. But the silence of early authors must not be exaggerated; when Muirchu wrote there were many biographies of the saint already in existence, and if the manuscript "Book of Durrow," which still exists, be really in the handwriting of the great Columba, as some high

[1] He derives his information about Palladius from Prosper.

authorities believe,[1] this saint held Patrick in the highest reverence. The following subscription is placed at the end of the first portion of this manuscript:— "I beseech thy beatitude, holy presbyter Patrick, that whosoever shall hold this little book in his hand may remember the writer Columba, who have myself written this Gospel in the space of twelve days by the grace of our Lord."

In 634, Cummian, writing to Segene, abbot of Hy or Iona, respecting the date of Easter, refers to Patrick as "our father,"[2] and in the same century, the "Luxeuil Calendar" mentions Patrick under the date of March 17, which fixes the day of the saint's death. The hymn of Secundinus is certainly early, and probably belongs to the fifth century; and the hymn "Celebra Juda," which is ascribed to St. Cummine Fota, and placed in the seventh century, contains a mention of Patrick. The ancient "Catalogue of the Saints of Ireland," which is considered to be at least as old as the middle of the eighth century, furnishes an interesting account of Patrick's Church, and, indeed, in the seventh and eighth centuries we meet with a considerable body of Patrician literature.

It must be admitted, however, that much of this literature is such as causes pain to the Christian and dismay to the historian. For there are two Patricks: the historic Patrick of the "Confession," unlearned, with a Celtic weakness for exaggeration, but zealous,

---

[1] Dr. Whitley Stokes accepts the tradition, cxiv. Miss Stokes' "Early Christian Art in Ireland," 18, doubts. See Reeves' Adamnan, "Hist. of Scot." vi. xciii. Columba died in 597.

[2] Papa noster.

full of love for human souls, and in all respects an ardent Christian; and the fictitious Patrick of the later legends, headstrong, passionate, and revengeful; vain-glorious, destitute of natural affection, a relic-stealer, a vulgar wonder-worker, who overthrew paganism only to set up in its place a religion of the Pai-Marire type, a blend of paganism and Christianity. Permanent injury has been done by late legends to the popular conception of the character of Columba of Iona, and the character and teaching of Patrick have at times been partially misconceived from the same cause. The evil had begun in the time of Muirchu and Tirechan, but it had not advanced to such a point as to deprive their biographies of value; it is still possible for a careful student to gather historical matter from their records, many pages of which bear the unmistakeable impress of honesty and truth. In Muirchu's Life fiction is plentifully added to fact, but has not quite overpowered it; in the later "Tripartite Life," and the work of Joceline, the fictitious Patrick has completely taken the place of the historic saint, and has transferred to himself some of the true incidents of the life of his namesake. In Tirechan's biography the historic element preponderates far more considerably than in the work of Muirchu.

Muirchu is called in the "Book of Armagh" Maccu-Mactheni, that is, son of Macthene or Cogitosus. In a somewhat elaborate preface, modelled after the style of St. Luke's preface to his gospel, he states that he wrote in obedience to the command of Bishop Aed of Sletty, who died in 698. He complains that many before him had taken in hand to set forth in order a narration according to what their fathers, and those who from the beginning were ministers of the word, had delivered unto them; but on account of the very great difficulty of the narrative, and the diverse opinions and numerous suspicions of very many, they had never arrived at one clear track of history. He therefore (so he informs us with some magniloquence) ventured his little boat in this troublous ocean with much diffidence, as he knew well the billows and whirlpools which were to be encountered.[1] The "suspicions of very many," to which he alludes, may have been doubts concerning some of the astounding miracles which were related of Patrick; for subsequently he has to rebuke scepticism respecting the twelve days without night, which he says followed upon Patrick's death.[2] The besetting sins of Muirchu were a childish credulity and an immoderate love of fine language. At times he can state plain facts in plain words, and then he is worthy of attention, despite his utter lack of the critical faculty, which was not a common possession in his age. But he accepts implicitly the most absurd miracles, and reproves doubters by suggesting that they should read their Bibles. He even further sets himself to heighten the colours of the wonders he narrates by

---

[1] Muirchu's Life. W. S. 269.
[2] Ib. 297. The "Hymn of Fiacc" states that there was no night for a year, an extreme form of the legend, which, as Dr. Todd remarks ("St. Patrick," 489 *note*), is an argument against the antiquity of the hymn.
"He put an end to night, for light was not consumed with him: To a year's end was radiance; this was a long peace-day."
Haddan & Stubbs' "Councils" ii. 359.

using all the embellishments of style at his command, and by plagiarising and quoting passages alike from the Scriptures and from the classical poets. In adopting inflated language he was following the fashion which prevailed in Ireland in his age, and which often irritates the modern student in his investigations among Celtic sacred legends. Of the early life of Patrick and the commencement of his missionary work in Ireland he furnishes a narrative, which is generally plain and consistent, but afterwards he forsakes all appearance of historical narration, and gives stories, more or less elaborated, such as recommended themselves to his taste, and leaves the greater part of the missionary journeys of Patrick altogther unrecorded.

Were Muirchu our only authority of the seventh century, we might despair of gathering much historical information respecting St. Patrick, besides what he himself supplies in his writings, for Muirchu has the faculty of destroying any good impressions he may have produced at the outset, by the absurdity of his subsequent narrative. The vanity of the author has damaged his work, for he seeks throughout his own self-glorification rather than historical truth; he aims at the artistic finish of an ethical treatise, and neglects to record the plain and ordinary incidents of missionary work. Yet when we tear off the tawdry frippery with which he has ornamented his narrative, we may recognise in the biography an early cycle of tradition, such as his date would cause us to expect. He knows nothing, for example, about a commission from Pope Celestine. In the early part of his work, where he is terse and restrained in his style, he certainly consulted the "Confession" of St. Patrick, and very probably also followed closely some earlier life of the saint, for Muirchu's individuality does not clearly manifest itself until he reaches the visit to Tara. It would therefore probably be unjust to reject the authority of the first portion of the biography because of the extravagance of the rest, and even in the latter and far larger portion it may be possible to discover truth amid fable.

The biography by Tirechan is a much superior work and has more pretensions to be historical. It is stated to have been written by the author from the dictation, or from a book, of Bishop Ultan, whose pupil he was. This Ultan was bishop of Ardbraccan, and died in A.D. 656. But Tirechan did his best to gather all the information he could, not only from Bishop Ultan, but from other quarters, and, like a plain honest man, seems to have set it down as he found it, without adding any improvements of his own. He refers to Patrick's own words in various places, and quotes the "Confession" as "his own writing." He adduces "old men" also as his informants, and appeals to the common traditions current among his contemporaries. "All things," he says, "which I have written from the beginning of this book ye know, because they happened in your district, except a few of them which I learnt to the advantage of my labour from many seniors and from the relation of Bishop Ultan of the Conchuburnenses, who fostered me." He speaks of stones, patens, and a book connected with Patrick's history which he had seen with his own eyes. He is terse, whereas Muirchu is generally diffuse, and in a history of almost exactly the same length he gives more than double the same information. He is credulous, but as he does not elaborate his narration of miracles, and does not admonish doubters, his credulity is less offensive than Muirchu's, and he does not omit genuine history in order to make space for fable. He states that his words are simple, but he does not apologise for his "vulgar style" with the use of every rhetorical artifice. "All things," he says in one place, "which I have written from the beginning of this book are simple. Everything which remains will be terser." Lord Bacon, in his Essays, says nothing briefer and plainer than this; Muirchu would have taken a page to say the same thing and then would have broken his promise. But though he uses no tricks of style, he has a keen sense of the beautiful. Muirchu piles Pelion upon Ossa in his endeavour to impress his readers by the wonders wrought by Patrick at Tara, and to modern taste he only makes the story insufferable; Tirechan narrates the story of the daughters of Laoghaire so that it is a "thing of beauty" for all time. It may not be his own composition, but at least it must be conceded that he had the grace to borrow wisely. Muirchu's faults seem less excusable, seeing that in the same age Tirechan felt no constraint upon him to yield to the same temptation, but could write a sensible narrative, which, though less valuable in some respects than Adamnan's "Life of Columba," or Jonas' "Life of Columbanus," as being written at a greater distance from the lifetime of the saint whose history it relates, yet contains passages which have rarely been surpassed for beauty, and is as a whole with all its defects a not unworthy tribute to the memory of Ireland's great apostle.

Tirechan furnishes very few particulars of Patrick's early life. He professes only to record his missionary life, and he does that very thoroughly, though briefly, up to the time of Patrick's visit to Munster. Then follow short notes on Patrick's three prayers for the Irish; on the chronology of his life, which is said to have resembled the life of Moses in length; on four points of resemblance between Patrick and Moses; on a contest for his body after his death; on his mission by Pope Celestine; and on the fourfold honour paid him in Irish monasteries and churches. Last of all comes a brief summary of contents.

There are certain peculiarities about these supplementary notes which have to be noticed. The chronology given is altogether inconsistent with the chronology of an earlier part of the work, and the story that Patrick was sent to Ireland by Pope Celestine, is put curiously out of its place, and was not mentioned before. The parallelism with Moses is also quite a novel idea; it had been previously noticed indeed that Patrick once fasted forty days and forty nights, in imitation of "the discipline of Moses, Elias, and Christ," but no further resemblance was ever suggested, and one of the stories referred to, wherein a parallel is found—namely, the statement that an angel spake to Patrick from a bush—is not recorded by Tirechan at all, though it is found among the marvels which pleased Muirchu. But this is not all;

the summary of contents does not suit Tirechan's biography. It enumerates "race, name, genealogy, boyhood, captivities, miracles, Christian servitude, *documentum*, industry, curses upon sinners, blessings on the pious, age." But Tirechan says not a word about Patrick's race, genealogy, or about his boyhood prior to his captivity, and he makes no mention of his second captivity. An author might possibly, in compiling a somewhat inartistic narrative from various sources, add notes at the end which were inconsistent with the rest of the work, but he could scarcely furnish a summary which included points which he had never taken up at all. Either the scribe of the "Book of Armagh" omitted parts of Tirechan's Life which corresponded with passages in Muirchu's work which he had already written down, or else this summary does not properly belong to Tirechan's work at all. Probably the latter is the case, for this summary is almost as remarkable for what it leaves out as for what it puts in. Tirechan takes especial note of Patrick's great baptisms of converts, and in any summary, however brief, would have been likely to make some mention of these, as indeed he does in a previous summary of Patrick's missionary labours, where he states that "God gave him the whole island, with the men thereof, by an angel of the Lord, and he taught them the law of God, and baptized them with the baptism of God, and pointed out the cross of Christ, and announced his resurrection."[1]

---

[1] I cannot believe that these supplementary notes are the work of the same hand which wrote Tirechan's biography. If they are Tirechan's, they cannot belong to Bishop Ultan, and the latter

If these supplementary notes are excluded from consideration, the value of Tirechan's biography is very greatly enhanced. The more it is studied, the greater impression it produces of care and accuracy. Not only in particulars noted by the author, but in others also, coincidences may be noticed between the statements of Tirechan and the writings of Patrick. Tirechan mentions various occasions on which Patrick selected boys to train for holy orders, and tells

must be credited with the greater portion of the work which bears Tirechan's name. But it is probable that they are later than Tirechan. If Tirechan had heard of the commission from Celestine, Muirchu, who probably wrote a little later, would have been likely to hear of it too, and it is not the kind of story which Muirchu would have neglected had he heard of it. Dr. Whitley Stokes has hinted a doubt whether Tirechan was the author of this story (cx. *note*). I would suggest that the supplementary notes were added by Ferdomnach, the scribe of the " Book of Armagh," just as he added supplementary notes, and the *Dicta Patricii* ("Sayings of Patrick") at the end of Muirchu's Life. There he marks the end of Muirchu's Life by the words *Finit. Amen.* There is nothing to mark the end of Tirechan's narrative. The summary, then, is not Tirechan's summary of his biography, but the scribe's loose summary of the whole of the preceding documents, including the works both of Muirchu and Tirechan. Then the words follow, "All which things done in God have been gathered and collected from the most skilful ancients." This would refer to the Lives by Muirchu and Tirechan, and to the supplementary notes to both. Then the scribe continues: " There begin a few other things found in late times, and to be narrated in their places." These words no doubt introduce supplementary notes from documents which the scribe considered to be of later date than the lives by Muirchu and Tirechan, and the former notes. It certainly is simpler to suppose the words "All which things," &c., and "There begin a few," &c., to be written by the same person, viz., the scribe Ferdomnach, than to suppose, as is usually done, that the first sentence was written by Tirechan, and marks the conclusion of his work, and the next was written by Ferdomnach.

the story of the little child Benignus. Patrick informs us, in curious corroboration of these statements, that he sent to Coroticus, as his deputy, a holy priest, whom he had taught "from infancy." Patrick relates the difficulty which he found in refusing the voluntary gifts of religious women, who threw off their ornaments upon the altar, and Tirechan, without directly referring to this passage, mentions the particular instance of Senmeda, daughter of Endae, who gave Patrick her "necklaces and wristbands, and anklets and bracelets," which in the Irish language were called "aros." The records of great baptisms are confirmed by Patrick's statement, that he baptised many thousands. There is also a distinct agreement between Patrick and Tirechan respecting the frequency with which "daughters of chieftains" became "virgins of Christ." Patrick's policy in paying court to the Irish princes, which Tirechan illustrates, is warranted as historical by the saint's own statement, that he gave presents to the kings and pay to their sons who escorted him.

Many things in Tirechan's narrative which at first sight appear improbable are really instances of ordinary Celtic or primitive usage. It seems unreasonable to suppose that Patrick consecrated so many bishops as Tirechan mentions; but all authorities testify to the substantial accuracy of his statements. Patrick himself speaks of having ordained clergy "everywhere." Similarly the building of so great a number of churches, and the grouping them in sevens and threes, are facts that need not be questioned, and are quite natural if viewed in connection with the fashion of their construction. Every word of Tirechan's narrative deserves careful study; its value as history should not be rashly impugned, lest the sceptic himself be convicted of ignorance; and even where a passage must be rejected as history, it may be accepted as early and interesting tradition possessing a considerable though inferior worth of its own.

Unfortunately, Tirechan had no followers, or, if he had, their works have perished. A few interesting and plausible stories, preserved by the scribe of the "Book of Armagh," are all the available matter of later date than Tirechan and Muirchu which we have for a sketch of St. Patrick's missionary labours. For Muirchu was the precursor of a company of legend-writers, who followed and surpassed him in the work of inventing a fictitious Patrick, who was eventually to oust the real Patrick from his place. Some of their works, as the "Hymn of Fiacc"[1] and the "Tripartite Life," were long supposed to be much more ancient than they really are, and have in consequence often obtained more credence than was their due. The earliest and least untrustworthy of such productions are the "Hymn of Fiacc" and the Patrician legend in Nennius' "History of the Britons," which may belong respectively to the eighth

---

[1] The "Hymn of Fiacc" cannot be the composition of Fiacc of Sletty, as the Irish in which it is written is not the Irish of his age. (See Whitley Stokes, cxii.). Moreover, it was written after the desolation of Tara, which happened in A.D. 563, when the Abbot of St. Ruan went in procession to the Palace of Tara and cursed it, because the sanctuary of his abbey had been violated and the criminal executed in Tara. From that time Tara ceased to be the residence of the kings. There are two passages in the hymn which refer to this.

and ninth centuries; but the "Tripartite Life" and the legends of Probus[1] and Joceline[2] are practically useless as authorities for the life of St. Patrick. Their value lies rather in their illustration of the sentiments of the centuries in which they were written, and sometimes in the preservation of curious customs and ideas earlier than their own date, but not necessarily prevalent in the time of St. Patrick.[3] For, as has been well said, the Irish life of a saint "too often bids defiance to truth, reason, and decency, and, instead of history, presents a specimen of the meanest fiction."[4] The wildness and extravagance of some of the fictions respecting St. Patrick have led one learned student to conjecture that in some cases the mythology of a heathen Celtic god has been transferred to him by a confusion of names. His baptismal name is said by the "Hymn of Fiacc" to have been Succat, which "is the modern Welsh Hygad (warlike), and was the appellation of a Cymric war-god."[5] If this be a correct theory, the transference may not be without parallel in Celtic legend. "The prestige of the goddess" Brigit may have "helped to make the

---

[1] Probus wrote his life as "a token of fraternal regard" for "brother Paulinus." His date is uncertain. Dr. Whitley Stokes places him in the tenth century.

[2] Monk of Furness, an expert legend-writer, who flourished about 1185. Hardy, "Descriptive Catalogue," i. 64. Colgan includes other lives in his "Triadis Thaumaturgæ Acta," 1647.

[3] A list of lives, &c., of St. Patrick is contained in Nicolson's "Irish Historical Library" (1724), pp. 102-106.

[4] Reeves' *Columba*. "Historians of Scotland," vi. 223.

[5] Mr. Whitley Stokes, cxxxvii. Tirechan and Muirchu mention the name, but do not say when it was given.

fortune of the saint who took her name,"[1] St. Bridget, or Bride; and the mythology of Bran may have supplied the basis of the wondrous legend of St. Brandan or Brendan,[2] the sailor saint, who went forth with his monks, seeking "the island which is called the Land of Promise of the Saints, where never cometh night nor endeth day."[3]

Such instances of confusion may explain, but cannot excuse, the monstrosities with which Celtic legends are filled, and which cause the historian to say, with the Romish apologist, *Legendæ sunt lugendæ*, "the legends are lamentable."[4] The extravagances of Celtic romances—their wondrous quests and magical achievements, their impossible heroes who can ford seas or keep their breath nine days and nine nights under water—are atoned for by a certain strange, indefinable charm, the "glamour" of the Celtic imagination; and we read of the warlike deeds of Cuchulainn, the beautiful hero of Ulster, and of his wooing of Emer, or of the marvels accomplished by Kulhwch to win his yellow-haired bride, Olwen, and can enjoy the wild and wondrous stories much after the same fashion as we enjoy "Kubla Khan" or "Christabel." The art is imperfect, but it is real art of its kind. But the Celtic writers of sacred legends are not merely extravagant—they are intolerably dull. Math in the romance forms a woman out of flowers, "the fairest and most graceful that man ever saw." Patrick

---

[1] Rhys, "Hibbert Lectures," 75.
[2] Nutt, "Studies on the Legend of the Holy Grail," 264-5.
[3] Rees, "Cambro-British Saints," 253.
   Abbé Feller, quoted in Kenelm Digby's "Morus."

in the legend forms Echu Redspot of a "clot of gore, and that spot was in his body as a sign of the miracle." No children save mis-births used to be born to Carthenn till this Echu was brought forth. In the former story the extravagance is full of beauty; in the other there is no beauty at all. What are we to say of the tale of St. Brynach the Irishman, who when he entertained a Welsh tyrant and lacked suitable provisions for him, plucked loaves from an oak, drew wine from a brook, and gathered its pebbles for fishes? Or what of the Legend of St. Aedh, the Irish bishop of Ferns? He was exceedingly merciful—so merciful as a boy that when he saw eight hungry wolves pass the sheep he was tending, he gave them eight of his wethers to eat. When he saw his aunt coming, the holy boy was afraid, and prayed, saying "Lord, help me." And the Lord, we are told, heard his prayer and sent eight wethers to the sheep, so that all was put right. At another time, when he had grown up, he heard some wolves crying (he seems to have been exceedingly fond of wolves), and he gave them a calf, and they ate it up. In the morning the cook came to look for the calf but found it not, and the saint said to him, "Don't look after it, I gave it to some hungry wolves while you were asleep." The cook was naturally concerned at this benevolent act, and enquired, "How shall we quiet the cows?" "Let me bless your head," said Aedh, and he blessed the cook's head, and said furthermore, "Go and show the cows your head." The cows licked the cook's head and were appeased, and afterwards had other calves. The same saint, according to his biographer, crossed the sea in a chariot without wetting the wheels, and on another occasion carried a friend of his to Rome in a fiery chariot. But though he was so kind and compassionate to wolves, he could be very revengeful towards those who offended him, and could curse so vigorously as to split a rock in two.[1]

These monstrous fables must have been written by persons of the meanest capacity for others who were no better than themselves. It is surely rather rash for anyone to assert that "many and wonderful as are the miracles recorded in the 'Lives of the Saints,' there is not one for which we may not find a parallel in the Acts of the Apostles."[2] But the same writer makes an admission in another place: "The miracles which are related to have been performed by St. Patrick are of a very striking character; and as they have been recorded in their naked simplicity, and often in uncouth and ill-chosen language, by his early biographers, they have scarcely been received with the credit they deserve, even by Catholic writers." This statement respecting the wiser Romish writers is correct; they ignore or dismiss the grosser extravagances of the legends. The early Bollandists, in recording the lives of the Irish saints, protested against much which

---

[1] Rees, "Cambro-British Saints," *Vita Sancti Aidui*, 232-250. The English translation is very inaccurate, as is usual in this book. Hardy, "Descriptive Catalogue," i. 188-189, says the manuscript is of the 12th century. It is printed in "The Acta Sanctorum," ii. 1111, and by Colgan in "Acta Sanctorum Hiberniæ," and abridged by Capgrave in the "Nova Legenda Angliæ." Colgan attributes it to St. Evinus, with but little reason. Hardy says, "This biography is marvellously absurd."

[2] "Life of St. Patrick" (Kenmare Series), 23.

they included, and the later editors went further and suppressed very much. But the extreme party perceive "a peculiar fitness" in such miracles as that of the increase of height bestowed on Eoghan by St. Patrick, and they blame the more moderate for "scepticism;" so far are the members of the Roman communion from attaining that uniformity of belief concerning which they make their boast.

No one would argue that Mr. Gladstone or the Marquis of Salisbury never lived because caricatures of them have been published; and the publication of ridiculous miracles attributed to Patrick neither contravenes the fact that Patrick lived and taught, nor the fact that miracles have been worked at various times in the world's history. The lying wonders of late Celtic legends are on quite a different plane, not only from the miracles of the New Testament, but even from those contained in Adamnan's "Life of Columba." Whether miracles were worked by early missionaries, such as Patrick and Columba, is a problem which a biographer of Patrick is not necessarily called upon to discuss, because he has no documents in Patrician literature which throw much light upon it. Patrick himself nowhere claims the power; but this may be due to the modesty which is an attribute of the saintly character, and to a feeling of the comparative unimportance of these signs and wonders in view of the great triumph of converting human souls from error to truth. More significant than Patrick's silence is the silence of Secundinus, who might have been expected to mention such mighty works, if any really occurred, in a poem extolling the life and work of Ireland's great apostle. Muirchu and Tirechan, who record miracles, wrote too long after Patrick's death to be trustworthy authorities in a matter of this kind, and the former was a man of execrable taste and small judgment. Tirechan weakens his testimony by including two extravagant stories. Patrick, he says, found a huge grave, one hundred and twenty feet in length, and, in response to the curiosity of his companions, raised from the dead its occupant, who declared that he had been buried a hundred years, and told his name, and how he had been a swineherd and had been slain by soldiers. And Patrick then baptized him, and he was placed again in his grave. He tells us also how the saint once found a cross on a grave, and inquired of its occupant who he was, and the dead man answered from the grave that he was a pagan, and that the cross had been placed on his grave by mistake. These stories supply us with a criterion of Tirechan's ability to sift the marvels that were current in his day. Otherwise there is little in his Life which savours of the miraculous except a few stories of the destruction of druids. The druids claimed to be magicians, like many other priests and prophets of the evil one, both in ancient and modern times ; and if they really possessed such powers as they professed, their overthrow by a Christian missionary in the name of God need not be cavilled at. But, unfortunately, neither Muirchu nor Tirechan are trustworthy witnesses in such a matter, so that it would be rash to assume from their evidence that Patrick treated the druids of Ireland as St. Paul treated Elymas and as St. Peter is

It would be tedious to examine in detail the monstrous prodigies recorded in the later legends of St. Patrick. But there is a worse fault than that of extravagant folly which they manifest, and which they share with many other Irish legends of the baser sort. They breathe throughout a pagan and anti-Christian spirit of revenge, and thereby distort and deprave the character of the saint whom they profess to magnify. No one objects to the introduction of an occasional episode in which vengeance is made to overtake the legendary tyrant, who is as stupid and mischievous a creature as the giant Blunderbore. It may have been well in an age of violence to impress a moral of this kind upon the princes and nobles, whom nothing but the dread of supernatural penalties could restrain, and who were often as wicked, though never quite as stupid, as the tyrants of the legends. But it surely was unnecessary to represent the saints as clothing themselves with cursing like as with a raiment, or to make them deal destruction upon mean men as well as upon the great. Giraldus Cambrensis, himself the author of legends, one of which is not overwise, remarks, with some surprise, the revengeful temper of the Irish saints.[1] His own fellow-countryman, Cadoc,

---

[1] The passage (*Giraldus Cambrensis, Topograph. Hibern.*) is so exceedingly curious as a mediæval illustration of the extravagance of these stories, and of the surprise they occasioned to strangers to Ireland, that I quote it in full from Bohn's translation (page 111.):—
LV.—*That the saints of this country appear to be of a vindictive temper.*

"It appears to some very remarkable, and deserving of notice, that, as in the present life the people of this nation are, beyond all others, irascible and prompt to revenge, so also in the life that is

who had a connection with Ireland, was similarly treated by his biographer. Cadoc, when a boy, we are told, was sent by his Irish tutor for some lighted coals. He asked them of a boorish servant, but was told in reply that he would have to carry them in his cloak. Thereupon he prayed that the man might be burned up, his threshing-floor be cursed so that it might not be used afterwards, and his offspring become slaves to foreigners, all of which came to pass.[1] A saint of this description would be a bane, and not a blessing, to a land.

According to the "Tripartite Life of Patrick," cursing was customary with that saint. Immediately upon his landing in Ireland he cursed Nathi, son of Garrchu, who came against him.[2] At Tara he not only destroyed wizards, but when the Irish king bade his household to slay him, he exclaimed, like Cromwell at Dunbar, " Let God arise, and let His enemies be scattered," and immediately there

after death, the saints of this country, exalted by their merits above those of other lands, appear to be of a vindictive temper. There appears to me no other way of accounting for this circumstance but this:—As the Irish people possessed no castles, while the country is full of marauders, who live by plunder, the people, and more especially the ecclesiastics, made it their practice to have recourse to the churches instead of fortified places, as refuges for themselves and their property ; and, by divine providence and permission, there was frequent need that the church should visit her enemies with the severest chastisements, this being the only mode by which evil-doers and impious men could be deterred from breaking the peace of ecclesiastical societies, and for securing, even to a servile submission, the reverence due to the very churches themselves from a rude and irreligious people."

[1] *Vita Sancti Cadoci* in Rees' " Cambro-British Saints," 29.
[2] " Tripartite Life," W.S. 33.

was a mighty earthquake, and the assembly rose up, each fighting against the other, so that fifty men fell slain.[1] He cursed the sons of Erc, who stole his horses, saying, "Your offspring shall serve the offspring of your brethren for ever."[2] He cursed Oengus, who came to him drunk, and said to him, "Thy successors will be ale-bibbers, and they will be parricides through thee."[3] He cursed the Grecraige, who flung stones at him and his household. "My God's doom:" said he, "in every contest in which ye shall be, ye shall be routed, and ye shall abide under spittles and wisps and mockery in every assembly at which ye shall be present."[4] He gave goats' beards as a perpetual heritage to the family of some thieves who had stolen and eaten two of his goats.[5] He caused fifty horsemen who came to a ford to slay him, to be drowned in crossing the stream.[6] When Faillen, the reeve of the fort of Naas, feigned to be sleeping in order to excuse himself from seeing Patrick, he caused his sleep to be one from which there was no waking.[7] When a train of jugglers asked him for food, he sent to Lomman and Mantan to furnish him with it, but they would not, so he procured it from a boy, "to save his honour." As the jugglers were eating the food, the earth swal-

---

[1] "Tripartite Life," W.S. 47.
[2] Ib. 109.
[3] Ib. 137. Tirechan, 319.
[4] Ib. 139.
[5] Ib. 181. This is the meaning given by Colgan. The curse in the text is rather indefinite.
[6] Ib. 183.
[7] Ib. 185.

lowed them up, and Patrick cursed the race of Lomman and the cloister of Mantan for their lack of respect to him.[1] His curses lighted not only on mankind, but on inanimate nature. Sechnall and he cursed the stones of Uisnech, and nothing good was made of them thenceforth, not even washing-stones.[2] The water of the sea opposed him once as he was sailing, and he solemnly cursed it.[3] He fell into the river Buall, and he cursed its eastern half, and thenceforth but little fish was caught there.[4] He cursed the river Dub, because the fisherman gave him no fish.[5] If his friends offended him, they suffered from his wrath equally with his foes. The two sons of Cairthenn consecrated a bishop without his knowledge, and he cursed their churches: in the one there should always be contention, and in the other poverty.[6] Bishop Olcan acted contrary to his wish, and he ordered his charioteer to drive over him.[7] His sister Lupait sinned, and he drove his chariot three times over the penitent and killed her.[8] In the blasphemous story of his fast on Cruachan Aigle his wrath is directed against the Almighty Himself. The angel said to him, "God gives thee not what thou demandest, because it seems to Him excessive and obstinate, and great are the requests." "Is that His pleasure?" said Patrick. "It is," said the angel. "Then this is *my* pleasure," he replied: "I will not go from this Rick till I am dead or till all the requests are granted

---

[1] "Tripartite Life," 205.
[2] Ib. 81.
[3] Ib. 183.
[4] Ib. 143.
[5] Ib. 147. Tirechan, 328.
[6] Ib. 159.
[7] "Ib. 167.
[8] Ib. 235.

to me." "Then," we are told, "Patrick abode in Cruachan in much displeasure." The angel at last returned to treat with him, and offered him certain privileges, but he demanded more, and refused to leave the Rick till the Day of Doom. It was not till "all creatures, visible and invisible, including the Twelve Apostles, besought the Lord" to grant Patrick's requests that he obtained what he wanted, and then left the Rick.[1]

Was it to be treated with ingratitude such as this that holy Patrick devoted his life and all the energies of a loving and impetuous nature to the conversion of the Irish people? A fouler travesty of a noble character could scarcely be published than is contained in these late legends. If I have bestowed more pains upon the investigation of them than they deserve, it has been to show how utterly worthless and morally detestable they are, so that Patrick may be fully acquitted of the foul charges which they advance against him. Of all the instances of impiety which I have quoted from the "Tripartite Life," Tirechan only records two[2] and Muirchu one.[3] It was reserved for later legend-writers to chronicle these relics of pagan sentiment. There is no excuse to be made for such stories; they are not even "the forgeries of jealousy," such as Muirchu puts forward for the

---

[1] "Tripartite Life," 113-121.
[2] The cursing of the sons of Erc (W.S. 319) and of the river Dub (W.S. 328). He gives a few other similar stories.
[3] The earthquake at Tara. Muirchu also tells a story how Patrick cursed some land, and made it barren (W. S. 292). Both he and Tirechan relate the destruction of druids. Muirchu also tells how Patrick cursed Coroticus, the tyrant.

glorification of the see of Armagh in opposition to other sees. They are simply the product of an evil imagination and of an inclination to revert to the heathenism from which the Apostle of Ireland sought to cleanse his adopted country.

For, in truth, the essential difference between the real and the fictitious Patrick is that the one was a Christian and the other a pagan. As the Celts of Applecross returned to the paganism from which their missionary Maelrubha had converted them, and worshipped Maelrubha himself, with heathen sacrifices, as "the god Mourie," even as late as the seventeenth century, so the mediæval reverence of Patrick was a pagan reverence. The garb of the legendary saint is that of a Christian bishop, but the face is the cruel, revengeful face of a heathen god.[1]

---

[1] One Irish cleric is said to have "performed fasting against the Lord," because he thought that a fellow-cleric had been better treated than he. See Dr. W. Stokes' "Lives of Saints from the Book of Lismore," p. xi.

CHAPTER XIV.

THE TEACHING OF ST. PATRICK.

THERE are two aspects in which Celtic Christianity is presented to us in history: a stern asceticism, which becomes gloomy and morbid in the person of Gildas; and a kindly and all-embracing charity, which some traditions attribute in a marked degree to the Welsh saint, Cadoc the Wise, of Llancarvan. Both the harsh and the gentle features are combined in the portraiture left to us of Columba of Iona, but perhaps we should reject the late stories of O'Donnell, which affix to him, in some degree, the guilt of bloodshed, and should accept only the record of his boundless love and his marvellous faith, as presented by his early biographer, Adamnan. The hymns and poems ascribed to him, whether rightly so ascribed or not, show what was the nature of that Irish Christianity of which he was so powerful an exponent. One of them, which depicts his feelings in gazing forth upon the Atlantic from his little island, is almost modern in its pathos, and approximates in its love of nature to that intimate feeling of sympathy with her various moods which we usually associate with our own century, and especially with the name of Wordsworth. Columba could, so Adamnan tells us, recognise "natural goodness"[1] even in an aged heathen who had never heard the tidings of the Gospel. Living in the midst of a heathen world, and with plentiful signs of the reign of evil frequently present to his eyes, he believed firmly in the supernatural powers of the druids, who were his foes, but resented their claim by virtue of their false god to lordship over air, wells, seas, and the other powers of the material universe; and instead therefore of accounting the world and all therein as unholy and profane, he taught that the earth was the Lord's and the fulness thereof, and by virtue of his commission reclaimed it for the Lord's service, and consecrated it anew. He believed that man is surrounded by an ever-present host of demons, but he held also that angels were ever ministering to the saints and defending them, and that at times he could discern them and their operations. Thus with all the rigour of monastic life, the Irish Christianity of Iona was eminently a joyous Christianity, with a full sympathy with human gladness and human sorrow, and no harsh judgment upon repentant sinners; it recognised beauty and hallowed the earth which it touched; it was not exclusive, but all-embracing, in its charity.

What we can read clearly in the writings of

[1] *Vita S. Columba*. i. sec. 27. "Strange to say, my sons, to-day, on this very spot an aged heathen, who has kept natural goodness through his whole life, will be baptized, will die, and will be buried."

Columba and his biographer, we may also, I think, discern by the help of careful study in the authentic records of St. Patrick, and we may infer that this character was given to early Irish Christianity by its first Apostle. "Thou fastest well," said the vision that bade him depart from his master, and his long fast upon the Mount of the Eagle may well be historic, but his stern repression of himself did not make him hard to others. It was no gloomy ascetic that won the love of the boy Benignus, that wept over the massacre of his converts at the hands of the soldiers of Coroticus, and that rejoiced with fatherly affection over the beautiful Irish maiden who devoted herself to the life of a "virgin of Christ." He too, like Columba, believed in "cruel, merciless" powers that assailed both body and soul, in "incantations of false prophets," in "black laws of heathenry," and in "spells of women, and smiths, and druids"; he had himself been buffeted by the arch-enemy so fiercely that he ever remembered the assault. But he trusted in the ever-abiding presence of Christ his Lord, and of the Holy Spirit who made intercession for him, and he knew that the "virtue of ranks of Cherubim," "the obedience of Angels," "the service of Archangels" were upon his side, and that he was but one of a great company of saints who sustained him and supported him in his conflict against evil by their sympathy and prayers and faith. So, in the midst of a relentless heathenism which arrogated the authority over nature to itself, Patrick raised the noble chant of the "Deer's Cry," and claimed for the Lord and for his Christ—

"The virtue of Heaven,
Light of Sun,
Brightness of Moon,
Splendour of Fire,
Speed of Lightning,
Depth of Sea,
Stability of earth,
Compactness of Rock."

He resented the claim of the prince of the power of the air to dominion over this world and the glory thereof, and considered it to be part of his commission to restore nature to its primeval condition, when all was " very good," and to realise the second blessing of this earth, whereby the Heavenly Vision declared that nothing therein was common or unclean. Nature, which hitherto, to the apprehension of the pagan Irish, had been full of cruel and merciless powers, now wore a wholly different aspect as framed and consecrated by the fatherly hand of God, and this new conception acted upon the minds of the susceptible Celts and produced a notable reaction. The "music" of the chanting waves and "the song of the wonderful birds" became each "a source of happiness"[1] to the Irish Christians of a later age, and their religious communities regarded the natural world as itself united to a spiritual world, in the midst of which they lived, and on whose mysterious wonders they were at times allowed to gaze.

The "Deer's Cry" has been sometimes thought to savour a little of pagan superstition. Certainly its author believed in the powers of the druids, just as natives of Africa believe in the powers of their

[1] See Columba's poem in Skene's *Celtic Scotland*, ii. 92.

medicine-men, and Hindoos in the power of the devil-priests of India ; just also as some of the early Fathers of the Church believed that the gods of the heathen world were powerful but malignant demons. Many Christians, both in ancient and modern times, have held that diabolic power has been exercised by wicked men who have sold themselves to work iniquity, and such a belief has not been usually considered unorthodox, even if it be mistaken. Patrick does not " invoke" the sun and the other powers of nature as themselves living and sentient agents, but he claims them as upon his side, because they were the Lord's and not the devil's. This is really not paganism, but very healthy Christianity. The essence of paganism is to claim the possession of the earth and all that is therein for some other than their rightful Possessor, and against this Patrick, Columba, and the other Celtic saints contended with all the earnestness of their Celtic nature. They liberated Nature, and they sanctified Art.

There is no indication of false teaching in either of Patrick's Epistles. His cry of "Helias" or "Eli" during his dream can hardly be distorted either into a survival of sun-worship or into a superstitious invocation of an Old Testament saint. His doctrines are set down in a passage of his "Confession," which is sometimes called his Creed, and in which it would be hard to detect anything superstitious or unorthodox. Strictly it is not a creed, for it omits several points which would be mentioned in such a document. But it is framed somewhat after the manner of a creed, and it declares, plainly and explicitly, the saint's belief in most of the cardinal doctrines of Christianity. It is as follows :—

"There is no other God, nor ever was, neither before, nor shall there be after Him, save God the Father, unbegotten, without beginning, from Whom is all beginning, upholding all things, as we say :—

"And His Son Jesus Christ, Whom indeed with the Father we testify to have always been before the origin of the world, spiritually with the Father, in an inexplicable manner,[1] begotten before all beginning; and by Himself were made things visible and invisible; and He was made man, and having conquered death, was received in the heavens to the Father. And He has given to Him all power above every name of things in heaven and things in earth and things under the earth, and that every tongue should confess to Him that Jesus Christ is Lord and God, in Whom we believe and expect His coming soon to be Judge of the quick and dead, Who will render to every man according to his deeds:

"And He hath poured upon us abundantly the Holy Ghost, a gift and pledge of immortality; Who makes the believing and obedient to be sons of God, and joint-heirs with Christ; Whom we confess and adore, one God in the Trinity of the Sacred Name."

It will be noticed that nothing is said by St. Patrick about the consubstantiality of the Son, about our Lord's burial and descent into hell, or about the resurrection of the body. But, as has been shown,[2]

---

[1] So Dr. Wright, 37. The "Book of Armagh" has *inerrabiliter,* "unerringly," but other MSS. "*inenarrabiliter.*"

[2] By Dr. Whitley Stokes, cxxxv.

we find some of these points in the second stanza of the "Deer's Cry":

> "I bind to myself to-day,
> The power of the Incarnation of Christ, with that of His Baptism
> The power of His Crucifixion, with that of his Burial;
> The power of the Resurrection, with the Ascension,
> The power of the Coming to the sentence of Judgment."

The "Hymn of Secundinus" also states:

> "Hymns with the Apocalypse and the psalms of God he sings,
> And handles them to the edification of the people of God;
> Which law he believes in the Trinity of the Sacred Name,
> And teaches the one Substance in three Persons."[1]

The authority of the Christian priesthood is affirmed by Patrick in the Epistle to the Subjects of Coroticus. Coroticus, He says, "fears not God, nor His priests, whom He hath chosen, and committed to them that highest and divine power, that whom they bind upon earth should be bound also in heaven.

"Wherefore," he continues, "I earnestly beseech you, holy and humble men of heart, not to flatter such men, nor take food or drink with them, nor ought their alms to be received, until they rigorously do penance[2] with tears poured forth, and make satisfaction to God, and liberate the servants of God, and baptized handmaidens of Christ, for whom He died and was crucified." Coroticus was nominally a Christian, so that his offence was the more grievous, and merited Patrick's sentence of excommunication. "Let every man fearing God know that they are

---
[1] *Hymnus S. Secundini.* H. and S. ii. 326.
[2] So Dr. Wright, "Writings of Patrick," 69. "Crudeliter effusis lacrymis pœnitentiam agentes."

aliens from me, and from Christ my God, for Whom I discharge an embassy."[1]

In various places Patrick declares his belief in the resurrection of the dead, the day of judgment, and the everlasting life of the world to come, of blessedness for the righteous, and of punishment for the wicked. "Without any doubt," he declares, "we shall rise again in that day, in the brightness of the sun,"[2] "we all together shall render account, even of the least sins, before the judgment seat of Christ the Lord;"[3] "he who shall have done His will shall not perish, but abide eternally, as Christ eternally abideth"[4]; but as for those "whom the devil has grievously ensnared, they will be chained equally with him in the everlasting Gehenna of punishment."[5]

There is nothing in Patrick's own writings about the "angel" Victor, or Victoricus, of whose appearances to Patrick many stories were told in later biographies and romances, and who is called "the angel of the Scotic race."[6] Patrick himself mentions once that he saw "a man, Victoricus by name," in a vision, but he gives no hint of a belief that it was an angelic visitation. He certainly believed in visions, and divine responses, and the watchful care of God, but in his "Confession" he says little about angels. Once only he adds solemnity to a statement by

---

[1] *Ep. ad Cor.* H. and S. ii. 315.
[2] "Confession," ib. ii. 132.
[3] Ib. ii. 298.
[4] Ib. ii. 313.
[5] *Ep. ad Cor.*, H. and S. ii. 315.
[6] Scholiast on "Fiacc's Hymn." W.S. 415.

adding that he speaks "in the presence of God and of his holy angels."[1] The references in the "Deer's Cry" to "the power of the ranks of cherubim," "the obedience of angels," and "the service of archangels," on the one hand, and to "the snares of demons" on the other, show a recognition on the part of its author of the existence of hosts of good and evil spirits, but there is nothing in Patrick's writings to suggest that in his teaching he gave such prominence to this subject as was given later in the Irish Church. The "Altus" of Columba rather contrasts in this respect with the "Deer's Cry."

Patrick lays great stress in his "Confession" upon the numbers he baptized, and from his other epistle we learn that chrism was used at baptism, and that the neophytes wore the white chrisom. It was "on the day after that in which they were anointed neophytes in the white garment, and while the faith was still shining on their foreheads," that Patrick's converts were butchered by the soldiers of Coroticus. The white chrisom was put on Ethne the Fair and Fedelm the Ruddy, after their baptism, according to the story related by Tirechan. In the Hymn of Secundinus Patrick's administration of the sacraments of Baptism and the Lord's Supper is thus spoken of:

"He boldly announces the name of the Lord to the nations;
To whom he gives the eternal grace of the laver of salvation;
For whose sins he daily prays to God;
For whom as to God he offers worthy sacrifices."[2]

---

[1] "Confession." H. and S. ii. 313.
[2] "Hymnus S. Secundini." H. and S. ii. 325.

There are some interesting references to the sacraments in Tirechan's Life. In the conversation with Ethne and Fedelm, Patrick declares the doctrines of the Trinity, of repentance after sin, of the life after death, of the resurrection in the day of judgment, and of the unity of the Church; he further requires the maidens to acknowledge that by baptism the sin of their father and mother is taken away, and he tells them that they cannot see the face of Christ till they have tasted death and received the sacrifice. The Eucharist is administered to them as a viaticum. In the "Tripartite Life," Patrick's words respecting the Eucharist are given thus: " Ye cannot see Christ unless ye first taste of death, and unless ye receive Christ's Body and His Blood;" which shows that the cup was not denied to the laity in the time of Patrick. The Hymn of Secundinus, moreover, relates that Patrick gave God's people to drink of a spiritual cup. Tirechan refers to the custom of mixing water with the wine. A child was baptized in its mother's womb by Patrick. "The water of the child's baptism, the same is the water of the woman's communion." [1]

I have already shown that it is unsafe to consult the later romances for particulars of Patrick's Christianity. Caution must be observed even in our study of the pages of Tirechan, for he wrote some two hundred years after Patrick's death. We may see in a mediæval picture the soldiers and senators of ancient Rome depicted in mediæval Italian costume, and similarly mediæval writers employ in their narra-

[1] Tirechan. W.S. 327.

tives of earlier events the language of their own times, and frequently attribute to the subject of their biography the opinions and practices familiar to themselves. We can only be sure that they are preserving an early tradition when we read in their pages the record of a custom which was foreign to their own experience, such as Joceline's narrative of the building of churches of planks and wattle, or his mention of Kentigern's consecration by a single bishop. An anachronism presented no difficulty to the minds of mediæval students.

We cannot, therefore, be quite certain the doctrines and practices attributed to Patrick by Tirechan were rightly so attributed. When he tells us that Patrick consecrated Olcan and "gave him part of the relics of Peter and Paul and others, and a cloth which covered the relics,"[1] or that Patrick gave Bishop Bron a tooth which fell out one day,[2] all that we need believe is that certain churches preserved relics in Tirechan's time, which they boasted had been thus presented. Still less need we believe the later note in the "Book of Armagh," which states that the "relics of Peter and Paul, Laurence and Stephen," at Armagh, were brought there through Patrick and Sachellus.[3] As little reason probably is there for trusting that supposed saying of Patrick which bids the "Church of the Scots" to be as the Romans in chanting "Lord, have mercy upon us,"[4] or the tra-

---
[1] Tirechan. W.S. 329.
[2] Ib. 327.
[3] W.S. 301.
[4] "Book of Armagh," W.S. 301.

ditional canon which states: "If any difficult questions arise in this island, let them be referred to the Apostolic See."[1] It was natural and easy for later innovators to consecrate their novelties by the sanction of a great and revered name. There is nothing in Patrick's acknowledged writings which gives any countenance, even so much as to a supposition that he acknowledged a harmless primacy of the Roman bishop, much less warrants anyone in asserting that he was a supporter by prophetic anticipation of the modern claims of the Papacy.

Equally untenable is the theory that Patrick made a compromise with paganism. "Nothing is clearer," states one author,[2] "than that Patrick engrafted Christianity on the Pagan superstitions with so much skill that he won the people over to the Christian religion before they understood the exact difference between the two systems of belief." There is not a tittle of evidence for this statement to be found in the writings of St. Patrick; unless we infer from his numerous baptisms that his requirements for that sacrament were not of an exacting character. Patrick's teaching in his "Confession" regarding the worship of idols and of the sun is unmistakeable and un-

---

[1] "Irish Canons," W.S. 506. See also "Book of Armagh," W.S. 356. I must acknowledge, however, that Dr. Whitley Stokes remarks as follows:—" He had a reverent affection for the Church of Rome; and there is no ground for disbelieving his desire to obtain Roman authority for his mission, or for questioning the authenticity of his decrees that difficult questions arising in Ireland should ultimately be referred to the Apostolic See." W.S. cxxxv.

[2] Dr. O'Donovan, quoted by Dr. Todd, "St. Patrick," 500.

compromising. "All those who adore the sun," he declares, "miserable ones, shall wretchedly be punished."[1] The doctrines of the Gospel are not disguised, nor its sterner truths minimised, in order to win converts. It is not the historic Patrick of the "Confession," but the fictitious Patrick of the late romances to whom a desire for compromise must be imputed, and the historian must beware of founding a theory of such a kind, which directly contravenes the testimony of Patrick's own words, upon the authority of worthless documents. There is a danger in their study, for the labour expended thereon at last dignifies the unworthy object, and the inquirer, when he turns up a paltry stone from the huge rubbish heap, is prone to fancy that he has discovered a precious jewel.

Tirechan's account of the death of Ethne the Fair and Fedelm the Ruddy, immediately after they received the Eucharist, may possibly indicate the existence in the early Irish Church of a lingering belief respecting the virtue of a voluntary death, which was a survival of the pagan idea of human sacrifice. But there is no reason to suppose that this formed part of Patrick's teaching, and it was probably only a literary relic, not an actual practice. A similar story is told of the maiden whom the Irish saint Enna loved before his conversion. St. Fanche gave her her choice either to wed Enna or "to love Him whom I love." She answered, "I will love whom thou lovest." Then St. Fanche said, "Come then with me into my

[1] *Conf.* H. and S. II. 313.

chamber, that you may rest there a little while." The girl went, and laying herself there on the bed, expired, and "gave up her spirit to God, the spouse whom she had chosen."[1] A more ghastly story, which almost seems to imply that the victim was buried alive, is told in the old Irish Life of Columba. Fortunately for the reputation of that holy man it is contradicted by implication in Adamnan's biography. The fable is related as an incident which happened immediately after the arrival of the missionary party in Iona. "Columkille said then to his people, ' It would be better for us that our roots should pass into the earth here.' And he said to them, ' It is permitted to you that some one of you go under the earth of this island to consecrate it.' Odhran arose quickly, and thus spake : ' If you accept me,' said he, ' I am ready for that.' ' O, Odhran,' said Columkille, ' you shall receive the reward of this ; no request shall be granted to any one at my tomb unless he first ask of thee. Odhran then went to heaven. He (Columkille) founded the church of Hy then."[2] Local tradition intensifies the horror of this tale by adding that when Odhran's tomb was opened subsequently, he was found alive, and uttered such terrible blasphemies that it became necessary to cover him up again.[3]

These stories certainly attest the persistence of pagan ideas in Ireland, but they lasted in spite of Patrick's teaching, not in consequence thereof. There

[1] Todd's " St. Patrick," 125 *note*.
[2] Reeves' Columba, " Historians of Scotland," vi. 288 *note*.
[3] Todd, 462 *note*, quoting from Pennant.

is trustworthy evidence that the second order of Irish saints attempted a compromise with paganism, but there is none that Patrick himself initiated such a policy.

CHAPTER XV.

ST. PATRICK'S CHURCH.

ACCORDING to the "Catalogue of the Saints of Ireland," which is referred by Dr. Todd to the middle of the eighth century, and which is generally accepted as an interesting and valuable record of the early Irish Church, there were three orders of Irish saints, the first most holy, the second very holy, the third holy ; the first burning as the sun, the second as the moon, the third as a star.

" The first order of Catholic Saints," we are told, " was in the time of Patrick. And then they were all bishops, famous and holy and full of the Holy Ghost, 350 in number,[1] founders of churches. They had one head, Christ, and one leader, Patrick. They observed one mass, one celebration, one tonsure from ear to ear. They celebrated one Easter, on the fourteenth moon after the vernal equinox ; and what was excommunicated by one Church, all excommunicated. They rejected not the service and society of women, because, founded on the rock of Christ, they

---

[1] Or 450 according to another MS.

feared not the blast of temptation. This order of saints lasted during four reigns, that is, for the time of Laoghaire, and Oilioll Molt, and Lugaidh, son of Laoghaire, and Tuathal. All these bishops were sprung from the Romans and Franks and Britons and Scots."[1]

The reigns referred to cover the period from Patrick's arrival in Ireland to about A.D. 540, and the description therefore applies to Patrick's Church. To modern readers the strangest and most striking feature in the narrative is the large number of bishops. There is no need to suppose, indeed, that the author intended the number of three hundred and fifty to be literally exact; it is equivalent to seven fifties and therefore probably signifies merely that the bishops were very numerous. In like manner, four reigns are assigned to each of the three orders of saints, although to maintain this artificial exactness several intermediate kings are left out, and only the names of the first and last of each four are intended to be seriously regarded. The same artificiality regarding numbers permeates early Irish literature. But in any case the author intends to state that Patrick's church differed from the church in later times by the great number of its bishops. The Second Order of Saints is distinguished as being an order " of Catholic Presbyters, for in this order there were few bishops and many presbyters, in number 300." In the Third Order of Saints there were " holy presbyters, and a few bishops."

[1] H. and S. ii. 292-294. Todd, 89, 90, *note.* Usher, " Antiq.," 913-915.

Tirechan's evidence goes to support the statement of the catalogue regarding the number of Patrick's bishops. He states that the saint came to Ireland with a multitude of holy bishops and minor clergy, and that he consecrated afterwards 450 bishops, a number which agrees exactly with one manuscript of the catalogue. He further gives the names of forty-four bishops in a list of Patrick's chief clergy, and mentions frequently the consecration of bishops in the course of his narrative. Later legends generally repeat the earlier statements with uninteresting variations of their own, but it is a little curious to notice that one ninth century story makes the number of Patrick's bishops the same as the number of his churches.[1]

[1] "Tripartite Life" (W.S. 261) states that Patrick consecrated 370 bishops, and ordained 3,000 priests and minor clergy. Nennius ("Historia Britonum," W.S. 500) mentions the writing of 365 alphabets or more, the founding of 365 churches, the consecration of 365 bishops or more, the ordination of 3,000 priests, the baptism in Connaught of 12,000 converts. The Chronological Tract in the "Lebar Brecc" quotes a statement that Patrick consecrated "seven fifties" of bishops, and "three hundred virginal elders, wrote 300 alphabets, and built 700 churches" (W.S. 553). The "Litany of Angus the Culdee' invokes "seven times fifty holy bishops, with three hundred priests, whom Patrick ordained." Dr. Skene, who treats the subject of the Church of St. Patrick in his "Celtic Scotland," ii. 14-26, quotes the statement of Angus, and adds:—"Upwards of half of his clergy seem, therefore, to have been bishops, and he appears to have placed a bishop, consecrated by himself, in each church which he founded. The difference in order between bishop and presbyter is here fully recognised, and there was nothing in this very inconsistent with the state of the primitive church, before it became a territorial church and its hierarchical arrangements and jurisdiction were adapted to and modelled upon the civil government of the Roman empire.'"

The multiplication of bishops in Ireland, which dated from the time of St. Patrick, was perpetuated for many centuries, so that St. Bernard complained that in his time "bishops were changed and multiplied without rule or reason, at the pleasure of the metropolitan (a thing unheard of from the very beginning of Christianity), so that one bishopric was not content with one bishop, but almost every church had its separate bishop." The early bishops had no territorial jurisdiction, and many were attached to monasteries and were under the authority of the abbot. This caused extreme astonishment to Bede, who records that the abbot of Hy was always a priest, and yet "the bishops themselves, by an unusual rule, had to be subject to him, after the example of the first teacher, Columba, who was not a bishop, but a priest and monk."[1] St. Bridget, who is said to have died thirty years after St. Patrick, is related in her legend to have felt the need of possessing a bishop connected with her monastery, "to consecrate churches and to settle the ecclesiastical degrees in them," and for this purpose she selected an anchorite, who was consecrated bishop. Mochta of Louth is said to have had in his monastery a hundred bishops, an exaggeration which nevertheless attests a fact. This Mochta is called by Adamnan "a pilgrim from Britain, a holy man, a disciple of St. Patrick the Bishop,"[2] and is

It is curious to note in the above numbers the prevalence of three, seven, and twelve. The same numbers are repeatedly found in the legendary accounts of St. Patrick. See W.S. 587, 589.

[1] Hist. Eccl. iii. 4.
[2] *Vita Sancti Columbae*. "Sec, Praef." See also Reeves' note, "Hist. of Scotland," vi, 248.

said to have landed at Omeath, in the county of Louth, with twelve followers. Mochta, therefore, would belong to the Church of St. Patrick, and to the first order of Irish saints, whereas Columba belonged to the second order, which derived much of its teaching from Welsh sources, especially from the three great saints of South Wales, David, Gildas, and Cadoc. Monastic bishops also existed in early times on the continent, as at Tours and St. Denis,[1] and in each of these cases a confirmation of the practice was subsequently obtained from papal authority. Tours was the celebrated monastery of St. Martin, and it is quite possible that Patrick, who had spiritual brethren in Gaul, for whose society he sometimes longed, even in the midst of his beloved Irish, had visited the monastery, and copied its customs in his religious foundations. The legends which represent him to have been a nephew or connection of St. Martin, and to have received the monachal tonsure at his hands,[2] may have arisen from some particular respect felt by St. Patrick for the Gallican saint, and the usages

---

[2] Todd, 51-69. He also specifies Laubes, in Belgium; Saltzburgh; Cassino in Italy; the monastery of Mount Sinai; Honaw, &c. At Tours the bishop was sometimes abbot, but generally the offices were divided. Pope Hadrian I confirmed the privilege at Tours, and Pope Urban II abolished it in 1096. In St. Denis the custom was abandoned in the beginning of the ninth century, after having been confirmed by Pope Stephen in 757, and by Pope Hadrian I in 786.

[1] *e.g.*, Marianus Scotus, W.S. 510. "St. Patrick, when he was 30 years old, coming to Tours, is tonsured by St. Martin with the monachal tonsure, because formerly he had the servile tonsure."

of his monastery. Martin died in Patrick's boyhood, so that Patrick can never have seen him; but the veneration felt for him in the Celtic communion is proved by the dedication of St. Ninian's church at Candida Casa, and of the little British church just outside Canterbury, to his memory, such instances of dedication being exceedingly rare among the Britons.[1]

In some places in Ireland there were groups of seven bishops. The arrangement of oratories in sevens has already been noticed as dating, according to Tirechan, from the time of Patrick; but the "Book of Armagh" says nothing about groups of seven bishops.[2] In the "Litany of Angus the Culdee" one hundred and fifty-three groups of seven bishops are invoked, and in many cases these groups consisted

---

[1] They generally called a church after its founder.

[2] Dr. Skene ("Celtic Scotland") supposes that collegiate churches of seven bishops were founded by Patrick towards the end of his life. "They were brought closer to the tribal system, based on the family, which prevailed in Ireland, by these bishops being usually seven brothers selected from one family in the tribe. We see the germ of something of the kind in Tirechan's 'Annotations,' where it is said that, towards the end of his career, Patrick passed the Shannon three times, and completed seven years in the western quarter, and came from the plain of Tochuir to Dulo Ocheni, and founded seven churches there." And again, "The seven sons of Doath, that is Cluain, Findglais and Imsruth, Culcais, Deruthmar, Culcais and Cennlocho, faithfully made offerings to God and Saint Patrick." But Angus the Culdee in his litany gives us a list of no fewer than one hundred and fifty-three groups sf seven bishops in the same church, all of whom he invokes. A few of these we can identify sufficiently to show that they usually consisted of seven brothers living together in one church, and that they belong to this period."

of brothers or near relatives. Six groups of seven bishops are mentioned in the "Martyrology of Donegal," and in three cases they are said to have been brothers.[1] In the legend of St. Forannan, a disciple of the great Columba, the seven bishops of Cluain Hemain, now Clonown, near Athlone, are said to have been present at Easdara on the occasion of a gathering of clergy in honour of Columba. These bishops are elsewhere represented as brethren, the sons of one mother, and are also invoked by Angus.[2] Several places in Ireland still preserve in their names the tradition of having been formerly the abodes of a party of bishops.[3] How long the institution of these groups lasted we know not, and its object can only be conjectured. The early Church of Ireland was essentially a missionary church, working in the midst of paganism, and Patrick and his successors adapted their methods to the circumstances of their mission. A regular diocesan episcopate under a central primacy was, perhaps, impracticable in a nation of small septs, which not infrequently were at variance with one another. There is certainly no trace of the primacy of Armagh in the earliest times; that was a subsequent development. The first bishops acted somewhat independently, though harmoniously. "What was excommunicated by one church, all excommunicated."

In later days the Celtic customs appeared exceedingly disorderly, when sharply contrasted with the

---

[1] Todd, 32.   [2] Ib. 34, 35.
[3] Ib. 33.

thorough organisation of the churches under the primacy of Rome, and this inferiority contributed largely to the failure of the Celtic churches in their struggle against the claims of the Papacy. The Irish Church was unsurpassed in planting new churches, but the Roman Church, from its superiority in organising, reaped the fruit of her rival's labours, and eventually secured that rival's submission. What, however, proved a defect in later centuries may, in Patrick's time, have been a source of strength and success. It must not be imagined that there was ever any confusion in Ireland between the various orders of the Christian Church. The presbyter-abbot was at times superior in jurisdiction to a bishop, but in orders he was universally, and at all times, regarded as the inferior. There was no such thing in the Irish Church as "Presbyterian orders." Holy orders were always conferred by a bishop, who also administered Confirmation and celebrated the Holy Communion with peculiar rites. This is proved by Adamnan's "Life of Columba," wherein we find that Abbot Findchan, when he wished a man ordained, did not venture to perform the rite himself, but sent for a bishop to confer the priesthood upon him.[1] Once a bishop from the province of the Munster-men came to Iona, and wished, from humility, to conceal the fact that he was a bishop. But on the next Lord's day, being invited by the saint, according to custom, to consecrate the Body of Christ, he asked the saint to join him, that, as two priests, they might break the body of the Lord together. But Columba perceived that he

[1] *Vita Sancti Columbæ*, i. 29.

was a bishop, and refused, saying, "Christ bless thee, brother; break this bread alone according to the episcopal rite; now we know that thou art a bishop. Why hast thou sought to hide thyself so long, and prevented our rendering thee the veneration due to thee?"[1] So far, then, was Columba—himself only a priest—from ignoring episcopal precedence, that he would not even presume to celebrate jointly with a bishop.[2]

It is quite uncertain whether, in the consecration of so many bishops, Patrick followed the custom of his own British Church. The only places in Britain at which we know there were Bishops in the time of Patrick are Londinium, Eburacum, "Colonia Londinensium," and Candida Casa, which correspond to the modern London, York, possibly Caerleon, and Whithorn. There were more than four British bishops at the Council of Ariminum in 359, but there is no certain proof of the existence of any very large number of bishops at any time in the early British Church, though there were probably monastic bishops, as

---

[1] *Vita Sancti Columbæ*, I, 35.   "Hist of Scot.," vi. 142, 263.

[2] Warren, "Liturgy and Ritual of the Celtic Church," 128, 129. "A very singular custom existed at Iona of two or more priests being ordinarily united in the Eucharistic prayer and act of consecration; to consecrate singly being the prerogative of bishops, or of individual priests specially selected and empowered to consecrate on account of their sanctity or eminence. . . . . . This custom of joint celebrants in the case of priests and of a single celebrant in the case of a bishop is peculiar to the Celtic rite, no similar practice existing in any other country or at any other time. There was something exactly opposed to it in the once general, but now nearly obsolete, rule of the Western Church, that when a bishop celebrated, the priests present should unite with him in the words and acts of consecration."

Paulinus of Whitland, after Patrick's time. The case
is different with regard to other churches. The
Council of Sardica found it necessary to check the
excessive multiplication of bishops in order to keep
up the dignity of the order, and consequently ordained
that it should not be lawful to place a bishop in a
village or small city where a single presbyter would be
sufficient. " In such places," it stated, " there is no
need to set a bishop, lest the name and authority of
bishops be brought into contempt." Yet, notwithstanding this rule, the custom continued. In Asia
Minor alone there were nearly four hundred bishops,
and among the Arabians and Cyprians it was a
custom to ordain bishops in villages as well as cities,
as also among the Novatian and Montanist heretics
in Phrygia. Every bishop had power, with the con-
sent of his metropolitan or the approval of a provincial
council, to divide his diocese and consecrate bishops
to certain portions ; and in Africa the orthodox party
and the Donatists, at the time of the schism, availed
themselves of this practice in order to outdo one
another in the number of their bishops ; so that the
Donatists even accused their opponents of appointing
bishops in places where there was no flock to feed.[1]
Besides absolute bishops there were Chorepiscopi or
country bishops, who are said to have been consecrated by one bishop only, the bishop of the city to
whose jurisdiction they severally belonged, and who
were quite subordinate to the City-Bishops. These

[1] Bingham, "Antiquities of the Christian Church," ii. 12, pp.
154-160, ed 1708. The pages in this edition, however, are incor-
rectly numbered, there being two sets of pages 153-160.)

were allowed to ordain the inferior clergy, but they could not ordain priests or deacons without the special leave of their superior bishop. In most respects they correspond to what are now known in England as suffragan bishops.[1]

It will appear from this evidence that, however strange the number of three hundred and fifty bishops in Ireland may appear to modern ideas, it was not a circumstance wholly without parallel; though the survival of the custom some centuries later caused as much astonishment to St. Bernard as its early record does to us.

But there were other primitive usages in the early Irish church with regard to the ecclesiastical orders besides the great multiplication of bishops, and these also may have been derived from Patrick himself. It was customary in the Celtic churches for consecration to be performed by a single bishop. According to Muirchu, Patrick himself was consecrated by Amatorex, and no mention is made of any assistant bishops. Patrick also appears to have consecrated others without any help. Kentigern, the saint of Glasgow, was in later days consecrated in like manner; and his biographer, Joceline of Furness, is rather scandalised by having to mention such an incident, and compensates for it by relating subsequently a fictitious visit of the saint to Rome, where his conse-

---

[1] Bingham, ii. 14, who further remarks: "Anciently, suffragan-bishops were all the city-bishops of any province under a metropolitan, who were called his suffragans, because they met at his command to give their suffrage, council, or advice in a provincial synod." The modern use of the term seems to have originated with the Act of the 26th of Henry VIII.

cration is confirmed by Gregory. Yet Joceline allows that "although the consecration to which the Britons were accustomed is scarcely consonant with the sacred canons, still it is agreed that it does not destroy the power and efficiency of the Divine mystery or of the episcopal ministration."[1] Besides the irregularity of consecration by a single bishop, Joceline further mentions that the British usage was merely to anoint the head of the elect by pouring on it the sacred chrism, with invocation of the Holy Spirit, and benediction and laying on of hands. The Scottish saints Ternan and Servanus are said to have been consecrated by one bishop only, as also the Welsh saints Dyfrig and Teilo. A very late story represents Columba as seeking to be ordained bishop at the hands of Bishop Etchen, who conferred on him priests' orders by mistake.

This legend, which is contained in the Annotations on the "Martyrology" of Angus the Culdee, is in all probability a fiction, but is nevertheless of considerable value, as its writer undoubtedly believed the ecclesiastical customs therein related to be consistent with the ecclesiastical discipline of his own time and of the early Church of Ireland. "Bishop Etchen," he says, "is venerated in Cluain-fota-Boetain, in Fera-Bile, in the south of Meath, and it was to him that Colum-kille went to have the order of a bishop conferred upon him. Colum-kille sat under the tree which is on the west side of the church, and asked where the cleric was. 'There he is,' said a certain

[1] *Vita S. Kentigerni*, xi. xvii. "Hist. of Scot.," v., ed. by Bp. Forbes. See also Bp. Forbes' note, 335-340.

man, 'in the field where they are ploughing below.' 'I think,' said Colum-kille, 'that it is not meet for us that a ploughman should confer orders upon us; but let us test him?'...... Then Colum-kille went up to the cleric, after having thus tested him, and told him what he came for. 'It shall be done,' said the cleric. The order of a priest was then conferred upon Colum-kille, although it was the order of a bishop he wished to have had conferred upon him. The cleric prayed until the following day, 'I regret,' said Colum-kille, 'that thou hast conferred this order upon me; but I shall never change it whilst I live; for this reason, however, no person shall ever again come to have orders conferred upon him in this church.' And this has been fulfilled, up to this time."[1]

The custom of single consecration prevailed in the Irish church to a comparatively late date, and was complained of by Lanfranc in a letter to the Irish king Torlogh in A.D. 1074, and by Anselm writing to king Muirchertagh or Moriarty in A.D. 1100.[2] Such consecrations, as Joceline admits, were always considered valid, though irregular. Instances occurred in other parts of Christendom, and no objection was raised in most cases to the validity of the act. Siderius, Bishop of

---

[1] I have borrowed the translation from Dr. Todd. See further, Todd, 70-77. Reeves' Adamnan. "Hist. of Scot.," vi. 226.

[2] Warren, "Liturgy," &c., 69. H. & S., i. 155. Todd, "St. Patrick," 1-3. Anselm says: " It is said, moreover, that bishops are chosen at random in your country, and appointed without a fixed place of episcopal jurisdiction; and that a bishop is ordained like a mere priest, by a single bishop." See further, "Ireland and the Celtic Church," p. 318. Lectures xv. and xvi. give a most graphic description of the Irish Church in the eleventh and twelfth centuries.

Palaebisca, was thus consecrated, yet Athanasius not only allowed his consecration and confirmed it, but afterwards raised him to the Metropolitical city of Ptolemais.[1] Several councils, however, prohibited such consecrations, and it is very curious that at the first Council of Arles, which in A.D. 314 enacted a canon on this matter, three British bishops were present and subscribed its decrees. By its twentieth canon this Council ordered that a consecrating bishop should have seven others with him, or if he could not procure seven he should not venture to ordain without the assistance of at least three.[2]

The legend of Columba's visit to Etchen also indicates that men were sometimes made bishops without having previously been priests. Columba asked to be made a bishop, but "the order of a priest was then conferred upon Columkille, although it was the order of a bishop he wished to have had conferred upon him." It is impossible to plead in this case that the orders of priest and bishop were conferred in one continued function analogous to the simultaneous administration of baptism and confirmation; for Columba is represented as saying, "I regret that thou hast conferred this order (*i.e.*, the priesthood) upon me." The author evidently believed that Columba wished to be consecrated *per saltum*, the priesthood being omitted as well as all minor orders. It matters little that the legend is probably a fiction, for

---

[1] Bingham, "Antiquities," ii. 11, p. 148, ed. 1708. So also the consecration of Evagrius of Antioch. There were other cases of consecration by two bishops only.

[2] H. & S. i. 7.

such a story could scarcely have arisen unless such irregular ordinations were occasionally performed. That they were considered valid by the early Church is shown by St. Jerome's maxim, "*In Episcopo et Presbyter continetur*" (In the Bishop the Priest also is contained).[1] The story of the consecration of Fiacc, which has been already related, attributes such ordinations to Patrick himself. Fiacc was not even a baptized Christian when Dubthach is said to have recommended him to Patrick as a suitable man for a bishop, and he was persuaded to accept the office by guile. "Patrick tonsured him and baptized him. He conferred a bishop's grade upon him, so that he was the bishop who was first consecrated in Leinster." The legend is not so old as Tirechan, and is uncertain, but it is not impossible. In some respects it resembles the story of the consecration of the great St. Ambrose. "When the people of Milan were so divided in the election of a bishop that the whole city was in an uproar, he being Praetor of the place, came in upon them to appease the tumult, as by virtue of his office he thought himself obliged to do; and making an eloquent speech to them, it had a sort of miraculous effect upon them, for they all immediately left off their dispute, and unanimously cried out they would have Ambrose to be their bishop. Which the Emperor understanding, and looking upon it as a providential call, he ordered

---

[1] *Ep.* cii. *ad Evang.* See also Hilary the Deacon in Ephes. chap. iv. 11: "In Episcopo omnes ordines sunt; quia primus sacerdos est, hoc est princeps est sacerdotum." (In the Bishop all orders are; because he is the first priest—that is, he is the chief of priests).

him to be baptized (for he was yet but a catechumen), and in a few days after to be ordained their bishop."[1] Eusebius, Bishop of Caesarea, was also only a catechumen when he was chosen bishop; and St. Cyprian was a neophyte.[2] There are stranger stories of ordination even than Fiacc's, which are better attested. The life of St. German, Patrick's instructor, was written by a contemporary, and not long after his death, and is therefore generally to be trusted. Yet this biography relates a curious story how German first took holy orders. He was wont to hang the spoils of the chase, of which he was passionately fond, upon an ancient tree, probably a relic of pagan superstition. Amator, Bishop of Auxerre, caused this tree to be cut down, and German threatened that he would take the bishop's life. But soon afterwards the bishop assembled the people in the cathedral. German came among others. The bishop ordered all to lay aside their arms, and caused the ostiarii to shut the doors of the church. Then with a band of clergy and nobles he seized the young soldier, German, and calling upon the name of the Lord, tonsured him, invested him in the clerical habit, and ordained him. This happened in 418, probably not quite half a century before the consecration of Fiacc, which, if performed by guile, was at least not accompanied by violence. Patrick may have been hard pushed at times for a man who

---

[1] Bingham, "Antiquities," ii. 10, 7. It seems probable, however, that Ambrose was previously made deacon, priest, etc.

[2] Ib. Eucherius, Bishop of Lyons, Nectarius of Constantinople, Philogonius of Antioch were also laymen.

would be acceptable to a particular tribe. A Roman, Briton, or Gaul was not always suitable, and the supply of these foreign missionaries was not inexhaustible. It was, doubtless, necessary in particular localities to have a native Irishman, and sometimes a member of the tribe in which he was to be placed. It is quite in accordance with what we know of Patrick's methods, and of primitive usages, that occasionally irregular ordinations of mere neophytes might be resorted to. A modern missionary would not baptize so indiscriminately as Patrick must have done, since he baptized "many thousands," and holy orders may also have been conferred with a lack of precaution that would be appalling to modern ideas.

The subsequent history of the church of Ireland strongly confirms this conception of the nature of Patrick's church. Though the clergy were at first largely drawn from foreign countries, from the Roman cities, and the country districts of Britain, and from Gaul, as is proved not merely by the "Catalogue of the Saints" and by the narratives of Patrick's labour, but also by the mention of Romans, Gauls, and Britons in the writings of Angus the Culdee, the church was from the very first the church of the Irish people. But this great advantage was accompanied by a corresponding disadvantage; the admission to baptism of whole tribes and the ordination of natives who had not shaken off old native prejudices of paganism, produced their natural result—pagan tares grew up among the Christian wheat. St. Bernard complained that in his time "instead of Christian piety there was everywhere introduced a cruel barbarism, nay, a sort of paganism, substituted under the Christian name." A brilliant scholar and student of Celtic Heathendom has been led by his researches to conclude that early Irish Christianity was little else than a veneered paganism. "Irish druidism," he says, "absorbed a certain amount of Christianity, and it would be a problem of considerable difficulty to fix on the point where it ceased to be druidism, and from which onwards it could be said to be Christianity in any restricted sense of that term."[1] This is a very strong statement, to which I am unable to subscribe, but there is a remarkable consensus of statements in ancient literature, that after the death of Patrick there was a considerable declension and a partial relapse into Paganism. This resulted, not from any faults in Patrick's teaching, of which there is no evidence, nor from any compromise with paganism in his policy, but more probably from a somewhat indiscriminate admission of candidates for baptism and holy orders. Many of the converts "feared the Lord, and served their own gods," and it was doubtful for a time whether druidism would not absorb Christianity.[2]

From this danger Ireland was saved by the infusion of a sterner monastic spirit. The Saints of the First Order "rejected not the service and society of women," or, according to another manuscript, "they excluded from the churches neither laymen nor

[1] Rhys, "Hibbert Lectures," 224.
[2] Todd, "St. Parick," 101-118. Haddan & Stubbs, "Councils." i., 115-116.

women." This does not mean that they had no monasteries, for we read of the monastery to which Assicus, Patrick's coppersmith, resorted as to an "island" of refuge from the rough storms of life, and there were others as well. But there was probably a large proportion of secular clergy in Patrick's church, and its monastic rules also were less rigorous[1] than those of the Second Order of Saints, which is thus described by the Catalogue:

"The Second Order was of Catholic Presbyters. For in this order there were few bishops and many presbyters, in number 300. They had one head, our Lord; they celebrated different masses, and had different rules, one Easter on the fourteenth moon after the equinox, one tonsure from ear to ear. They refused the services of women, separating them from the monasteries. This Order lasted hitherto for four reigns, that is, from the last years of Tuathal, and during the whole reign of king Diarmait, and that of the two grandsons of Muredach, and of Aedh, the son of Ainmire. They received a mass from Bishop David, and Gillas,[2] and Docus,[3] the Britons. Whose names are these: two Finians, two Brendans, Jarlath

---

[1] See Todd, 90-92. Dr. Skene remarks: "The first order, too, 'rejected not the services and society of women'; or, according to another MS., 'they excluded from their churches neither laymen nor women,' which indicates their character as secular clergy, in contradistinction to those under a monastic rule." See also "Tripartite Life," W. S. 89, where it is said that in consequence of a false rumour about Bishop Mel, who lived in one habitation with his kinswoman, Patrick said, "Let men and women be apart," &c.

[2] Viz. Gildas.

[3] Cadoc of Llancarvan, otherwise called Cattwg the Wise.

of Tuam, Comgall, Coemgen, Ciaran, Columba, Cainech, Eoghan mac Laisre, Lugeus, Ludeus, Moditeus, Cormac, Colman, Nessan, Laisrean, Barrindeus, Coeman, Ceran, Coman, [Endeus, Ædeus, Byrchinus], and many others."

Ireland, after Patrick's death, was influenced greatly by the monasteries of Whitherne, in North Britain, and by Menevia and Llancarvan, in what is now South Wales. Whitherne acted chiefly on the Christianity of the north of the island, and possibly commenced its work earlier than the Welsh monasteries, for one of its abbots, Bishop Cairnech, is said to have come to Ireland in the fifth century.[1] The Welsh monasteries acted chiefly on the centre and south of Ireland, and their work began in the sixth century, and is attested largely by the legends both of Irish and of Welsh saints. The most notable act of all, perhaps, was the mission of Gildas, who is said to have been invited to Ireland by king Ainmire, and who landed there about A.D. 565, and carried on a most successful work.[2]

It is unnecessary to relate here the history of this revival, or the subsequent labours of the Second Order of Saints. The monastic spirit which was infused into the Church of Ireland by Gildas and others speedily arrested decay, and produced an outburst of zeal and enthusiasm which has few parallels in history. Ireland sent forth missionaries

---

[1] Skene "Celtic Scotland" ii. 46.
[2] See Todd, 99-113; also "History of the Ancient British Church" (S.P.C.K.), 87-96, 134-140; the Legends of St. David and of St. Cadoc in Rees' "Cambro-British Saints," etc.

all over Western Europe, and planted her monasteries even in Italy, where the great Columbanus carried on the Church's campaign against Arianism and Papal autocracy. Irish monks were renowned for their adventurous daring, their learning, and their artistic skill. In their labours among pagans at home and abroad they carried out the policy which has on very imperfect evidence been ascribed to St. Patrick; they advanced, as he did, the claim that the earth was the Lord's and the fulness thereof; but they attempted also what he did not attempt, namely, to "engraft their own faith upon the ancient objects of pagan veneration."[1] Adamnan states that Columba on one occasion converted a sacred well of paganism into a Christian holy well,[2] and on another occasion endowed a white pebble with magical healing power.[3] The poems and sacred books and reliquaries of the saints now began to receive that reverence which the druids had before imparted to rings, and stones, and talismans.

It was the error of their time and of their birthplace, for the saints were themselves infected by the prevailing superstitions; but it was in some degree a fault which leaned to virtue's side, for it sprung also from a large-hearted charity and the belief that "in every nation he that feareth God and worketh righteousness is accepted with Him." "It was the Holy Ghost," so the Celtic clergy held, "that spoke and prophesied through the mouths of the just men

---

[1] Todd, 127.   [2] *Vita S. Columbæ*, ii. 10.
[3] Ib. ii. 34.

who were formerly in the island of Erin, as he had prophesied through the mouths of the chief prophets and noble fathers in the patriarchal law; for the law of nature had prevailed where the written law did not reach."[1] The Celtic love of fatherland and people forbade them to hold that their forefathers were accursed and their national customs abominable. Like Laoghaire they could not forsake their fathers or be untrue to their traditions; but, unlike him, they thought they could be Christians and yet remain patriots.

With all its defects their Christianity was a great and noble thing, which claimed the earth for its rightful Possessor; which sanctified art, beauty, and culture; and which toiled for the conversion of human souls with untiring zeal and all-embracing charity. Its error in tolerating pagan survivals must not be exaggerated, as it may be if attention is exclusively concentrated thereupon. It was not paganism that sent forth the Irish missionaries to the islands of the Atlantic and all over the continent, planting everywhere homes of religion and schools of learning.

---

[1] *Senchus Mor*, which continues as follows:—"Now the judgments of true nature which the Holy Ghost had spoken through the mouths of the Brehons and just poets of the men of Erin, from the first occupation of this island down to the reception of the faith, were all exhibited by Dubhthach to Patrick. What did not clash with the Word of God in the Written Law and in the New Testament, and with the consciences of the believers, was confirmed in the laws of the Brehons by Patrick and by the ecclesiastics and the chieftains of Erin; for the law of Nature had been quite right, except the faith, an its obligatoins, and the harmony of the Church and the people. And this is the Senchus Mor."

Paganism is the religion of dread, not of love; and Irish Christianity, as represented by Columba, was full of compassion for human frailty, of tenderness for human ignorance, and of love for human souls.

* * * * *

This love for human souls is the secret of the history of St. Patrick, and of the golden age of that Church which he founded. Ireland and her Church have suffered changes since the days of Patrick; Tara has lain desolate for thirteen hundred years, and

> "The high house of O'Neill,
> Is gone down to the dust,"

but the love of the great British saint still lives in the memory of the people whom he loved. There are few spectacles in history more heroic and admirable than the persistent resolution of the unlearned rustic in the face of danger and delay, and under pressure of suffering of mind and body; or than the faith in the Unseen which finally carried him through all to his appointed task, and enabled him, purified by trial, to win a nation to his Lord. Youth, which is sometimes bidden to learn from examples of worldly success, may have its ideals raised and purified by the contemplation of Patrick's perseverance in a loftier ambition than that of the self-made man, and may be nerved to greater effort by his dauntless faith and unfailing hope; yet, great as are faith and hope, a greater than these is Charity. "We live by admiration, hope, and love;" and Patrick's life may stimulate all these emotions in us, and make our lives the richer in consequence; but the loveableness of his character, which won the love of children and attracted to him princes and peasants, noble maidens and young poets, was the secret of his power. His mission began in the exercise of that hardest proof of charity, forgiveness; for the nation which he sought to bless was that which had carried him into captivity from his father's home. The modern poet, who has so lovingly related the Legends of St. Patrick, sums up in this virtue of forgiveness the essence of his teaching:

> "All ye who name my name in later times,
> Say to this People, since vindictive rage
> Tempts them too often, that their Patriarch gave
> Pattern of pardon ere in words he preached
> That God who pardons. Wrongs if they endure
> In after years, with fire of pardoning love
> Sin-slaying, bid them crown the head that erred;
> For bread denied let them give Sacraments,
> For darkness light, and for the House of Bondage
> The glorious freedom of the sons of God."

INDEX.

ADAMNAN, 162, 171, 181, 189, 190, 202, 207, 211, 224
Aed of Sletty, 167
Aedh, St., 48, 179
Aengus, 143
Agricola, 18
Ailbe, 57
Ailill, 141
Alban, 3
Alclud, 10, 14, 158
Aloo, 157. See Alclud
Alphabets written by Patrick, 110, 111
Altars of stone, 58, 123, 145; of copper, 124; of wood, 123
Altus of Columba, 72, 197
Altus, 55
Amalgaidh. See Awley
Amator, 219
Amatorex, 40, 44, 45, 49, 50, 214
Ambrose, St., 218
Ancestors, worship of, 64
Anselm, St., 216
Antoninus, 14, 18
———, wall of, 13, 14, 18, 20
Aquileia, 21
Aralensis, 33
Ardbraccan, 170
Arles, 33; Council of, 217
Armagh, Ferta of, 115, 118; Church called Sabhall, 120, 144; foundation of churches at, 143, 144; primacy of, 85, 210; bishops of, 82, 85, 115, 145, 150, 153; Book of, described, 152-157, 160
Arthur, 12
Assicus, 124, 125, 222
Auxilius, 45, 75, 141
Awley, sons of, 101, 102, 115, 131, 136, 137

BALLYLIGPATRICK, 25
Banda, 140
Banna, 12
Bannavem Taberniae, 5, 7, 8, 12, 13, 22, 23, 24, 35
Baptism, at fountain Loigles, 101, 137; of Ethne and Fedelm, 107; of Conall, 101; at the well Sini, 135, 137; at Oenadare, 136, 137; Festival of Patrick's, 137; referred to in the Confession, 137, 145, 197, 175, 220; of the sons of Dunling, 141; of Fiacc, 142; of the men of North Munster, 143; of a Scotic lady, 146; chrism used at baptism and chrisom worn, 197; mentioned in Hymn of Secundinus, 197, 198; Patrick's Doctrine of Baptism, 106, 198; books of, 113.
Baslick, 131

230 INDEX.

Bede, 165, 207
Bells, Celtic, 112, 113, 123, 125-127
Beltaine, 62, 63, 69, 92
Benen, 12, 81, 82, 87, 150, 175, 191, 161
Benignus. See Benen
Bernard, St., 207, 214, 220
Bernicius, 131
Beuno, 48, 134
Bile Torten, 141
Bishops, numerous in Patrick's church, 204-214; consecration of, by a single, 199, 214-217; consecration, *per saltum*, 142, 217, 218; country bishops, 213; bishops in Ireland before Patrick, 57, 58
Book of Lecan, 53
Books given by Patrick, 111-113
Boulogne not St. Patrick's birthplace, 5
Braid, 25
Bran, 178
Brandan, St., 178
Branwen, 83
Brene, 77
Brigid, St., 12, 52, 123, 178, 207
Britons with Patrick, 75, 76, 205, 220
Bron, 199
Brittany, 5, 164
Broichan, 60
Brynach, 48, 179
Buall, 186

CADOC, ST., 48, 114, 133, 151, 183, 184, 189, 208, 222
Cadwaladr, 48
Caelestius, 56
Cainnech, 136
Cairnech, 161
Cairthenn, 186

Calpurnius, 4, 16
Candida Casa, 159. See also Whithorn
Cannibalism, 88
Caplit, 104, 107, 108
Cashel, 60, 122, 142, 143
Catalogue of the Saints of Ireland, 166, 204, 205, 222, 223
Cathures, 14
Cedd, 133
"Celebra Juda," 166
Celestine, 30, 33, 44, 57, 48-51, 150, 169, 172
Cenn Cruaich, 61, 69, 103
Cereticus, 158
Cermand Celstach, 67
Chasuble, its primitive shape, 128
Chi-Rho monogram, 138
Chorepiscopi, 213
Chronology of Patrick's life, 32, 51-54, 147-151
Churches founded by Patrick, 113-123
Church, Northern, 120
Clebach, 104, 108, 115
Cleghile, pillar-stone of, 65, 66
Cochmaiss, 123
Coirpre, 99, 100
Coirthech. See Coroticus
Colman, 58
Columb, 113
Columba, St., 2, 54, 60, 67, 114, 121, 133, 162, 165, 166, 167, 171, 181, 189, 190, 191, 193, 197, 202, 207, 208, 210, 211, 212, 215, 216, 217, 223, 224, 226
Columbanus. St., 47, 125, 165, 171, 224
Columkille. See Columba
Conall, brother of Laoghaire, 100, 140, 118
Conall, son of Enna, 101

INDEX. 231

Concessa, 4, 17
Confession of Saint Patrick, quoted, 3, 4, 22, 23, 26-28, 30-31, 33, 34, 36, 37, 40, 41-43, 58, 64, 91, 102, 137, 145-147, 157, 191, 193, 194, 196; known by Muirchu, 8, 154, 170; quoted by Tirechan, 154, 170; silent on the subject of any commission from Pope Celestine, 49; fixes Patrick's age at his consecration, 32, 54; contained in the Book of Armagh, 152-154; its genuineness admitted by all competent scholars, 154; proofs of its genuineness, 154, 155; mentions no miracles, 154; a defence of the author's mission, 156; coincidences between it and the Epistle to the Subjects of Coroticus, 159, 160; contrasts with late legendary lives, 166, 167.
Connaught, Patrick in, 104-110, 114, 131-140.
Consecration by a single bishop, 214-217; *per saltum*, 217, 218
Constantine, the usurper, 24
Cormac, Mac Art, 87
Cornwall, 145
Coroticus, King of Aloo, 157, 158, 191; story about him related by Muirchu, 159, 187; Patrick's Epistle to the Subjects of, 157-160; also referred to, 6, 17, 148, 175, 191, 195, 196, 197
"Corslets," 162, 164
Cothraige, 18; stone of, 66, 103; rock of, 142

Crochan, 104, 109
Cromduff, 62
Crosiers, 127, 128
Cross, 64, 65, 138, 139
Cruachan Aigle, 132, 186, 191
Cumbria, possible labours of St Patrick in, 38
Cummian, 166
Cummine Fota, St., 166
Cybi, 134

DAIRE, 143, 144
Dalaradia, 25, 140
Dalriada, 140
Darerca, 4, 103, 123, 164
David, St , 7, 151, 208, 222
Death, Voluntary, of Miliuc, 78; of Ethne and Fedelm, 107; of the maiden loved by St. Enna, 201; of Odhran, 202
Declan, 57
Deer's Cry, 94-98, 191, 192, 195
Dharna, 78
Dichu, 25, 77, 79, 81 137
Downpatrick, 147
Druids, 63, 190, 224; claims of, 59; their worship of the well Slan, 67, 135; their spells, 71, 97 ; overthrown by Patrick at Tara, 90, 91, 184; Mael and Caplit, 107, 108; their *airbacc giunnae*, 108; their garments, 130; taught about the day of Erdathe, 93
Dub, 186
Dubthach, 91, 141, 142, 218, 225
Dulo Ocheni, 121
Dumbarton, 10, 11, 22, 158
Dunbrettan, 10

Dunling, sons of, 141
Dunseverick, 140
Durrow, Book of, 165
Dyfrig, St., 215

EBMORIA, 44
Echu Redspot, 179
Enna, sons of Awley, 101, 102, 131
Enna, St., 201
Erc mac Dego, 101, 137
Erdathe, 93
Erem, 61
Etchen, 215, 216, 217
Etech of Mochae, 113
Ethne, 103, 104, 109, 115, 131, 197, 198, 201
Eucharist, Doctrine of the, 107, 197, 198, 201

FAED FIADA, 94. See also Deer's Cry.
Faillen, 185
Fanche, St., 201
Fasting of Patrick in Ireland, 26; of Patrick on Cruachan Aigle, 132, 186, 191; of Celtic bishops before consecrating a church, 133; of Celtic saints, 134
Fechach, 103
Fedelm, daughter of Ailill, 141
Fedelm, daughter of Laoghaire, 104, 109, 115, 131, 197, 198, 201
Feidlimidh. See Phelim
Ferdomnach, 152, 153
Fertae Martyrum, 144
Fiacc, 110, 127, 134, 141, 218, 219
Fiacc, spurious hymn of, 9, 60, 149, 168, 176, 177
Finan, 133
Findchan, 211

Fire, worship of, 70; Paschal lighted by Patrick, 91
Fochlut, 41, 100, 101, 138
Foirtchernn, 83-85
Forannan, St., 210
Franks with Patrick, 75, 131, 205

GALL, ST., 125
Gallarus, oratory of, 117
German, St., 39, 40, 43, 44, 49, 127, 219
Gildas, St., 21, 22, 162, 189, 208, 222, 223
Gilla Coemain, Poem of, 53, 54
Giraldus Cambrensis, his opinion of the Irish saints, 183
Glastonbury, 12, 145
Grecraige, the, 185
Gregory, Pope, 215
Gregory of Tours, 154
Guasacht, 78, 103
Gundleus, 114. See also Gwynllyw
Gwithian, 117, 123
Gwynllyw, 133. See also Gundleus

HELIAS, Patrick's cry of, 28-29, 31, 193
Hercaith, 112, 113
Heremon, 65
Hermon, Mount, 40, 49
Hernicius, 131
Honorat, 33
Honorius, 21, 24

IBAR, 57
Idols, worship of, 60; at Cashel, 60, 142, 143; Cenn Cruaich, 61, 103; Cermand Celstach, 67
Illan, 141
Illtyd, 7

INDEX. 233

Inbher Ailbine, 81
Inbher Colpthi, 81
Ihbher Dea, 76
Indract, 12
Inis Patrick, 76
Ireland, Church of, did it exist before Patrick? 55-59; Patrick's Church, 204-220; subsequent history, 220-226
Iserninus, 45, 75, 141
Island means monastery, 33

JAMES, ST., 55
Jarlath, 150
Joceline, his date, 177; his Life of Kentigern, 114, 199, 214, 215; his Life of Patrick, 40, 51, 149, 177
Jonas, 171
Justus, 113

KENTIGERN, ST., 48, 114, 134, 135, 151, 199, 214
Kieran, 57
Kilpatrick, Old, 11, 13
Kirkmadrine, 138

LANFRANC, 216
Laoghaire, 53, 83, 90-94, 100, 102, 104, 118, 140, 148, 162, 171, 184, 205
Lebar Brecc Homily, 10
Legends of Celtic saints criticised by Dr. Reeves, 177; by Giraldus Cambrensis, 183; extravagant, 177-182; revengeful, 183-188
Leinster, Patrick in, 141, 142
Lerins, 33
Letha. See Brittany
Lia Fail, 65
Liamain, 4, 119, 164

Liturgy of Patrick, 113
Llancarvan, 189, 223
Llantwit Major, 7, 122
Loch Selce, 132
Loigles, 101
Loiguire. See Laoghaire
Lollius Urbicus, 14, 18
Lomman, 82-87, 103, 185, 186
Lucetmael, 90
Lugnademon, 135
Lugnassad, 62, 63, 100
Lugnath, 119
Lupait, 4, 123, 186
Lupus, St., of Troyes, 33, 39, 127
Luxeuil Calendar, 166

MABRAN, 103
Mactaleus, 141
Macthene, 167
Mael, 104, 107, 108
Maelrubha, St., 67, 188
Mag Inis, 81
Mag Selce, 66, 131, 138
Mag Slecht, 61
Mag Tochuir, 58
Magnus Maximus, 21, 24
Magonus, 7, 18
Mangan, James Clarence, translation of the Deer's Cry, 94-98
Mansuetus, 56
Mantan, 185, 186
Maree, Loch, 67
Martin, St., 4, 17, 40, 153, 208, 209
Maun, 7
Mawon, 7
Medan, St., chapel of, 117
Mel, 103, 123
Mellon, 3
Menevia, 223
Menhir, developed into Christian cross, 138
Milchu. See Miliuc

Miliuc, 25, 37, 53, 54, 76, 77, 78, 79, 103, 108, 140
Miracles ascribed to Patrick discussed, 180, 181
Mochae, 113
Mochta, 76, 207, 208
Mochuda, 128
Mog Ruith, 66
Mogain, 141
Moses, Patrick likened to, 150, 151, 172
Mourie, the god, 67, 188
Moy, River, 138
Mugdoirn, 140
Muirchu, his Life of St. Patrick discussed, 167-170; referred to, 4, 8, 11, 17, 26, 32, 40, 43, 44, 53, 60, 64, 76, 77, 78, 82, 90, 93, 120, 125, 127, 140, 143, 144, 153, 157, 158, 159, 165, 171, 176, 187, 214; does not mention any mission of Patrick by Pope Celestine, 48
Mune, 112, 137
Munster, Patrick in, 142, 143

NAAS, 185
Nathi, 184
Nemthor, 8, 9; said to be Dumbarton, 10, 11; conjectured to be St. Michael's Tor, 12
Nennius, his dates of Patrick's arrival in Ireland, 52
Niall, 93
Ninian, St., 13, 16, 116, 138, 159, 209
Nitria, 131
Numbers, Sacred, 121, 122, 205, 206

OCHA, Battle of, 53
Odhran, 202

Odissus, 4
Oen-adare, 136, 137
Olcan, 140, 186, 199
Oudoceus, 48

PADRIG MAENWYN, traditional name of Patrick, 7
Paganism, no relapse at BannavemTaberniae into 23; in Ireland, 27, 59-74, 78, 79, 92, 146; not to be laid to the charge of Patrick, 29, 192, 193; a religion of dread, 69-71, 226; attacked by Patrick in its strongholds, 91, 92, 99, 100, 103; found in the later legends of Patrick and other Celtic saints, 144, 166, 177-188; no compromise with it made by Patrick, 200-203; later attempts at compromise, 66-70, 203, 224, 225; relapse after Patrick's death, 220, 221
Palladius, 18, 33, 44, 46, 48, 50, 51, 52, 53, 54, 57, 73, 76, 81, 165
Patrick, St., birth, 3; parents, 4; birthplace discussed, 4-13; *ingenuus*, 17; also named Succat, 17; other names, 18; his sin, 23; carried captive to Ireland, 25; his repentance, prayers and fasting, 26; his escape, 26-30; probable second captivity, 30; theory of his early labours in Ireland as priest discussed, 34-37; his wanderings, 35, 37; with relations in Britain, 4, 37, 41; his mission opposed, 37; possible labours

in Cumbria, 38; visit to Gaul, 39; probably instructed by St. German, 39, 43; opposition to his consecration, 42; consecrated bishop, 44; sailed for Ireland, 45; not sent by Pope Celestine, 48-51; date of his landing in Ireland, 51-54; his companions, 75; landed at mouth of Vartry, 76; sailed thence northward, 76; his conversion of Dichu, 77; visit to Slemish, 77; his policy discussed, 79-81; left Dichu, 81; baptism of Benignus, 82; visit to Laoghaire at Tara, 89-93; his Irish Hymn, 94-98; visit to Teltown, 99; conversion of Conall, 100; baptism at the fountain Loigles, 101; league with the sons of Awley, 102; visit to Uisnech, 66, 103; ordination of Bishop Gosacht, 103; entered Mag Slecht, 103, 61; crossed Shannon, 103; converted Ethne and Fedelm, 104-109; stayed seven years in Connaught, 110; trained pupils and wrote *abgitoria*, 110-112; built churches, 113-122; halted in Mag Selce, 131, 66; entered Sligo, 132; fasted on Cruachan Aigle in Mayo, 132-135; baptized many thousands at the well Sini, 135; came to the well Findmag, 135; came to Tirawley, 136; baptized many, 136-137; erected a stone in sign of the cross of Christ, 138; came into Ulster, 140; returned to Meath, 140; visited Leinster, 141; consecrated Fiacc, 141, 218; entered Munster, 142; founded churches at Armagh, 143-144; legend of his visit to Glastonbury, 145; conversion of a Scotic lady, 146, death at Saul, 147; burial at Downpatrick, 147; date of his death, 148; his age at time of his death, 149-151; his "Confession," 154-157; his "Epistle to the Subjects of Coroticus," 157-160; his "Sayings," 161; his Irish Hymn, 162-164; 94-98; mention of St. Patrick in early literature, 165, 166; life of the saint by Muirchu, 167-170; by Tirechan, 170-176; other lives, 176; legendary misrepresentations of his character, 177-188; no paganism in his teaching, 192, 193; his Creed and practices, 194-200; no compromise with paganism, 200-203; his Church, 204-226; number of bishops, 205-214; consecration by one bishop 214; his Latin, 29

Patrick, seat of, 7
——, well of, 11; near Patterdale, 38; at Naas, 141
——, stone of, 141
——, tent of, 141
——, rock of, 140
——, bell of, 125, 126

INDEX.

Patrick, footmark of, 25
Patrick of Culwen, 38
Patrickdale, 38
Patrick, Bampton, 38
Patrick, Preston, 38
Paulinus, 213
Pelagian heresy, 3, 39
Pelagius, 56
Perranzabuloe, 116, 117, 123
Phelim, 83, 85
Pilgrimages popular among Celts, 47
Piran, 116, 145
Porth Curnow, church of, 117
Potitus, 4
Probus, 34, 36, 40, 149, 177
Prosper, 39, 50, 165

RESTITUTUS, 164
Rhydderch, 14
Rivers, worship of, 70
Romans with Patrick, 75, 205, 220
Rosina, Valley of, 7

SABHALL, a barn, 77, 120, 144. See Saul
Sachellus, 199
Samhain, 62, 69
Sardica, Council of, 213
Saul, 77, 119, 120, 147. See Sabhall
Scirit. See Skerry
Scothnoe, 83
Sechnall. See Secundinus
Secundinus, Hymn of, 150, 164, 166, 181, 186, 195, 197
Segene, 166
Segitius, 44, 49
Senchus Mor, 162, 225
Senior, 36, 40
Senmeda, 175
Servanus, 215
Seven churches, 121; companies, 122; Bishop-Houses, 122; Bishops, 121, 123, 209, 210; fifties, 205, 206
Side or Sidhe, 60, 64, 105
Siderius, 216
Simeon Stylites, 47
Sinell, 137
Sini, 135
Sixtus, Pope, 113
Skerry, 25, 140
Slain, 77
Slan, a well, 67, 135
Slane, 89
Slemish, 25, 26, 77, 140
Sletty, 141, 167
Snam da En, 103
Staff of Jesu, 61, 128, 135
Stones, worship of, 65-67, 103, 132, 145; inscribed by Patrick and his companions, 132
Sucat, 17
Succat, 17, 177
Succet, 17
Sun, worship of, 62-64, 99

TAILLTIN. See Teltown
Tara, 65, 79, 80, 81, 82, 87, 99, 101, 129, 136, 137, 141, 184
Tassach, 124, 128, 147
Teilo, 29, 215
Teltown, 63, 99, 100
Tempull Phaidrig, 119
Ternan, 215
Theodosius, 21
Tigris, 123
Tirawley, 104, 136, 137
Tirechan, his Life of St. Patrick discussed, 170-176; referred to, 17, 33, 53, 60, 64, 66, 75, 81, 82, 91, 93, 99, 100, 102, 103, 104, 105, 109, 111, 112, 113, 115, 121, 124, 125, 127, 131, 132, 136, 138, 140, 141, 150, 153, 164, 165,

187, 198, 199, 201, 206, 209; supplementary note respecting the mission of Patrick by Celestine, 48; doubt whether these notes were by Tirechan, 173-174
Tirglass, 143
Tlachtga, 63
Tonsure, priestly, 120, 129, 142
——, druidical, 108, 129
Torbach, 153
Trim, 82, 85, 144
Tripartite Life, of little historical value, 176, 177; its monstrous stories, 184 to 187.
Tudno, 133
Tyrrhenian Sea, 33, 37, 161

UISNECH, 66, 103, 186
Ulster, Patrick in, 77, 140, 145, 147
Ultan, Bishop, 17, 170
Usk, 12

VERE, Mr. Aubrey de, Legends of Saint Patrick, quoted, 25, 43, 107, 132, 143, 227
Verulamium, Synod of, 39

Victor, angel of the Irish nation, 41, 48, 196
Victoricus, a man, 41, 196
Victoricus, an angel, 26, 196. See Victor
Victoricus, Bishop, 140
Vincent of Lerins, 33
Visions of St. Patrick, 26, 28, 30, 41, 42, 43, 156, 196

WELLS, worship of, 67-70; Slan or Findmag, 67, 135; Chollerford, 67; the god Mourie's, 67; St. George's, 68; St. Elian's, 68; Baranton, 68; St. Madron's, 68; Ffynon Tegla, 69; Chapel Uny, 69; St. Patrick's, 11, 38, 141; baptism at Loigles, 101; Ethne and Fedelm at Clebach, 104, 105, 108; baptism at Sini, 121, 135; at Oen-adare, 136; Pagan well made a Christian holy well by Columba, 224
Welsh traditions of Patrick, 7
Whitherne } 116, 138, 209,
Whithorn } 212 423

PRINTED BY THE HANSARD PUBLISHING UNION, LIMITED, LONDON AND REDHILL.

PUBLICATIONS
OF THE
Society for Promoting Christian Knowledge.

Church History Cartoons.

From Pictures drawn by W. J. MORGAN. Each picture illustrates an important event in the History of the Church of England. The Cartoons are bold and effectively coloured. Size, 45 in. by 35 in.

No. 1. Gregory and the English Slaves, A.D. 589.
2. St. Augustine before King Ethelbert, A.D. 597.
3. Manumission of a Slave by a Saxon Bishop.
4. The Martyrdom of St. Alban.
5. Columba at Oronsay, A.D. 563.
6. St. Aidan preaching to the Northumbrians.
7. The Venerable Bede translating St. John's Gospel, A.D. 735.
8. Stonehenge.
9. Iona at the Present Day. Founded A.D. 565.
10. Murder of Monks by the Danes, Crowland Abbey, about 870 A.D.
11. The Martyrdom of St. Edmund, A.D. 870.
12. St. Dunstan reproving King Edwy, A.D. 955.
13. Norman Thanksgiving after the Battle of Hastings, A.D. 1066.
14. The Murder of Thomas A'Beckett, A.D. 1170.
15. The Crusaders starting for the East.
16. Archbishop Langton producing before the Barons the Charter of Henry I., A.D. 1213.
17. Preaching at St. Paul's Cross, A.D. 1547.
18. The Seven Bishops sent to the Tower, A.D. 1688.
19. The Consecration of Matthew Parker as Archbishop of Canterbury, Dec. 17th, 1559.

1s. 4d. each on thick paper. | 3s. mounted and varnished.
2s. mounted on canvas. | 4s. ditto ditto, on roller.

WORKS ON CHURCH HISTORY, &c.

Ancient British Church, A Popular History of the. With special reference to the Church in Wales. By E. J. NEWELL, M.A. With Map. Fcap. 8vo. Cloth boards. 2s. 6d.

[*A lucid book on a department of history hitherto much neglected.*]

Church in England and its Endowments, A Brief SKETCH OF THE HISTORY OF THE. With a List of the Archbishops, tracing their succession from the present time up to the Apostles, and through them to Christ. By the Rev. GEORGE MILLER. Post 8vo. Paper cover. 4d.

[*A clear and simple statement of the history of Church endowments. For General Readers.*]

Church History in England. By the Rev. A. MARTINEAU. From the Earliest Times to the Dawn of the Reformation. 12mo. Cloth boards. 3s.

[For reference and general use.]

Church History (A Chapter of English): being the Minutes of the S.P.C.K. for the years 1698–1703, together with Abstracts of Correspondents' Letters during part of the same period. Edited by the Rev. EDMUND McCLURE, M.A. Demy 8vo. Cloth boards. 5s.

Church History, Illustrated Notes on English. By the Rev. C. A. LANE, Lecturer of the Church Defence Institution. Vol. I.—From the Earliest Times to the Dawn of the Reformation. Vol. II.—Its Reformation and Modern Work. Crown 8vo. Cloth. 1s. each.

[Deals with the chief events during the period. The illustrations, amounting to over 100 in each Volume, add to its popular character.]

Church History, Sketches of. From the First Century to the Reformation. By the late Rev. J. C. ROBERTSON, M.A. Post 8vo. Cloth boards. 2s.

[A simple and attractive account of the leading events in Church History, from A.D. 33 to the Reformation: for general readers; suitable also for use in Sunday and day schools.]

Church History in Scotland, Sketches of. By the Rev. JULIUS LLOYD. Post 8vo. Cloth boards. 1s. 6d.

[An account of Church affairs in Scotland from St. Columba's Mission to Iona until the present time.]

Works on Church History, &c.—*Continued.*

Church History, Turning Points of English. By the Rev. E. L. CUTTS. Crown 8vo. Cloth boards. 3s. 6d.

[The leading events in the Church of England from the earliest period of British history to the present day, showing the Church questions that have arisen, and yet remain as our inheritance; for Churchmen in general.]

Church History, Turning Points of General. By the Rev. E. L. CUTTS. Crown 8vo. Cloth boards. 5s.

[The leading events in General Church History from the time of the Apostles to the present day; useful for a text-book in schools, &c., and for general readers.]

Dictionary (A), of the Church of England. By the Rev. E. L. CUTTS. With Numerous Woodcuts. Crown 8vo. Cloth boards. 7s. 6d.

[A manual for the use of clergymen and schools.]

History of the English Church, in Short Biographical Sketches. By the Rev. JULIUS LLOYD. Post 8vo. Cloth boards. 1s. 6d.

[Leads the reader, by a series of selected lives, to a general idea of the Church History of England.]

Lectures on the Historical and Dogmatical Position of the Church of England. By the Rev. W. BAKER, D.D. Post 8vo. Cloth boards. 1s.

[Supplies in short compass a clear account of the historical position of the Church of England: for general readers.]

John Wiclif, His Life, Times, and Teaching. By the Rev. A. R. PENNINGTON, M.A. Fcap. 8vo. Cloth boards. 3s.

[This work embraces the result of recent researches: for general reading.]

Great English Churchmen; or, Famous Names in English Church History and Literature. By W. H. DAVENPORT ADAMS. Cloth boards. 3s. 6d.

Grosseteste, Robert, Bishop of Lincoln, The Life and Times of. By the Rev. G. G. PERRY. Post 8vo. Cloth boards. 2s. 6d.

["Grosseteste chiefly as a reformer in a corrupt period of the Church, and his quarrel with the Pope": for general reading.]

Churchman's Life of Wesley (The). By R. DENNY URLIN

PUBLICATIONS ON "CHURCH DEFENCE."

Disestablishment and Disendowment: What they MEAN AND WHAT MUST COME OF THEM. An Address by the Right Rev. W. C. MAGEE, Lord Bishop of Peterborough. Post 8vo, stitched, 5s. per 100.

The Case for "Establishment" stated. By the Rev. THOMAS MOORE. Post 8vo, paper cover, 6d., cloth boards, 2s.

The Englishman's Brief on behalf of his National CHURCH. By the Rev. T. MOORE. Post 8vo, paper cover, 6d.

Talks on Tithes: Why pay them? By Farmers HOPGOOD, CORNFIELD, AND STOCKWELL. Edited by the Rev. T. MOORE. Post 8vo, paper cover, 6d.

Tithes and the Poor (No. 2136). By the Rev. T. MOORE. 12mo, 4s. per 100.

Hear the other Side (2129). A word about Disestablishment and Disendowment. By the Rev. J. TRAVISS LOCKWOOD. 12mo, 8s. per 100; paper cover, each 2d.

Tithes. By the Rev. JAMES HAMILTON, Vicar of Doulting, Somerset. 12mo, 4s. per 100.

Church Endowments. A Lecture delivered at Swindon by Sir JOHN CONROY, Bart. Post 8vo, paper cover, 2d.

The Church of England, Past and Present. A popular Lecture. By the Lord BISHOP OF CARLISLE. Post 8vo, paper cover, 4d.

The Church and the People. By the Rev. H. W. REYNOLDS. Post 8vo, paper cover, 2d.

The Work of the Church of England, for the Benefit OF ENGLAND'S PEOPLE. By the Rev. GUY MILLER. (No. 2195). 12mo, 4s. per 100.

Church Property, Not National Property. A Lecture delivered at Swindon by Sir JOHN CONROY, Bart. Post 8vo, paper cover, 2d.

The Union of Church and State. By the late Rev. PROFESSOR BLUNT, B.D. Fcap. 8vo, paper cover, 2d.

Notes on Church and State. By EDWARD HAWKINS, D.D. Post 8vo, paper cover, 2d.

STORIES FOUNDED ON CHURCH HISTORY.

The Church in the Valley. By ELIZABETH HARCOURT MITCHELL. With four page Woodcuts. Crown 8vo. Cloth boards, 3s.

[A story which introduces much Church History, and is well calculated to spread useful information upon the Disestablishment question.]

Conquering and to Conquer. A Story of Rome in the Days of St. Jerome. By the author of " The Schönberg-Cotta Family." Crown 8vo. Cloth boards. 2s. 6d.

[Presents a fair Picture of Society in Jerome's time: for General Readers.]

The First Rector of Burgstead. A Tale of the Saxon Church. By the Rev. E. L. CUTTS. Fcap. 8vo. Cloth boards. 1s. 6d.

[For General Readers.]

Gaudentius. A Story of the Colosseum. By the Rev. G. S. DAVIES. Crown 8vo. Cloth boards. 2s. 6d.

[A Picture of Roman Morals yielding to the pressure of Christianity: for Educated Readers.]

Lapsed, not Lost. A Story of Roman Carthage. By the author of " The Schönberg-Cotta Family," &c. Crown 8vo. Cloth boards. 2s. 6d.

[A Story of the time of St. Cyprian : for General Readers.]

Mitslav; or, The Conversion of Pomerania. By the late Right Rev. R. MILMAN, D.D. Crown 8vo. With Map. Cloth boards. 3s. 6d.

Narcissus. A Tale of Early Christian Times. By the Right Rev. W. BOYD CARPENTER, Lord Bishop of Ripon. Crown 8vo. Cloth boards. 3s. 6d.

St. Cedd's Cross. A Tale of the Conversion of the East Saxons. By the Rev. E. L. CUTTS. Post 8vo. Cloth boards. 2s.

[The Story is based upon Bede's " Ecclesiastical History," Chap. 22, Book III. : for General Readers.]

Stories for the Saints' Days. By S. W., author of "Stories for every Sunday in the Christian Year." Fcap. 8vo. Cloth boards. 1s. 6d.

[An Epitome of the Lives of certain Saints and Fathers : for Ordinary Readers]

Jack Dane's Inheritance. A Tale of Church Defence. By FRANCES BEAUMONT MILNE. With one page Woodcut. Post 8vo. Limp cloth. 6d.

[A story upon the rights and liberties of the Church of England.]

DIOCESAN HISTORIES.

Bath and Wells. By the Rev. W. HUNT. With Map. Fcap. 8vo. Cloth boards. 2s. 6d.

Canterbury. By the Rev. R. C. JENKINS. With Map. Fcap. 8vo. Cloth boards. 3s. 6d.

Chichester. By the Rev. W. R. W. STEPHENS. With Map and Plan of the Cathedral. Fcap. 8vo. Cloth boards. 2s. 6d.

Durham. By the Rev. J. L. LOW. With Map and Plan. Fcap. 8vo. Cloth boards. 2s. 6d.

Hereford. By the Rev. Canon PHILLOTT. With Map. Fcap. 8vo. Cloth boards. 3s.

Lichfield. By the Rev. W. BERESFORD. With Map. Fcap. 8vo. Cloth boards. 2s. 6d.

Norwich. By the Rev. A. JESSOPP, D.D. With Map. Fcap. 8vo. Cloth boards. 2s. 6d.

Oxford. By the Rev. E. MARSHALL, M.A. With Map. Fcap. 8vo. Cloth boards. 2s. 6d.

Peterborough. By the Rev. G. A. POOLE, M.A. With Map. Fcap. 8vo. Cloth boards. 2s. 6d.

Salisbury. By the Rev. W. H. JONES. With Map and Plan. Fcap. 8vo. Cloth boards. 2s. 6d.

St. Asaph. By the Venerable Archdeacon THOMAS. With Map. Fcap. 8vo. Cloth boards. 2s.

St. David's. By the Rev. Canon BEVAN. With Map. Fcap. 8vo. Cloth boards. 2s. 6d.

Winchester. By the Rev. W. BENHAM, B.D. With Map. Fcap. 8vo. Cloth boards. 3s.

Worcester. By the Rev. I. GREGORY SMITH, M.A., and the Rev. PHIPPS ONSLOW, M.A. With Map. Fcap. 8vo. Cloth boards. 3s. 6d.

York. By the Rev. Canon ORNSBY, M.A. With Map. Fcap 8vo. Cloth boards. 3s. 6d.

NON-CHRISTIAN RELIGIOUS SYSTEMS.

Fcap. 8vo. Cloth boards. 2s. 6d. each.

Buddhism. Being a Sketch of the Life and Teachings of Gautama, the Buddha. By T. W. RHYS DAVIDS. With Map.

Buddhism in China. By the Rev. S. BEAL. With Map.

Confucianism and Taouism. By Professor ROBERT K. DOUGLAS, of the British Museum. With Map.

Hinduism. By Professor MONIER WILLIAMS. With Map.

Islam as a Missionary Religion. By CHARLES R. HAINES. (2s.)

Islam and its Founder. By J. W. H. STOBART. With Map.

The Corân: its Composition and Teaching and the Testimony it bears to the Holy Scriptures. By Sir W. MUIR, K.C.S.I.

THE FATHERS FOR ENGLISH READERS.

Fcap. 8vo. Cloth boards. 2s. each.

Leo the Great. By the Rev. CHARLES GORE, M.A.

Gregory the Great. By the Rev. J. BARMBY, B.D.

Saint Ambrose: his Life, Times, and Teaching. By the Rev. ROBINSON THORNTON, D.D.

Saint Athanasius: his Life and Times. By the Rev. R. WHELER BUSH. (2s. 6d.)

Saint Augustine. By the Rev. EDWARD L. CUTTS, B.A.

Saint Basil the Great. By the Rev. R. T. SMITH, B.D.

Saint Bernard, Abbot of Clairvaux, A.D. 1091-1153. By the Rev. S. J. EALES, M.A., D.C.L. (2s. 6d.)

Saint Hilary of Poitiers and Saint Martin of Tours. By the Rev. J. GIBSON CAZENOVE, D.D.

Saint Jerome. By the Rev. EDWARD L. CUTTS, B.A.

Saint John of Damascus. By the Rev. J. H. LUPTON, M.A.

Saint Patrick: his Life and Teaching. By Rev. E. J. NEWELL, M.A. (2s. 6d.)

Synesius of Cyrene, Philosopher and Bishop. By ALICE GARDNER.

The Apostolic Fathers. By the Rev. Canon HOLLAND.

The Defenders of the Faith; or, the Christian Apologists of the Second and Third Centuries. By the Rev. F. WATSON, M.A.

The Venerable Bede. By the Rev. G. F. BROWNE.

THE HOME LIBRARY.

Crown 8vo. Cloth boards. 3s. 6d. each.

Black and White. Mission Stories. By H. A. FORDE.

Charlemagne. By the Rev. E. L. CUTTS, B.A. With Map.

Constantine the Great. The Union of the Church and State. By the Rev. E. L. CUTTS, B.A.

Great English Churchmen; or, Famous Names in ENGLISH CHURCH HISTORY AND LITERATURE. By W. H. D. ADAMS.

John Hus. The Commencement of the Resistance to Papal Authority on the Part of the Inferior Clergy. By the Rev. A. H. WRATISLAW.

Judæa and her Rulers, from Nebuchadnezzar to Vespasian. By M. BRAMSTON. With Map.

Mazarin. By the late GUSTAVE MASSON.

Military Religious Orders of the Middle Ages: the Hospitallers, the Templars, the Teutonic Knights, and others. By the Rev. F. C. WOODHOUSE, M.A.

Mitslav; or, the Conversion of Pomerania. By the late Right Rev. R. MILMAN, D.D. With Map.

Narcissus: a Tale of Early Christian Times. By the Right Rev. W. BOYD CARPENTER, Bishop of Ripon.

Richelieu. By the late GUSTAVE MASSON.

Sketches of the Women of Christendom. Dedicated to the Women of India. By the author of "The Chronicles of the Schönberg-Cotta Family."

The Church in Roman Gaul. By the Rev. R. TRAVERS SMITH. With Map.

The Churchman's Life of Wesley. By R. DENNY URLIN, Esq., F.S.S.

The House of God the Home of Man. By the Rev. Canon JELF.

The Inner Life, as Revealed in the Correspondence of Celebrated Christians. Edited by the late Rev. T. ERSKINE.

The Life of the Soul in the World: its Nature, Needs, Dangers, Sorrows, Aids, and Joys. By the Rev. F. C. WOODHOUSE, M.A.

The North-African Church. By the Rev. JULIUS LLOYD, M.A. With Map.

Thoughts and Characters; being Selections from the Writings of the author of "The Chronicles of the Schönberg-Cotta Family."

THE HEATHEN WORLD AND ST. PAUL.

This Series is intended to throw light upon the writings and labours of the Apostle of the Gentiles.

Fcap 8vo. Cloth boards. 2s. each.

Saint Paul in Greece. By the Rev. G. S. DAVIES, M.A., Charterhouse, Godalming. With Map.

Saint Paul in Damascus and Arabia. By the Rev. GEORGE RAWLINSON, M.A., Canon of Canterbury. With Map.

Saint Paul in Asia Minor and at the Syrian Antioch. By the Rev. E. H. PLUMPTRE, D.D., Vicar of Bickley, Kent. With Map.

Saint Paul at Rome. By the Very Rev. Charles MERIVALE, D.D., D.C.L., Dean of Ely. With Map.

ANCIENT HISTORY FROM THE MONUMENTS.

This Series of Books is chiefly intended to illustrate the Sacred Scriptures by the results of recent Monumental Researches in the East.

Fcap. 8vo. Cloth boards. 2s. each.

Sinai, from the Fourth Egyptian Dynasty to the Present Day. By HENRY S. PALMER, Major R.E., F.R.A.S. With Map.

Babylonia (the History of). By the late GEORGE SMITH. Edited by the Rev. A. H. SAYCE, Assistant Professor of Comparative Philology, Oxford.

Greek Cities and Islands of Asia Minor. By the late W. S. W. VAUX, M.A., F.R.S.

Assyria, from the Earliest Times to the Fall of Nineveh. By the late GEORGE SMITH, Esq.

Egypt, from the Earliest Times to B.C. 300. By the late S. BIRCH, LL.D., etc.

Persia, from the Earliest Period to the Arab Conquest. By the late W. S. W. VAUX, M.A., F.R.S.

Publications of the Society.

THE PEOPLE'S LIBRARY.

Crown 8vo. Cloth boards. 1s. each.

A Chapter of Science; or, What is a Law of Nature? Six Lectures to Working Men. By Professor J. STUART, Cambridge. With Diagrams.

A Six Months' Friend. By HELEN SHIPTON, author of "Christopher." With several Illustrations.

Biographies of Working Men. By GRANT ALLEN, B.A.

British Citizen (The): his Rights and Privileges. A Short History by J. THOROLD ROGERS, M.P.

Factors in Life. Three Lectures on Health—Food—Education. By Professor SEELEY, F.R.S.

Guild of Good Life (The). A Narrative of Domestic Health and Economy. By B. W. RICHARDSON, M.D., F.R.S.

Household Health. A Sequel to "The Guild of Good Life." By B. W. RICHARDSON, M.D., F.R.S.

Hops and Hop-Pickers. By the Rev. J. Y. STRATTON. With several Illustrations.

Life and Work among the Navvies. By the Rev. D. W. BARRETT, M.A. With several Illustrations.

The Cottage Next Door. By HELEN SHIPTON. With several Illustrations.

Thrift and Independence. A Word for Working Men. By the Rev. W. LEWERY BLACKLEY, M.A.

LONDON:

Society for Promoting Christian Knowledge:
NORTHUMBERLAND AVENUE, CHARING CROSS, W.C.;
43, QUEEN VICTORIA STREET, E.C., 97, WESTBOURNE GROVE, W.
BRIGHTON: 135, NORTH STREET.
NEW YORK: E. & J. B. YOUNG & CO.